yates-brewery.co.uk
PO38 1XG
YATES' BREWERY
ISLE OF WIGHT
500
WIGHT
Bottle 5.0%
WINTER
ABV
WINTER ALE BREWED AT
THE INN AT ST LAWRENCE
BEST BEFORE: End Aug 2004
W910
KU-511-011
Ashcott
ABV 4.3%
Somerset
A light brown fruity beer, with malty
Richmond Ale
ABV
50 cl
W.J.KING & CO.
BREWERS
KING'S OLD ALE
ABV 4.5%
BOTTLE CONDITIONED
Summer™
Lightning
AWARD WINNING
HOP BACK BREWERY
Golden Ale
ABV 5%
500 mL ℮
FROM THE TALBOT AT KNIGHTWICK
TEME VALLEY BREWERY
HEARTH WARMER
BREWED USING ONLY WORCESTERSHIRE HOPS
WARWICKSHIRE BEER COMPANY
BEST BITTER
ABV 3.9%
WHITTINGTONS BREWERY
Purveyors of the Purrfect Pint
Finest Bottle Conditioned Gloucestershire Bitter
CATS WHISKERS

HOLE HEARTED
A Golden Ale for the Hole in the Wall
Brewed with 100% Cascade Hops
The Oakleaf Brewing Co. Ltd.
Gosport
ABV 4.7%
500ML℮

EMPIRE PALE ALE

'The Friendly Ale'
Butty Bach

"Town Crier"
BREWED BY
Hobsons
BREWERY CO.
Bottle Conditioned Beer
Alc. 4.

EDWIN TUCKER'S
DEVONSHIRE
Edwin Tucker
PRIZE ALE

500ml℮

WOODFORDE'S
WHERRY
HOPS · BISTOS
WHERRY
CHAMPION BEER OF BRITAIN
WOODFORDE'S
NORFOLK
ALES
Alc. 3.8%
BOTTLE
CONDITIONED
REAL ALE

O LUX
Brewed with the ad...
English Damsons from ...
fermentation was temperat...
unique flavour of the fruit...
fermentation took place in...
the champagne-like natural b...
rich, lion, fruit ale.
33cl
DAMS N
OLD LUXTERS BREWERY · HAMBLEDEN · HE...
OXFORDSHIRE · TEL (01 491) 638...

BRAKSPEAR
BOTTLE CONDITIONED
English Target hops give this beer a remarkable aroma.
Late copper hopping with Goldings & fermentation by the Brakspear
yeast creates the noble bitter palate. Bottle Conditioning
preserves the fruity, zesty aroma & gives
a crispy natural sparkle
Organic
Beer
4.6% Vol.

RINGWOOD
BOLD FORESTER
SPRING
ALE
4.2% ABV
BREWERY

GOOD BOTTLED BEER GUIDE

Jeff Evans

Sponsored by

ASDA

CAMRA BOOKS

Contents

Published by CAMRA Books, 230 Hatfield Road,
St Albans, Hertfordshire AL1 4LW.
Tel. (01727) 867201 Fax (01727) 867670
e-mail: camra@camra.org.uk

© CAMRA Books 2004 · ISBN 1-85249-197-3
Author: Jeff Evans
Design: Rob Howells
Cover design: Paul Welti Cover photograph: Gus Filgate

Great effort has gone into researching the contents of this book, but no responsibility can be taken for errors.

Conditions of sale
This book shall not, by way of trade or otherwise, be lent, resold, hired out or otherwise circulated without the publisher's prior consent in any form of binding or cover other than that in which it is published and without similar conditions being imposed on the subsequent purchaser. All rights reserved. No parts of this publication may be reproduced, stored in retrieval systems, or transmitted in any form or by any means, electronic, mechanical, photocopying or otherwise, without the prior consent of CAMRA Books.

Foreword

BEER HAS A HUGE PART TO PLAY in the British psyche and at last we are really beginning to understand the full extent to which it can be enjoyed. We have always appreciated the simplicity of that first beer after a long day and are now further enjoying the opportunities that the many styles of beer offer – with food, for instance.

A continued improvement in the standard of presentation of bottles has certainly helped beer to be seriously considered as an alternative to wine. Up to now, the beer inside has been of the highest standard but often brewers have failed at the final hurdle – in the packaging. With this enhancement, I am looking forward to seeing beer back where it belongs – on peoples' dinner tables, and the final confirmation of beer's rightful place will be when more restaurants and bars offer beer menus alongside wine lists.

The past year has been eventful, with further consolidation of the brewing industry at one end but, more excitingly, a continued emergence of the craft brewer at the other. The arrival of exotic beers from Europe and elsewhere in the world is offering us even more diversity, and the fact that many of these breweries have existed for hundreds of years is testament to the longevity of the product. It makes one realise that, long after we are all gone, beer will continue to be brewed in the traditional way and that the palates of future generations will be offered delicacies that are still only in the minds of the current brewers.

Asda will continue to work with brewers large and small to develop the beer on offer. Our connections with SIBA (Society of Independent Brewers) have enabled us to source beers from craft brewers to satisfy everyday needs at a local level. The *Asda Beer Competition* – won first by RCH's Double Header – is in its second year and will offer opportunities for all, and as the new industry training body, The Beer Academy, grows we will continue our patronage.

Asda is also delighted to sponsor the CAMRA *Good Bottled Beer Guide* for the first time and I hope that you will enjoy working your way through these different beers as much as I will.

Ged Futter
Category Buyer, Beer, Asda Stores

Introduction

IT'S NOT JUST THE NUMBERS, YOU KNOW: it's what's going on around them. It's easy to evaluate the success of real ale in a bottle by simply counting how many examples are now on sale, and how many breweries produce them. We're talking well over 600, from 143 breweries, up more than 100 bottles and 30 breweries since the last edition of this book, just a year ago, and a world away from the time when CAMRA was formed in 1971 and just five bottled real ales were in regular production (see Classic Revival, pages 10–12). But the headline figure, while impressive, is only a partial indicator of the bottled beer renaissance. In many ways, of more significance is the activity surrounding it, initiatives that are preparing the ground for yet more expansion in future.

Take, for instance, the way in which specialist bottled beer shops are developing (see Shopping Around, pages 13–15). In truth, they are still rather thin on the ground, but the more that open every year, clearly the more opportunities drinkers will have to buy bottled real ales. As getting hold of bottles has always been the major stumbling block for most real ale enthusiasts, it's a major advance that, when coupled with the progress made in mail order sales – from shops, from breweries and from internet businesses – promises to encourage yet more brewers to turn to the bottle.

High street highs

Elsewhere in the high street, there are further signs of progress, with supermarkets taking more beers from small brewers, albeit for sale at a local level. There are concerns that Safeway's excellent selection may be compromised by its take-over by Morrisons, but we hope the pioneering spirit of retiring beer buyer Glenn Payne will be maintained under the new ownership. Sainsbury's is certainly moving in the right direction, and there are signs that Tesco has turned the corner and recognises the value in stocking a good and interesting range of bottled beers once again. Off-licence chain Unwins now ensures that real ale in a bottle accounts for at least 25% of its bottled ale range, and has written to its staff to outline the role bottle-conditioned beer can play in their branches. The *Good Bottled Beer Guide*, meanwhile, is delighted to welcome Asda as its sponsor, and applauds beer buyer Ged Futter's efforts to expand the store's selection.

Asda has been proactive already in promoting good quality bottled beers, particularly when, in 2003, it launched its *Asda Beer Competition*. Open to all brewers, this contest selects four finalists that each enjoy six weeks' exposure in Asda, giving customers the chance to vote for their favourite, which is then offered a six-month launchpad in store. Double Header, a bottle-conditioned beer from RCH Brewery, was the first winner. Asda's initiative follows on from the well-established *Tesco Beer Challenge*, which also offers an exclusive in-store contract to winning beers. To add to the theatre now being constructed around good bottled beer, Tesco has announced two further awards – for the 'Best Innovation in Brewing' and the 'Best New Imported Beer'.

Major retailers such as these are not, it seems, just paying lip service to beer, but are actually recognising the opportunities the sector presents and the way in which it has been down-played over the years, particularly in relation to wine. To help correct the situation, they are sending staff on the new courses that have been developed by The Beer Academy, an industry-funded body that seeks to educate and inspire people working in the trade. The way in which the courses illustrate the wonders of beer can only result in a wider choice of beers on sale in future, better presentation and more information for customers.

In search of enlightenment

Working on that premiss that better information leads to a more enlightened consumer, who is more inclined to opt for quality, the Campaign for Real Ale, too, has stepped into the retail arena. With the publication of this edition of the *Good Bottled Beer Guide*, CAMRA is launching a major initiative: the Real Ale in a Bottle accreditation scheme. Drawing on the support of both brewers and retailers, it aims to end the confusion that often exists between what is, and what is not, a real ale in a bottle, helping drinkers who want to try bottled real ale to make the right choices.

CAMRA is confident that, once good bottled real ale has been sampled, consumers will appreciate that it tastes so much better than pasteurised, filtered, artificially-carbonated bottled beer. CAMRA came into being because pasteurised, filtered beer was being served in pubs in place of traditionally-brewed, 'real' ale that is allowed to mature naturally in the cask for fuller, fresher, more complex flavours. As a result of CAMRA's efforts, cask-conditioned real ale has been preserved and, while it is not sold in every pub (thanks to the indifference of major pub companies and powerful international breweries), it is very much the life-blood of the regional and small brewery sectors, as well as being universally recognised as the connoisseur's choice.

The bottled side of the beer industry has suffered even longer. The traditional way of bottling was not to filter the beer and pasteurise it, but to allow the yeast to continue fermentation in the bottle, for a natural effervescence and multi-dimensional flavours. Sadly, from about the 1920s, technology got the better of good bottled beer, leaving us with that sorry statistic of just five bottled real ales in 1971. CAMRA has always championed bottle-conditioned beer, but, with bigger battles being fought in the bar rooms and brewery boardrooms, the bottling line has not always been given the fullest attention. However, amends are being made. In 1991, CAMRA added the *Bottle-Conditioned Beer* category to the *Champion Beer of Britain* competition, and in 1998 the

Why Only Bottle-Conditioned Beers?

The fact that the *Good Bottled Beer Guide* features only bottle-conditioned beers (real ales in a bottle) is sometimes queried. The majority of bottled beers to be found on the high street, after all, are filtered, and very often pasteurised. But therein lies the problem.

CAMRA is a consumer organisation that campaigns for, among other things, tradition and quality. In fact, these two are closely related, in that, very often, things done traditionally are often of the best quality – think of farmhouse cheeses or bread from family bakeries. Beer is no exception. When produced in the proven, traditional fashion, to provide flavour and character for the customer and not just profit and convenience for the manufacturer, it is, simply, so much better.

CAMRA has proven this time and again with draught real ale ('cask-conditioned beer') and now wants to do this with bottled real ale ('bottle-conditioned beer'). Just as the best-selling *Good Beer Guide* highlights only draught real ale, so its little companion, the *Good Bottled Beer Guide*, highlights only bottled real ale.

This may have been seen as an extremely small niche publication when it first arrived – there were only around 150 beers listed in the first edition – but the point has been made and now, with well over 600 bottled real ales featured, there's no doubting that the *Good Bottled Beer Guide* has established that there is very definitely a market for real ale in a bottle and has no need to include processed bottled beers that, frankly, with very few exceptions, do not taste so good.

first edition of the *Good Bottled Beer Guide* was released. Now, with the launch of the accreditation scheme, the battle for better bottled beer is being taken into the high street.

Another major development that is set to benefit bottled beer is the beer with food concept that has been embraced by brewers large and small. Celebrity chefs have been commissioned to provide interesting menus to match to beer, special tastings have been organised, and some breweries now even send out key personnel to pubs to host beer and food dinners. They see it as a way of encouraging customers to think more about the beer they are drinking. As bottled beer is particularly suited for dining, the belief is that shoppers will choose bottled beers more carefully, rather than just picking up a six-pack or some nationally-advertised brand.

Missed opportunity

One area in which brewers can do better, however, is in the labelling of bottled beers. CAMRA is offering help with the new accreditation scheme, but there is so much more that can be said about each beer, and the beer label, for most breweries, is very much a wasted opportunity. The next time you're in an off-licence take time to study some labels closely. In very few instances will you find much information about the beer itself. Will there be a full listing of ingredients, including the variety of malts and strains of hops? Probably not. Will the label tell you about the style of beer and its history? Unlikely. What about how the beer is brewed, the background of the brewery, some ideal food accompaniments, perhaps? Only rarely. What you may well find is some crass, totally unhelpful statement such as 'Brewed from the finest ingredients by our masterbrewer', which is about as insulting to the intelligence of the customer as it gets. Do we honestly expect the beer to be made by an office boy from whatever is left over in the brewhouse?

Why are breweries so blind to the possibilities the label presents? Unlike in the pub, off-trade shoppers have time to study the label before buying, and when they are in the comfort of their own home, enjoying a leisurely glass, they have even more time to contemplate the brewer's message. It's time the label was used to inspire and educate customers. It has worked brilliantly for the wine industry, after all.

Such a small improvement, in conjunction with all the other positive activities that have been outlined, can only have a beneficial impact on British bottled beer. It will be interesting to see the results – defined by the quantity and variety of beers featured in the next edition of this book.

The Stamp of Authenticity

ALTHOUGH THERE IS NO SHORTAGE of bottled real ales now on sale, it is still not always easy to identify such beers. For instance, many well-known draught real ale brands are filtered and pasteurised when they are bottled, rather than being allowed to mature naturally like their pub equivalents.

Adding to the confusion, rather than introducing clarity, is the language of the bottle label. Technical terms are difficult to understand. Is there any difference between 'bottle-conditioned' and 'brewery-conditioned'? Importantly, yes. A 'bottle-conditioned' beer will contain yeast and continue to ferment in the bottle, making it a real ale. A 'brewery-conditioned' product, on the other hand, is likely to be both filtered and pasteurised prior to bottling.

To help overcome such confusion, and to help shoppers select natural, live beers, CAMRA has now launched an accreditation scheme for real ale in a bottle. The initiative is comprised of two parts: the creation of an accreditation logo that can be used on bottles, and standardised text outlining the idiosyncrasies of real ale in a bottle and the best means of storing and serving such beers.

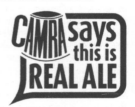

CAMRA says this is REAL ALE

When spotted on bottle labels, the 'CAMRA says this is Real Ale' logo will clearly show that the method of production has been recognised by CAMRA and that the beer is a bottle-conditioned product. The logo is therefore a technical endorsement and should not be seen as an award that reflects on the taste, style, ingredients or any other aspect of the beer. Apart from in its well-publicised award schemes, such as the *Champion Beer of Britain* competition, CAMRA leaves such assessments to the personal tastes of the drinker.

It is hoped, in time, that this logo will become an industry-standard hallmark and CAMRA is working hard with both breweries and retailers to achieve this. In spring 2004, all breweries known to produce real ales in a bottle were contacted and offered the chance to support the scheme by using the accreditation logo on their bottle labels. The response was overwhelmingly positive and some brewers were hoping to carry the new logo on their products by the time of the scheme's launch in August 2004. Other breweries, while keen to embrace the hallmark, have large stocks of printed labels that need to be used up, so, while the number of bottles in circulation carrying the new logo may be limited at first, many more should be spotted as months go by.

Words of advice

Bottle-conditioned products seem to have a reputation for being difficult to look after. People tend to be wary of the sediment in the bottle, and worry that it will ruin the taste. It is important to emphasise once again that yeast is vital to the fresh taste of the beer, its light drinkability, and the way in which it matures. It offers nothing to be afraid of: it will not harm you if consumed, although, by making the beer hazy in the glass, it may marginally spoil the appearance.

To overcome such concerns, and to allow drinkers to get the best out of real ales in a bottle, CAMRA, in consultation with brewers, has devised the second part of the accreditation structure, namely concise instructions on how to serve and pour beer that can be added to a beer label. These read: 'Yeast is the hallmark of a natural beer and produces a sparkle and sediment characteristic of all living beers. Store upright, serve lightly chilled and pour with care to leave the natural sediment in the bottle.'

The accreditation scheme has been devised in direct response to the increased number of enquiries to CAMRA about what constitutes a bottle-conditioned beer, and, perhaps more importantly, where such beers can be bought. That's why CAMRA is also engaging the support of shops. The aim is to see these products stocked as a separate category and promoted in retail outlets. It is also hoped that product knowledge among staff will be enhanced, and that shops will endorse the programme by using point of sale materials.

With the growth of the take-home market, CAMRA believes it is important to address this issue and encourage armchair drinkers to try different bottle-conditioned products. After all, they are the next best thing to a pint of real ale in the pub. But you, too, can help CAMRA highlight the demand for choice. Next time you visit your off-licence, check for, and ask for, your favourite bottle-conditioned products. Let the shop know that you support 'Real Ale in a Bottle'.

For a list of partners, and for updates on the scheme, see www.camra.org.uk/raib or contact CAMRA on (01727) 867201.

Classic Revival

FIVE BEERS STAND OUT in the history of British bottled beers. They are the five, resilient bottle-conditioned beers that were still standing their ground when CAMRA came into existence in 1971. They came from diverse backgrounds, they had different pedigrees and, sadly, since the early days of CAMRA, they have also suffered varying fates. As a Famous Five, they proved to be too adventurous for an increasingly narrow-minded brewing industry, and now we must content ourselves with a modest, but still defiant, Three Musketeers. Their stories have been told many times before, but are always worth the re-telling, especially when there's a new chapter to be unveiled.

Stout sacrifice

We begin with Guinness Extra Stout, the biggest seller of the five, accounting for nearly one quarter of Guinness's bottled beer business. Naturally maturing in the bottle, it offered so much more in the way of character than the chilled, nitrogen-flattened Guinness sold on draught, and its rich, fresh taste marked it out as the obvious choice for discerning drinkers stranded in a keg-only pub. All this wasn't enough, however, for Guinness. In 1993, the company announced that bottle conditioning was to end and Guinness Original (as it had then become known) was to be pasteurised, and pasteurised it remains. Disheartened we certainly should be that such a great beer has been emasculated in this way, but the bottled beer revival has at least thrown up some brilliant alternatives. For a real bottled stout, try Wye Valley's Dorothy Goodbody's Wholesome Stout, Titanic's Stout, or Hop Back Entire Stout, to suggest but three. They may not be found in virtually every pub, as the great Guinness used to be, but they shouldn't be too hard to track down.

There's better news from Hampshire. In the 1920s, a Yorkshire brewer named Steel took up an appointment at George Gale in Horndean and brought with him a recipe for an old ale of 9% alcohol. Prize Old Ale has been a fixture at Gale's ever since, despite never being a massive seller. The beer is still in production and, although no longer matured in oak casks, is conditioned at the brewery for at least six months before being packaged in its famous corked bottle. It is an inspirational beer with a worldwide reputation, though its deep, sherry-like flavours and giddy potency mark it out as a beer that will not appeal to all palates. All the same, this is one of the great beers you can tuck away and retrieve on a rainy day some years into the future, when the wonders of bottle conditioning can truly be experienced.

Seasoned travellers

Another beer that matured magnificently in the bottle was Courage's Imperial Russian Stout. This is the beer that warmed the hearts of the imperial Russian court. Hogsheads of the dark, nourishing, heavily-hopped, 10% brew regularly rolled off ships at the end of a turbulent crossing of the Baltic in the 18th and 19th centuries. It was originally a London beer, but its last days were spent in Tadcaster, the John Smith's brewery producing the final ever brew back in 1993. So far Scottish Courage has failed to respond to calls for another bottling, but there was some encouragement when, for 2003's Great British Beer Festival, the company commissioned a one-off draught version from its soon-to-be-closed Edinburgh brewery. Those who sampled it appreciated once again the rich, dark, smooth, liquorice-accented, raisiny, bittersweet flavours, but the word from the top was unequivocal: there was to be no bottling. Content yourselves, therefore, with some admirable replacements, the likes of Teignworthy's Empress Russian Porter, Pitfield's 1792 Imperial Stout, Harveys Imperial Extra Double Stout, Durham's Temptation and Good King Henry from Old Chimneys.

Another seasoned traveller has fared rather better of late. Worthington's White Shield was created in the 1820s, as a bottled version of the India pale ales that were shipped to the subcontinent. It gained a cult following over the years, and certificates were awarded to drinkers who could pour a bottle without letting the fine sediment slip into the distinctive Worthington glass. Like Guinness Extra Stout, it became a reliable standby in pubs where the draught beer was undrinkable. Sadly, Bass, its brewer, mucked about with it, moved it out of the Burton Unions wooden cask fermentation system, shipped it from brewery to brewery and finally lost interest when sales dipped to around 1,000 barrels a year. After a hue and cry among devotees, however, the beer was allowed to live on, but not with Bass. The brewing and marketing rights were assigned to King & Barnes in Horsham, who promptly ensured the beer won CAMRA's *Bottle-Conditioned Beer* gold at the *Champion Beer of Britain* contest. Success was shortlived, however, when K&B was taken over by Hall & Woodhouse and the brewery was closed.

The rights now belong to Coors, who bought the brand when Bass finally gave up the brewing ghost in 2000. The beer has returned to its rightful home in Burton upon Trent, and there has been much to celebrate. It is now brewed in what was until recently called the Museum Brewery, the working exhibit at the Bass Museum (now Coors Visitor Centre) where brewer Steve Wellington lovingly re-creates lost beers from the archives. It is a sign of Coors's commitment to the beer that the brewery has been re-named The White Shield Brewery and the beer has been taken into the wider Worthington's portfolio. A new label design, aimed at the younger drinker, has been launched and sales are on the up. The White Shield is gleaming much more brightly than it has been for a long, long time.

Laurels for Hardy's

There is similar joy down in the West Country with the news that Thomas Hardy's Ale is back. This near-12% beer was created by Dorset brewer Eldridge Pope in 1968, to mark the 40th anniversary of the death of the Wessex novelist. Famously, a quotation from Hardy's book *The Trumpet-Major* was re-printed on each label. The beer grew in esteem as fans squirrelled away bottles and then unveiled them years later to compare the various vintages. Even Eldridge Pope staged a vertical tasting of several vintages in the early 1990s, which is hard to believe when you consider that the company was only too keen to wash its hands of brewing completely not so many years later.

This ultimately led to Hardy's Ale facing the axe. In 1999, the final Dorchester-brewed vintage was produced, and the book seemed closed. Thankfully, some forward thinking by a company that imports beer into the USA, has seen Hardy's Ale rise from the ashes. In 2002, Phoenix Imports commissioned O'Hanlon's brewery in Devon to re-create the beer. With a little help from former Eldridge Pope brewers, O'Hanlon's followed the original recipe and finally released the first new batch – to much acclaim – in autumn 2003. It's a tale of fortune and misfortune of which Hardy himself would have been proud, but Hardy's Ale is back, to the delight of the madding crowd.

All we need now is for Phoenix Imports, or a similar body, to acquire the rights to bottle-conditioned Guinness Extra Stout and Courage Imperial Russian Stout, and we could happily turn the clock back three decades – with one difference, of course. The Famous Five classics would find they have far more competition on their hands these days.

Shopping Around

WHEN MARTIN KEMP AND ROB JONES took over a small London off-licence in 1981, they were venturing into unknown territory. The Two Brewers already sold a good variety of beers but, by renaming it The Beer Shop, they set out to provide a service quite different from the run-of-the-mill offie, specialising in bottled beers from around the world. Twenty-three years on, The Beer Shop is still in business, which must say something about the bottled beer trade.

What is surprising is not that The Beer Shop has succeeded and prospered for more than two decades, but that it has taken so long for other specialist beer shops to catch on. There are certainly others that have stood the test of time, The Ale Shop in Leeds and The Archer Road Beer Stop in Sheffield, for instance, but for most of the period that The Beer Shop has been in business, it has had few rivals anywhere in the country.

The tide has certainly turned, however. The way in which the public has caught the wave of the bottled beer revival has inspired dozens of other beer shops to open their doors. The fact that supermarkets have whetted the appetite by at last giving shelf room to quality bottled beers has made shoppers

Cutting out the Middle Man

One of the most inventive ways in which brewers have sought to sell their beers has been through the expanding farmers' markets system. Struggling to find a place for their draught beers in pubs where only big brewers survive, thanks to the massive discounts demanded by pub companies, small brewers have needed to look elsewhere for trade. They've turned to the bottle in a big way and have recognised that cutting out the middle man and taking a stand at a farmers' market can be a quick and easy way of selling their products.

Itchen Valley Brewery has been operating this way for years. It may mean no Sunday morning lie-in, but the brewers are keen to turn out and offer samples of their wares to discerning local shoppers, happy in the knowledge that, once tasted, their beers can seldom be resisted. It's a great way to raise the profile of the brewery and interact with the public, and hundreds of bottles can be sold in just one morning.

To find your nearest farmers' market, check out the website: www.farmersmarkets.net.

sit up and consider that there really is wonderful variety and choice out there, and now they're seeking out stores where they can buy something a little out of the ordinary.

Anywhere goes

The great thing about bottled beer is that it can be sold almost anywhere. It can be bolted on to a fine selection of cheeses in a delicatessen, or muscle its way between chutneys and jams in a country craft centre. The shelf life is relatively long, and the returns to the producer minimal. If it doesn't sell, then the retailer has only forked out for a case, so there's no financial risk involved. You only have to consider some of the beer shops listed at the back of this book to see how versatile a product it is.

Tucker's Maltings in Devon is a case in point. Here we have a traditional floor maltings that was looking to use up some spare capacity to offer tours. What could be a better add-on to the fascinating exhibits but a bottled beer shop, so visitors could actually buy some of the finished product they'd seen started, with the malting process, on their tour?

A similar thought process was behind the addition of a beer shop to Hogs Back Brewery in Surrey, when it was founded in 1992. By stocking an excellent range of beers from all over the world, it gave people a reason to stop by the brewery and take an interest in what was going on, and added to the profitability of the company at the same time.

A trip to East Anglia reveals yet more enterprise, as shops like Barwells in Bury St Edmunds and Memorable Cheeses in Ipswich recognise the added colour a range of locally-brewed beers provides in their craft food shops. A similar service is provided in Scotland by Peckham's. At the other end of the scale is Binns, a department store in Darlington, where the beers section puts other such large establishments to shame.

There are also warehouse-style operations such as Beers of Europe in Norfolk, vast barns offering more beers than you can shake a bottle opener at, not to mention farm shops like Devon's Green Valley Cider and The Real Ale Shop at Wells-next-the-Sea in Norfolk. And retailers don't even need a permanent base to grab a piece of the action. Utobeer is a company that operates a market stall called The Beer Cage. Trading on Friday afternoons and Saturdays, the site, within Borough Market, near London Bridge, is a magnet for shoppers stocking up for the weekend.

There are plenty of independent retailers out there – from the traditional off-licence, to the pub with a 'jug and bottle', to the homely corner shop – but some refuse to see the light.

All it takes is the imagination to clear a couple of shelves of some of the more obvious brands and stock up with interesting bottled ales, and they'd have an instant point of difference from similar retailers. If they could see beyond big brewers' discounts and the tempting offers of free chiller cabinets, they'd be able to offer a product that genuinely brings people in. Let's face it, if you only stock the same old brands as everyone else, who's going to go out of their way to come to your shop, especially when the major multiples sell them so much cheaper?

The domination of the six-pack is going to be hard to challenge, but the growing number of beer shops proves that there is, nevertheless, real demand for bottled beers.

Buying and Storing Real Ale in a Bottle

Because it is a living, working product, real ale in a bottle needs a little extra attention before you drink it. Just like cask ale in a pub, it benefits from care and respect, but a few ground rules make it simple:

Buy fresh stock
Although bottle-conditioned beers sometimes mature beautifully in the bottle (particularly strong, malty ales), buy the freshest beer you can (check the best before dates) and, with only a few exceptions, drink it sooner, rather than later.

Keep it dark
Most beer bottles are dark brown. This is for a purpose. The opacity of the glass protects the beer from being 'sunstruck' – a chemical reaction caused by bright light that leads to unpleasant flavours and 'skunky' aromas. To help the bottles do their job, store them in as near a light-free zone as possible. Be particularly careful with clear- or green-glass bottles, which may look nice but are woefully inadequate in protecting beer.

Keep it cool
Low temperatures preserve beer. When it comes to serving temperatures, follow the advice on the label.

Keep it upright
Unless the bottle has a cork, in which case it is best stored lying down, to keep the cork moist, bottled beers should be stored vertically. If you do lay down a beer, remember to put it back upright a few days before drinking to give the sediment time to settle.

From Brewhouse to Bottle

BY THE TIME YOU FLIP THE CAP off your bottled beer, a lot of water has flowed under the bridge – most of it through the brewhouse on the way. But, even though water is the major component, there's far more to beer than Adam's ale.

The process of brewing begins with malt, often described as 'the soul of beer'. Malt is barley grain that has been partially germinated to help release sugars needed for the brewing process and then kilned to prevent further germination. The degree of kilning also dictates the character of the malt; the more 'baked' the malt, the darker the colour and the more roasted the taste. Some malts are toasted black for bitter, coffeeish flavours; others are just lightly crisped for a sweeter, nuttier taste. At the brewery, the malt is crushed and then combined in a vessel called a mash tun with hot water (known as 'liquor' in the trade), which has usually been treated to remove unsuitable chemicals or to emulate the brewing waters of towns like Burton upon Trent.

Hopping to it

After roughly an hour and a half's mashing and stirring, a thick, sweet liquid called wort is formed. This is run off from the mash tun and diverted into a boiler known as a copper. Here the wort is boiled up with hops which add bitterness and sometimes herbal, spicy, citrous or floral characters. Like malts, hops come in many varieties. Some are very bitter; others milder. Some make themselves known in the aroma; others are expressed in the taste. Hops also act as a preservative. They can be added as whole hop flowers or as compressed pellets. Some brewers use hop oils (concentrated extract), but these can be astringent. The hops are added at various stages of the boil and sometimes 'adjuncts' are introduced in the copper, or earlier in mash tun, too. These include sugars, which add to the fermentability of the wort, and maize, which helps produce a good head on the finished beer, but such additives are opposed by purists.

After an hour or two in the copper, the hops are strained out and the wort is run off and cooled, before being pumped into a fermenting vessel, where yeast is added ('pitched').

How real ale in a bottle is brewed

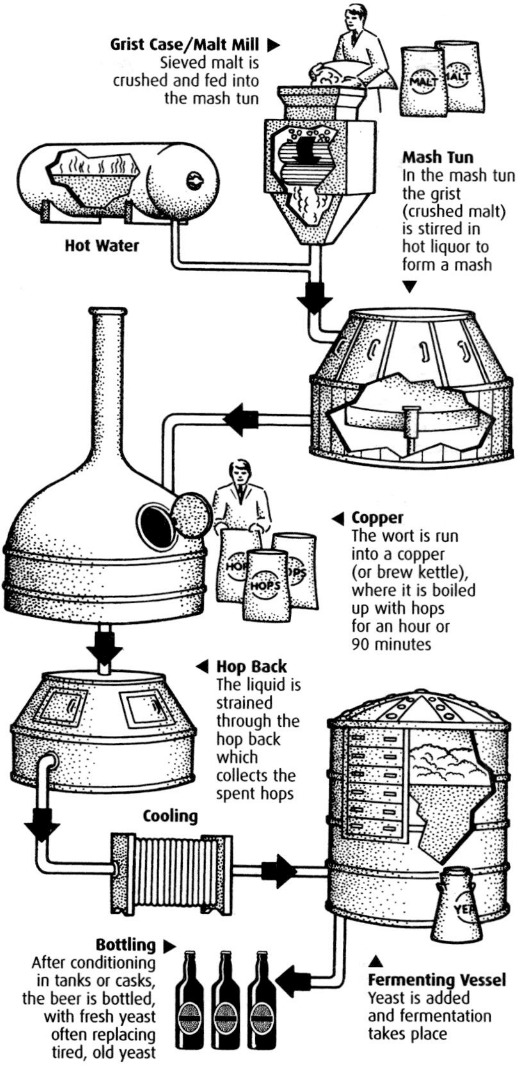

Grist Case/Malt Mill
Sieved malt is crushed and fed into the mash tun
MALT
MALT
Hot Water
Mash Tun
In the mash tun the grist (crushed malt) is stirred in hot liquor to form a mash
Copper
The wort is run into a copper (or brew kettle), where it is boiled up with hops for an hour or 90 minutes
HOPS
Hop Back
The liquid is strained through the hop back which collects the spent hops
Cooling
Fermenting Vessel
Yeast is added and fermentation takes place
Bottling
After conditioning in tanks or casks, the beer is bottled, with fresh yeast often replacing tired, old yeast

Yeast is a single-celled fungus that turns the sugars in the wort into alcohol and carbon dioxide (the gas that gives beer its natural effervescence). Each yeast, however, also has its own character which is harnessed and preserved by brewery chemists. Many breweries use the same yeasts for decades, ensuring that the brewery maintains its own individuality.

During the first few days of fermentation, the yeast works furiously with the wort, growing quickly and covering the top with a thick, bubbly layer of foam. Most is skimmed off, but some sinks into the brew and continues to work, eating up the sugars and generating more carbon dioxide and alcohol. Lager beers are known as 'bottom fermenting', because the yeast they use sinks to the bottom of the wort, rather than lying on the top. A few days later, this 'primary fermentation' is deemed over and bottle-conditioned beers and other, 'processed' bottled beers go their separate ways.

Parting of the ways

Processed, or 'bright', beers are chilled, filtered and pasteurised, killing off and removing any yeast still in the brew. They are then put into bottles and carbonated. Some of these beers are given time at the brewery beforehand to mature. Other breweries follow a halfway-house system whereby the beer is sterile filtered to remove the yeast, but is not pasteurised. Such beers, strictly speaking, do not condition in the bottle and have a fairly short shelf-life, but they do have a fresher taste than heavily pasteurised beers.

For bottle-conditioned beers, however, the next stage varies from brewery to brewery. Some adopt the simplest form of bottle conditioning, siphoning the beer from a cask or tank into the bottle, yeast and all. This can be a rather hit and miss affair, as not enough yeast may get into the bottle to ensure a good secondary fermentation and the beer may be rather flat when opened. Other breweries take greater pains to ensure their beers have the right level of fizz. They fine or filter out the tired old yeast and replace it with fresh yeast, which may be a special strain that works well in bottles. The technically precise check the yeast and fermentable sugar levels to guarantee that the right amounts are present.

Some brewers 'kräusen' the beer ready for bottling. This involves adding some partially fermented wort to the beer to give the yeast new sugars to react with. Others prime the beer, using sugar solutions for the same purpose. Once capped and labelled, bottles are often warm-conditioned at the brewery for a few weeks before going on sale, to ensure that the secondary fermentation gets off to a good start.

The Bad Bottled Beer Guide

If you want boring consistency, choose a pasteurised beer (but look out for the wet paper or cardboard notes that all too often indicate that pasteurised beer has become oxidised). If, on the other hand, you want the ultimate bottled beer experience, choose a bottle-conditioned beer.

However, by definition, real ale in a bottle is a living product and part of the trade off for the ripe, deep, fresh flavours is the fact that sometimes things can go wrong. Most often this is a result of lack of care at the brewery or during bottling. The most successful bottle conditioners have learned that absolute sterility in the brewhouse is paramount, to avoid unwanted bacteria turning the beer sour. These bacteria may not have much effect in a cask beer, which is drunk within a month or so of leaving the brewery, but left to their own devices in a bottle for several months, they can cause havoc. When this is the case, it is usually obvious from the first sniff and you won't feel inclined to take even a sip!

Scrupulous bottlers ensure that any yeast in the bottle is clean and pure and they bottle under the most rigid circumstances. Sterile filtration is the only option for some brewers, who want to ensure their beers have a long shelf-life, as this takes out even the tiniest bits of bacteria and infected yeast. By re-seeding the beer with fresh yeast before bottling, they still manage to ensure a good, reliable secondary fermentation in the bottle.

Keeping out damaging oxygen is another issue. Although the yeast can eat up some oxygen that has entered the beer (something that is not possible with filtered, pasteurised beers), some brewers go a step further and seal their bottles with oxygen-eating caps. These look like standard crowns but have a special internal layer that is activated when moist and contains granules that soak up excess oxygen. When they cost only 0.2p each more than standard caps, it makes you wonder why more brewers don't use them.

Sometimes, however, the bottler's work is all in vain as failure to look after the bottles somewhere in the supply chain (or even in your own larder) can lead to disappointment. That said, there shouldn't be too much concern if the beer is hazy in the glass. A characteristic of real ale in a bottle is that it contains a sediment. The sediment is mostly comprised of yeast and natural proteins and is certainly not harmful.

Observe the golden rules – keep bottles upright, cool and away from the glare of bright lights – and you'll be well on your way to appreciating the joy of good bottled beer.

How the Guide Is Organised

THE *GOOD BOTTLED BEER GUIDE* contains details of all known bottle-conditioned beers being brewed in the UK at the time of going to press. The beers are listed by brewery (which is briefly described), and within each brewery beers are listed in increasing order of strength. For each beer the following information is given: alcohol by volume percentage (ABV – the beer's strength), bottle size and ingredients. Suggested serving temperatures have been simplified to 'cold', 'cool' and 'room temperature', as gauging the precise temperature of a beer is always difficult. Cool is estimated to be around 12°C, or the correct temperature for cask ale in a pub.

Beers featured in this book are mostly sold locally, through farmers' markets, small grocers, craft shops and delicatessens. Some breweries also sell direct to the public, but this may be by the case only, and some offer a mail order service, which is mentioned if relevant. Otherwise beers can be obtained through specialist off-licences or mail order companies (see the Beer Shops section at the back of the book). If a beer has a listing with a major retailer (supermarket or off-licence chain), this is indicated. However, where beers are actually sold is subject to change, so it is suggested that readers contact the breweries for up-to-date details of retailers.

The tasting notes are purely the views of the author. Because bottle-conditioned beers are likely to change character during their shelf life, these notes are therefore offered only as a basic guide.

Acknowledgements

Much appreciation is offered to numerous people for their assistance in the compilation of this book. These include CAMRA's brewery liaison officers, brewers who kindly forwarded details of their beers and sample bottles, CAMRA's Research Manager, Iain Loe, and beer importers James Clay and Pierhead Purchasing (for help with beers from overseas).

Brewers who would like to make sure their beers are featured in the next edition are invited to contact the author, Jeff Evans, via CAMRA at: 230 Hatfield Road, St Albans, Hertfordshire AL1 4LW (e-mail: camra@camra.org.uk).

ALEWIFE

Alewife Brewery, Starston, Harleston, Norfolk IP20 9NN.
Tel. (01379) 855267
E-mail: alewifebrewery@yahoo.co.uk
Website: www.alewifebrewery.co.uk
Mail order service

This tiny brewery was set up by Jane Taylor in 2000 after encouragement from friends who admired her home brewing skills. She named the brewery – based in a little village off the A143 in Norfolk – after the historic alewife, a woman brewer who in centuries past produced beer at home as part of her household duties and placed a broom by the gate to show when her ale was ready. The broom now forms part of the brewery's logo. Jane seldom brews draught beer, because of the weight of casks, but focuses instead on bottles and runs a mail order service from her website. The malts used in her beers are organically produced, although in some cases Jane has been using instead traceable malt grown at a Norfolk farm (bottle labels show which malt has been employed).

Harvest Ale

■ **ABV 4.5%** ■ **BOTTLE SIZE 500 ml** ■ **SERVE cool**
■ **INGREDIENTS Pale malt/crystal malt/Challenger hops**

This was Jane's first commercial beer and it remains her most popular. She bottles it direct from a cask or the conditioning tank, like her other beers.

Dark Skies Stout

■ **ABV 4.6%** ■ **BOTTLE SIZE 500 ml** ■ **SERVE cool**
■ **INGREDIENTS Pale malt/chocolate malt/Styrian Golding hops**

A stout first produced in early 2001. It makes a perfect match for curries and other spicy food, according to Jane.

Festival Ale

■ **ABV 6.5%** ■ **BOTTLE SIZE 500 ml** ■ **SERVE cool**
■ **INGREDIENTS Pale malt/chocolate malt/roasted barley/Golding hops**

Originally a celebration beer for the new millennium, Festival Ale, says Jane, makes a great accompaniment for a slice of rich fruit cake. The beer is matured for several months before bottling.

Hunters Moon

■ ABV 6.8% ■ BOTTLE SIZE 500 ml ■ SERVE cool
■ INGREDIENTS Pale malt/crystal malt/hops undeclared
Brewed only for special occasions, this complex, potent brew incorporates a mix of English hops.

Tasting Notes

A complex ruby ale with a creamy, malty nose laced with a hint of bubblegum. Dark malt and a sharp, raspberry fruitiness feature in the mouth, with fruit and chocolate in the finish.

ANGLO DUTCH

The Anglo Dutch Brewery, Unit 12, Saville Bridge Mills, Mill Street East, Dewsbury, West Yorkshire WF12 6QQ.
Tel. (01924) 457772
Website: www.anglo-dutch-brewery.co.uk
Brewery founded in 2000 by Mike Field (Anglo) and Paul Klos (Dutch), using brewkit from the Rat & Ratchet brew pub in Huddersfield and based in a former dye house. The beers are bottled and marketed by Clarke's Organic (see separate entry).

Kletswater

■ ABV 4% ■ BOTTLE SIZE 500 ml ■ SERVE cool
■ INGREDIENTS Maris Otter pale malt/crystal malt/wheat malt/Pilgrim and First Gold hops
The Dutch word 'klet' means to waffle, to talk endlessly, so this is, effectively, 'waffle water'.

Tasting Notes

Pale gold in colour, with light malt and gently perfumed hop in the nose. Tangy, perfumed hop dominates the otherwise sweet taste, before a dry, hoppy aftertaste.

Tabatha

■ ABV 6% ■ BOTTLE SIZE 500 ml ■ SERVE cool
■ INGREDIENTS Lager malt/Pilgrim, First Gold and Fuggle hops/coriander
A strong golden, Belgian-style ale, named after Mike Field's cat. A little coriander added into the copper along with the Fuggle late hops adds a touch of spice.

Tasting Notes

Another pale golden beer with a malty aroma and taste, backed with some sweetness and a light hop tang. Gently warming, bittersweet, drying, malty finish.

B&T

B&T Brewery Ltd., The Brewery, Shefford, Bedfordshire SG17 5DZ. Tel. (01462) 815080 Fax (01462) 850841
Mail order service

This Bedfordshire brewery was founded as Banks & Taylor in 1981 and rescued from receivership by new ownership in 1994, when the company name was shortened to B&T. Key brewery personnel were maintained to ensure consistency, and the name Banks & Taylor is still used on the bottle labels. Bottling takes place on site after one month's maturation in the cask. The beer is allowed to drop bright and then re-seeded with new yeast and primed with sugar.

Black Dragon Mild

- **ABV 4.3%** ▪ **BOTTLE SIZE 500 ml** ▪ **SERVE cool**
- **INGREDIENTS Mild ale malt/crystal malt/black malt/roasted barley/wheat malt/Golding hops**

Brewed initially as a cask beer for CAMRA's May Mild Month in 2001, and bottled for the first time that same year.

Tasting Notes

A near-black beer with dark malts leading in the aroma before a bittersweet, roasted malt and barley taste supported by fruity hop. Bitterness builds in the dry, roasted finish.

Dragonslayer

- **ABV 4.5%** ▪ **BOTTLE SIZE 500 ml** ▪ **SERVE cool**
- **INGREDIENTS Pearl pale malt/wheat malt/Challenger and Golding hops**

Based on the legend of St George, Dragonslayer was first brewed in cask form in 1992 and is a particularly suitable accompaniment for white meats and pasta dishes, say the brewers. The best before date is set at six months.

Tasting Notes

A straw-coloured ale with a spicy, fruit cocktail aroma. The bittersweet taste is malty and fruity, yet also crisp, with a little spicy hop and liquorice. Dry, spicy hop and malt finish.

Edwin Taylor's Extra Stout

- **ABV 4.5%** ▪ **BOTTLE SIZE 500 ml** ▪ **SERVE cool**
- **INGREDIENTS Pearl pale malt/brown malt/roasted barley/Challenger hops**

Named after the great-grandfather of brewery founder Martin Ayres, Edwin Taylor's Extra Stout has been on sale in cask form since 1991. This bottled version was launched in 1998 and is said to be ideal with oysters and strong meats like game. Before bottling, the beer is given a month longer to mature in cask than the other beers. A seven-month best before date is applied. The aforementioned Mr Taylor was, as the label grandly declares, involved in brewing in London in the 1890s. His great-grandson chuckles about the more modest reality of his profession – he was a drayman for Fremlins.

Tasting Notes

A near-black beer with a chocolatey and coffeeish aroma, preluding a nicely balanced taste of sweet malt, coffee, hop and roast bitterness. Lingering, dry, roast finish.

SOS

- **ABV 5%** ▪ **BOTTLE SIZE 500 ml** ▪ **SERVE cool**
- **INGREDIENTS Pearl pale malt/crystal malt/Golding and Fuggle hops**

B&T won the *Tesco Beer Challenge* in 2002 with a bottled version of its cask ale called SOS. The beer was brewed by B&T and bottled by Brakspear for its six-month exclusivity in Tesco, but the demise of the Henley brewery coincided with the end of the Tesco contract and this bottled beer is now bottled at B&T for sale in independent off-licences.

Old Bat

- **ABV 6%** ▪ **BOTTLE SIZE 500 ml** ▪ **SERVE cool**
- **INGREDIENTS Pearl pale malt/crystal malt/brown malt/Fuggle hops**

Originally known by the jokey name of 2XS (drink 2XS, get it?) when first appearing in cask in 1990, this strong bitter was renamed Old Bat when the first bottles appeared back in 1998. The best before date is set at ten months. Good with cheese, according to the brewers.

Tasting Notes

A chestnut-coloured strong ale with a very malty and fruity (bananas) aroma, backed by a little savoury yeastiness. The same banana notes come through in the taste, which is malty and sweet. The finish is sweetish, malty and fruity, but with a little bitterness for balance.

Black Old Bat

- **ABV 6.5%** ▪ **BOTTLE SIZE 500 ml** ▪ **SERVE cool**
- **INGREDIENTS Pearl pale malt/crystal malt/black malt/Fuggle hops**

This winter brew is described by B&T as a 'barley wine-type porter', which perhaps sums up its complexity. It was new in cask and bottle in 1998 and is another beer to try with strong meats and cheeses. A ten months' best before period is posted on the bottle.

BALLARD'S

Ballard's Brewery Ltd., The Old Sawmill, Nyewood, Rogate, Petersfield, Hampshire GU31 5HA.
Tel. (01730) 821301 Fax (01730) 821742
E-mail: info@ballardsbrewery.org.uk
Website: www.ballardsbrewery.org.uk
Mail order service

Founded in 1980 at Cumbers Farm, Trotton, Ballard's has been trading at Nyewood in West Sussex since 1988 and bottle conditioning for a number of years. Recently, it has been producing special beers for the British Museum, to tie-in with exhibitions. These have been sold in the museum's Digby Trout restaurant and cafeteria, as well as in the usual Ballard's outlets. All the beers are fined in a conditioning tank, sterile filtered and re-seeded with dried yeast before bottling. They carry a nine-month best before date, although the strongest beer should mature beautifully well beyond this time.

Best Bitter

- **ABV 4.2%** ▪ **BOTTLE SIZE 500 ml** ▪ **SERVE cool**
- **INGREDIENTS Pearl pale malt/crystal malt/Fuggle and Golding hops**

Ballard's first ever beer, and its consistent best seller, was only introduced in bottled form in 2001. One to drink with red meat and cheeses, according to brewery founder Carola Brown.

Tasting Notes

An amber beer with a malty, fruity nose. The taste is quite dry and bitter with a little malt sweetness to start and some ale-fruit character. Dry, bitter finish.

King's Table

- **ABV 4.2%** ▪ **BOTTLE SIZE 500 ml** ▪ **SERVE cool**
- **INGREDIENTS Pearl pale malt/torrefied wheat/Fuggle and Golding hops**

Known as Golden Bine in its draught form, King's Table is bottled specially for Historic Royal Palaces (Hampton Court, the Tower of London and Kensington Palace). The same beer has also appeared under different names for the British Museum's restaurant. A beer to savour with fish or spicy foods, perhaps.

Tasting Notes

A golden ale with a crisp, lemony, bittersweet character and a dry, hoppy, bitter finish.

Nyewood Gold

▪ABV 5% ▪BOTTLE SIZE 500 ml ▪SERVE cool
▪INGREDIENTS Pearl pale malt/Phoenix hops

It's amazing what you learn just by drinking beer. For instance, 'Nye', as in the brewery address and the name of this beer, is apparently a collective noun for a group of pheasants – which, of course, appear on the label. This beer was first brewed for the 1997 *Beauty of Hops* competition, where it took top honours in the category for Phoenix hops. The same draught beer then claimed the *Best Strong Bitter* prize at the *Champion Beer of Britain* contest in 1999. It was a logical progression to bottle it for the first time the same year. Ballard's recommends serving Nyewood Gold at a slightly lower temperature than its other beers and, again, perhaps enjoying a glass with a fish dish or a curry.

Tasting Notes

A golden ale with a soft malt and fruit nose before a bittersweet taste of malt, fruit and hop. Mellow, bittersweet, fruity finish, with soft malt lingering.

Wassail

▪ABV 6% ▪BOTTLE SIZE 500 ml ▪SERVE cool
▪INGREDIENTS Pearl pale malt/crystal malt/Fuggle and Golding hops

Wassail is a drinking salutation, translating as 'Be whole' from Old English. This winter warmer of the same name first appeared in cask in 1980, and in bottle in 1995, and is now produced every two months or so. The label shows Hengist, the 5th-century leader of the Jutes, toasting Vortigern, King of the Britons. Rowena, Hengist's daughter, who seduced Vortigern, is also depicted. The brewery suggests taking a glass or two with cheese, or with strong meats such as game.

Tasting Notes

A russet-coloured strong ale with a meaty, malt and fruit nose. Soft in the mouth, it tastes fruity, malty and alcoholic. The gently bitter, fruity, hoppy finish leaves a little tingle on the gums.

WMD

■ **ABV 9.4%** ■ **BOTTLE SIZE 275 ml** ■ **SERVE cool**
■ **INGREDIENTS Pearl pale malt/crystal malt/Fuggle and Golding hops**

WMD is the latest in the Ballard's series of 'Old Bounder' beers. The brewery has been producing these for 16 years now and, until recently, adopted the novel approach of matching the alcohol by volume percentage to the last two digits of the year for which the beer was brewed. Old Bounder itself appeared in 1988, at 8.8%, and the last beer to follow this pattern was Pleasure Domes, at 10%, in 2000. However, with duty so high on such strong beers, the brewery decided to move back to the year before the series began, producing Early Daze (8.7%) and then jumping ahead to Alchemist (9.2%), before moving onto Foxy (9.3%) and arriving at WMD at 9.4%. The first batch of each of these beers rolls out on the first Sunday in December (as part of a charity 'beer walk') and the brew is then repeated throughout the next 12 months. There is a draught version, too (available over Christmas), which is aged for at least two months before dispatch to the pub. Although each bottle carries a nine-month best before date, the beer is likely to remain drinkable for much longer. Enjoy it with game, beef or cheese, add a little to a Christmas pudding, or treat it like port, says Carola.

Tasting Notes

A red beer with a malty, fruity aroma. The silky, warming taste is sweet, malty and fruity, leaving a mouth-numbing, warming, creamy, malty finish with emerging bitterness.

BARTRAMS

Bartrams Brewery, Rougham Estate, Rougham, Bury St Edmunds, Suffolk IP30 9LZ. Tel. (01449) 737655
E-mail: marc@captainbill007.fsnet.co.uk

Marc Bartram set up his own brewery in an industrial unit in 1999 and was scheduled to move into new premises, on an old airfield, in 2004. An earlier Bartrams Brewery operated in Tonbridge, Kent, between 1894 and 1920. It was run by Captain Bill Bartram, whose image Marc wanted to use on his beer labels and pump clips. No photograph was found, however, so Marc grew a beard, became Captain Bill and now features on all his beers. Each beer is filtered and re-seeded with fresh yeast prior to bottling. Marc now hopes to gain Soil Association accreditation for the beers he brews using organic ingredients. As well as the numerous beers mentioned here,

Marc is also working on a series of beers based around the signs of the zodiac (all 4.2% but different styles). The bottles are mostly sold in East Anglian farmers' markets.

Marld

▪ABV 3.4% ▪BOTTLE SIZE 500 ml ▪SERVE cool
▪INGREDIENTS Mild ale malt/amber malt/roasted barley/flaked barley/Galena and Golding hops
Marc's dark ruby mild.

Tasting Notes
Spicy malt and a hint of chocolate in the aroma are followed by a malty taste, with a faint fruit note, before a lightly roasted, dry finish in which bitterness grows.

Rougham Ready

▪ABV 3.6% ▪BOTTLE SIZE 500 ml ▪SERVE cool
▪INGREDIENTS Pale malt/crystal malt/hops vary
A light beer, made from organic ingredients. The name is a pun on the brewery's new home.

Premier Bitter

▪ABV 3.7% ▪BOTTLE SIZE 500 ml ▪SERVE cool
▪INGREDIENTS Maris Otter pale malt/crystal malt/ chocolate malt/Challenger, Fuggle and Golding hops
Caricatures of PMs Thatcher and Churchill have featured on the pumpclips for the cask version of this ale, as did the contenders at the last General Election.

Little Green Man

▪ABV 3.8% ▪BOTTLE SIZE 500 ml ▪SERVE cool
▪INGREDIENTS Pale malt/First Gold hops/coriander
A more quaffable version of the 4% Green Man (see below), like its inspiration produced with organic ingredients.

Tasting Notes
A golden, bitter ale with the peppery, orangey notes of subtle coriander and hops throughout. Dry, bitter, spicy, hoppy finish.

Red Queen

▪ABV 3.9% ▪BOTTLE SIZE 500 ml ▪SERVE cool
▪INGREDIENTS Maris Otter pale malt/crystal malt/ chocolate malt/Challenger, Fuggle and Golding hops
A rich amber-coloured session ale.

Tasting Notes
Chocolate maltiness gives way to a little hop spice and citrous notes in the aroma, before balanced malt and bitterness combine in the taste, together with a clean, sweet, hoppy-citrous edge. Bitterness grows in the lightly fruity, hoppy finish.

Green Man

- **ABV 4%** ▪ **BOTTLE SIZE 500 ml** ▪ **SERVE cool**
- **INGREDIENTS Pale malt/First Gold hops/coriander**

A golden best bitter made with organic ingredients. Marc may change the organic components he uses slightly, depending on what becomes available in that form.

Tasting Notes
A fuller-bodied version of Little Green Man, with more malty sweetness in the taste. Sappy hops lose ground to a peachy/orangey fruitiness in the nose but re-emerge in the mouth. Dry, bitter, lightly fruity and spicy, hop finish.

Headway

- **ABV 4%** ▪ **BOTTLE SIZE 500 ml** ▪ **SERVE cool**
- **INGREDIENTS Pale malt/crystal malt/hops vary**

Headway is an organic charity beer, with 10p per bottle sold being donated to Headway, the brain injury association.

Pierrot

- **ABV 4%** ▪ **BOTTLE SIZE 500 ml** ▪ **SERVE cool**
- **INGREDIENTS Maris Otter pale malt/caramalt/Fuggle, Golding, Saaz and Tettnang hops**

An ale inspired by a visit Marc made to a Croatian brewery.

Tasting Notes
A golden ale with a complex, hoppy nose, hops and bitterness well balanced by malt in the taste, and plenty of body for its strength. Long, hoppy finish. A hint of bubblegum throughout adds a something of a Belgian ale character.

The Bee's Knees

- **ABV 4.2%** ▪ **BOTTLE SIZE 500 ml** ▪ **SERVE cool**
- **INGREDIENTS Maris Otter pale malt/carapils malt/ Challenger, Ahtanum and Fuggle hops/wildflower honey/coriander**

As for Pierrot above, a very pale-coloured malt forms the basis of the mash for this honey-flavoured beer.

Tasting Notes

An amber beer with a floral, honeyed, hoppy aroma. There's a honey softness throughout the taste, which is otherwise crisp and bitter, with good malt balance. Dry, bitter finish with the smoothness of honey.

Catherine Bartram's IPA

- **ABV 4.3%** ■ **BOTTLE SIZE 500 ml** ■ **SERVE cool**
- **INGREDIENTS Pale malt/First Gold and Fuggle hops**

One Catherine Bartram was apparently a survivor of the Siege of Lucknow (1857–8) and her diary helped paint a picture of what went on during the conflict. Her Indian connections inspired this IPA.

Tasting Notes

A golden ale with an initial malty aroma which soon gives way to light, fruity hop. Tangy hop leads over malt in the taste and dominates the dry and increasingly bitter aftertaste.

Jester Quick One

- **ABV 4.4%** ■ **BOTTLE SIZE 500 ml** ■ **SERVE cool**
- **INGREDIENTS Maris Otter pale malt/crystal malt/ chocolate malt/Ahtanum hops**

A sweet, reddish bitter using American hops. Its name comes from the 'signature' (a drawn jester) used by one of the local artists who produce Marc's pumpclips.

Coal Porter

- **ABV 4.5%** ■ **BOTTLE SIZE 500 ml** ■ **SERVE cool**
- **INGREDIENTS Pale malt/crystal malt/barley extract/ hops vary**

Another organic beer, originally a one-off for a beer festival.

Stingo!

- **ABV 4.5%** ■ **BOTTLE SIZE 500 ml** ■ **SERVE cool**
- **INGREDIENTS Pale malt/Hallertau and Perle hops/ honey/coriander**

Another honey beer, made using organic ingredients. A Norwich Beer Festival winner in its cask version.

Tasting Notes

A sweetish and fruity bitter with a hoppy nose and a floral honey note on the swallow. Light honey softens the mostly bitter aftertaste.

Captain Bill Bartram's Best Bitter

▪ ABV 4.8% ▪ BOTTLE SIZE 500 ml ▪ SERVE cool
▪ INGREDIENTS Maris Otter pale malt/crystal malt/Fuggle and Golding hops

A tawny beer named after the man who inspired the brewery.

Tasting Notes

Red berry fruits lead in the nose, edging out lightly toasted, slightly treacly malt. Fruit, malt and bitterness are all to the fore on the palate and nicely balanced. Toasted malt, hops, lingering fruit and just a hint of almond contribute to the finish.

The Captain's Cherry Stout

▪ ABV 4.8% ▪ BOTTLE SIZE 500 ml ▪ SERVE cool
▪ INGREDIENTS Mild ale malt/crystal malt/black malt/ chocolate malt/smoked malt/Galena, Fuggle and Golding hops/cherries

A multi-award-winning ruby beer, based on the stout below but flavoured with cherries. Marc is obviously pleased with the way in which he processes the fruit and includes it in this beer and the Damson Stout mentioned below, but he declines to reveal his secret.

Tasting Notes

Cherry fruit leads over dark, lightly smoky malt in the aroma. The flavours of Captain's Stout are all here, too, but with light cherry adding a touch more sweetness. Subtle cherry lingers in the aftertaste, which is bittersweet, smoky and marked by roasted malt.

Captain's Stout

▪ ABV 4.8% ▪ BOTTLE SIZE 500 ml ▪ SERVE cool
▪ INGREDIENTS Mild ale malt/crystal malt/black malt/ chocolate malt/smoked malt/Galena, Fuggle and Golding hops

A ruby-coloured stout made using Bavarian smoked malt and (in part) American hops.

Tasting Notes

Biscuity dark malt leads in the lightly smoky aroma with just a hint of vanilla. There is plenty of roasted malt character in the taste, with coffee notes and a whiff of smoke, but a light, sweet fruitiness ensures it is neither too bitter nor heavy. Bittersweet, roasted malt and a lingering smokiness run into the aftertaste.

Damson Stout

■ ABV 4.8% ■ BOTTLE SIZE 500 ml ■ SERVE cool
■ INGREDIENTS Mild ale malt/crystal malt/black malt/ chocolate malt/smoked malt/Galena, Fuggle and Golding hops/damsons

A variation on the Cherry Stout featured earlier, incorporating different fruit.

Beer Elsie Bub

■ ABV 4.8% ■ BOTTLE SIZE 500 ml ■ SERVE cool
■ INGREDIENTS Maris Otter and Halcyon pale malt/amber malt/torrefied wheat/Challenger, Golding and Fuggle hops/wildflower honey/coriander

A strong honey beer originally brewed for a pagan wedding ceremony and now produced for other pagan festivals, including Hallowe'en. The back label features an amusing, not entirely (if at all) truthful, account of how the beer got its name.

Tasting Notes

A dark golden ale with a mellow honey note to the citrous, floral nose. Slightly earthy bitterness leads over spicy orange in the mouth, with more honey emerging softly on the swallow to linger lightly in the bitter, hoppy aftertaste.

Suffolk 'n' Strong

■ ABV 5% ■ BOTTLE SIZE 500 ml ■ SERVE cool
■ INGREDIENTS Pale malt/crystal malt/hops vary

Another new, organic strong ale.

Xmas Holly Daze

■ ABV 5% ■ BOTTLE SIZE 500 ml ■ SERVE cool
■ INGREDIENTS Maris Otter pale malt/crystal malt/ Golding and Fuggle hops

A light-coloured bitter only on sale at Christmas.

New Year Daze

■ ABV 5.2% ■ BOTTLE SIZE 500 ml ■ SERVE cool
■ INGREDIENTS Maris Otter pale malt/crystal malt/ roasted malt/Golding and Fuggle hops

A deep reddish bitter made available only over the Christmas and New Year period.

Mother in Law's Tongue Tied

▪ABV 9% ▪BOTTLE SIZE 500 ml ▪SERVE cool
▪INGREDIENTS Maris Otter pale malt/Galena, Tettnang and Hallertau hops

Brewed to celebrate Marc's mother-in-law's 90th birthday. He's now looking forward to her century.

BARUM

Barum Brewery Ltd., Pilton, Barnstaple, Devon EX31 1PD. Tel. (01271) 329994 Fax (01271) 321590
E-mail: info@barumbrewery.co.uk
Website: www.barumbrewery.co.uk

Barum was founded in 1996 with the purchase of the Combe Brewery in Ilfracombe. Relocated to near Barnstaple, it now produces a wide range of beers. The four bottle-conditioned beers are bottled direct from casks by Keltek Brewery.

Original

▪ABV 4.4% ▪BOTTLE SIZE 500 ml ▪SERVE cool
▪INGREDIENTS Pipkin pale malt/crystal malt/roasted malt/Fuggle, Challenger and Golding hops

Barum's first ever beer: a dark golden ale.

Breakfast

▪ABV 5% ▪BOTTLE SIZE 500 ml ▪SERVE cool
▪INGREDIENTS Pipkin pale malt/roasted malt/wheat malt/Challenger and Golding hops

Barum Brewery's enigmatic slogan is: 'Beer's not just for breakfast anymore', so they just had to call one of their beers Breakfast. The label shows a cartoon chef frying up a pint.

Tasting Notes

A heavily-hopped amber ale with a fruity aroma, a taste full of tangy, fruity hops and a bitter finish with the same characteristics.

Challenger

▪ABV 5.6% ▪BOTTLE SIZE 500 ml ▪SERVE cool
▪INGREDIENTS Pipkin pale malt/roasted malt/wheat malt/Challenger hops

As its name suggests, this is a single-varietal hop beer, focusing on Challenger hops.

Barnstablasta

- **ABV 6.6%** ▪ **BOTTLE SIZE 500 ml** ▪ **SERVE cool**
- **INGREDIENTS Pipkin pale malt/crystal malt/chocolate malt/wheat malt/Challenger and Golding hops**

A winter beer, as implied by the Santa Claus on the label who is about to be flattened by a falling grand piano.

Tasting Notes

A ruby/brown beer with an aroma of light chocolate, malt and fruit. The big, sweet taste features tangy, fruity hops, with a strong hint of roasted malt in the fruity hop finish.

BATEMAN

George Bateman and Son Ltd., Salem Bridge Brewery, Wainfleet, Lincolnshire PE24 4JE.
Tel. (01754) 880317 Fax (01754) 880939
E-mail: enquiries@bateman.co.uk
Website: www.bateman.co.uk

The Bateman brewery was established by the current chairman's grandfather back in 1874. Boardroom turbulence led to worries over its future in the 1980s, but the family retained control and secured the company's independence in a famous financial battle. It remains one of the UK's most revered breweries. All Bateman's own bottled beers are filtered, but it has occasionally turned out a bottle-conditioned beer for other parties, such as the ale for Booths listed below, which is bottled by Integrated Bottling Solutions (the business formerly run by Wessex Craft Brewers).

Pour with Care

- **ABV 4.5%** ▪ **BOTTLE SIZE 500 ml** ▪ **SERVE cool**
- **INGREDIENTS Maris Otter pale malt/crystal malt/wheat malt/Challenger and Golding hops**

Booths is a family-owned grocery chain based in North-West England, founded more than 150 years ago. Its 25 stores stock well over 100 bottled ales, many of them bottle conditioned, which earned the group the British Guild of Beer Writers' *Beer Supermarket of the Year* award in 2000. This 'own label' beer – launched in 2001 – is the brainchild of beer buyer Dave Smith, who hopes its descriptive title will encourage supermarket shoppers to try bottle-conditioned beer and understand more about serving this style of beer. At the bottlers, excess yeast is sedimented out in conditioning tanks before packaging, with no further yeast added.

Tasting Notes
A red-amber ale with a malty, banana-toffee nose. The taste is slightly salty, with loads of banana and toffee-malt flavour and a good, bitter balance. Drying, bitter, banana-malt finish.
Major stockist Booths

BATH

Bath Ales Brewery Ltd., Units 3–7, Caxton Business Park, Tower Road North, Warmley, Bristol BS30 8VV.
Tel. (0117) 952 7580 Fax (0117) 952 7590
E-mail: hare@bathales.co.uk
Website: www.bathales.com

Founded in 1995 near Wincanton and moved to a new 15-barrel site in 1999, Bath Ales was forced to relocate yet again in 2004, as business continued to expand. The company now runs a handful of excellent pubs in the Bath and Bristol areas and produces two bottle-conditioned beers (brewed and bottled under contract by Hepworth & Co. in Horsham).

Gem

- **ABV 4.8%** ▪ **BOTTLE SIZE 500 ml** ▪ **SERVE cool**
- **INGREDIENTS Maris Otter pale malt/Challenger and East Kent Golding hops**

Conceived as a beer for sale to restaurants and the hotel trade, Gem is considerably stronger than the 4.1% cask beer that bears the same name. The label carries the Bath Ales emblem of a hare, drawn in the style of the chalk figures that adorn hillsides in the West Country. Challenger hops are used in the brew kettle, with Goldings introduced later for aroma.

Tasting Notes
A dark amber bitter with malt and fruit in the nose (strawberry, pineapple and a little pear drop). The same strawberry fruitiness features in the taste, balanced with malt sweetness and hoppy bitterness. Dry, bittersweet hop finish.

Festivity

- **ABV 5%** ▪ **BOTTLE SIZE 500 ml** ▪ **SERVE cool**
- **INGREDIENTS Maris Otter pale malt/crystal malt/chocolate malt/roasted barley/wheat malt/Challenger and Bramling Cross hops**

A gold medallist as a cask beer in CAMRA's *Champion Winter Beer of Britain* contest in 2002, and runner-up overall, Festivity was launched in bottle in summer 2003 to draw attention to Bristol's (ultimately unsuccessful) bid to become *European City of Culture*. Likely to be only a seasonal, short-run bottling from now on.

Tasting Notes

A deep ruby ale with sweet coffee in the nose. The taste is also sweetish, with coffee-flavoured malt balanced by a bitter edge and a hint of cherry. There's a little chocolate on the swallow before a dry, bitter finish with a trace of cherry.

BEARTOWN

Beartown Brewery Ltd., Bromley House, Spindle Street, Congleton, Cheshire CW12 1QN.
Tel. (01260) 299964 Fax (01260) 278895
Website: www.beartownbrewery.co.uk

The town of Congleton received a charter in 1272 and at the time the three highest officials in the borough were the mayor, the ale taster and the bear warden (charged with procuring fighting bears for fairs). When this brewery was set up in 1994, the last two positions were combined to create a bear beer theme for all its brews, and to reflect Congleton's nickname of 'Beartown'. Now, following a brewery move, four regular bottled beers have been introduced. Each is racked bright into a cask, kräusened and filled on site using a four-head bottling machine. Other Beartown beers may be bottled from time to time.

Kodiak Gold

- **ABV 4% ■ BOTTLE SIZE 500 ml ■ SERVE cool**
- **INGREDIENTS Maris Otter pale malt/wheat malt/ Challenger and Northdown hops**

A bitter named after the giant grizzly bear from Kodiak Island. First brewed for cask in 1995.

Tasting Notes

A straw-coloured ale with a hoppy, lemony nose. The taste is clean, hoppy and lemon-sharp, with light malty sweetness in support. Dry, pleasantly bitter, hoppy finish.

Bearskinful

- **ABV 4.2% ■ BOTTLE SIZE 500 ml ■ SERVE cool**
- **INGREDIENTS Maris Otter pale malt/crystal malt/wheat malt/Challenger hops**

A tawny beer, the first ever beer from Beartown, although initially sold under a couple of other names.

Polar Eclipse

- **ABV 4.8%** ▪ **BOTTLE SIZE 500 ml** ▪ **SERVE cool**
- **INGREDIENTS Maris Otter pale malt/crystal malt/ chocolate malt/wheat malt/oat malt/Challenger and Northdown hops**

An oatmeal stout, introduced in autumn 1995.

Black Bear

- **ABV 5%** ▪ **BOTTLE SIZE 500 ml** ▪ **SERVE cool**
- **INGREDIENTS Maris Otter pale malt/crystal malt/ chocolate malt/wheat malt/Challenger and Northdown hops**

A ruby-coloured strong mild. The cask version was bronze medallist in its category at CAMRA's *Champion Winter Beer of Britain* competition in 2002. Originally created as a special brew for the Macclesfield Beer Festival in 1999.

Tasting Notes

A red beer with a chocolatey, malty aroma, a malty, nutty, chocolatey taste, with good hop-bitter balance, and a dry, bitter, roasted grain finish.

BELVOIR

Belvoir Brewery Ltd., Woodhill, Nottingham Lane, Old Dalby, Leicestershire LE14 3LX.
Tel./Fax (01664) 823455
E-mail: sales@belvoir-brewery.go-plus.net
Website: www.belvoirbrewery.co.uk

Established in 1995 by Colin Brown, who used to brew with both Shipstone's and Theakston, this brewery sits in the Vale of Belvoir (pronounced 'beaver'). As well as three regular cask ales, four bottled beers are now in production, each being filtered and re-seeded with fresh yeast prior to bottling on site (although some bottling may be contracted out in the near future).

Star Bitter

- **ABV 3.9%** ▪ **BOTTLE SIZE 500 ml** ▪ **SERVE cool**
- **INGREDIENTS Maris Otter pale malt/crystal malt/ chocolate malt/torrefied wheat/Target, Golding and Progress hops**

A new beer, introduced in spring 2004, the star in the name alluding to the emblem of Colin's former employer, the much-missed Shipstone's Brewery in Nottingham. Also in cask.

Tasting Notes
A dark golden beer with a hoppy nose and taste, and a dry, hoppy, bitter finish.

Beaver Bitter

- **ABV 4.3%** ■ **BOTTLE SIZE 500 ml** ■ **SERVE cool**
- **INGREDIENTS Maris Otter pale malt/crystal malt/ chocolate malt/Challenger, Progress, Bramling Cross and Golding hops**

One of the brewery's first ever cask beers, making a play on the often-mispronounced name of the brewery.

Peacock's Glory

- **ABV 4.7%** ■ **BOTTLE SIZE 500 ml** ■ **SERVE cool**
- **INGREDIENTS Maris Otter pale malt/crystal malt/ Target, Progress and Golding hops**

The agricultural pastures of the Vale of Belvoir are overlooked by the battlemented Belvoir Castle (seat of the Duke of Rutland) and there the grounds are home to a fine collection of peacocks. Their splendour is echoed in the name of this brew which was launched as a cask beer back in 1997.

Tasting Notes
A golden ale with a sherbety, hoppy aroma. Robust and full-bodied to taste, it features lots of bitter hops but also good malty balance. Dry, bitter, hoppy aftertaste.

Old Dalby

- **ABV 5.1%** ■ **BOTTLE SIZE 500 ml** ■ **SERVE cool**
- **INGREDIENTS Maris Otter pale malt/crystal malt/ chocolate malt/Challenger, Progress, Bramling Cross and Golding hops**

Old Dalby is the name of the village where Belvoir Brewery has set up home. Another beer first introduced in cask in 1997, this is generally only made available in winter.

BLACK ISLE

Black Isle Brewery, Old Allangrange, Munlochy, Highland IV8 8NZ. Tel. (01463) 811871 Fax (01463) 811875
E-mail: greatbeers@blackislebrewery.com
Website: www.blackislebrewery.com
Mail order service

Converted farm buildings in the Highlands of Scotland provide a home for Black Isle Brewery, which was set up 1998. The Black Isle itself is not an island but a peninsula across the Moray Firth from Inverness, with an ancient history of barley production and a spectacular coastline. The brewery runs a busy mail order service, selling the following organic (Soil Association-accredited) beers by the case and also two other bottled beers (filtered but not pasteurised). The beers are also sanctioned by the Vegetarian Society. The ones listed below are kräusened in a conditioning tank prior to bottling. Best before dates are marked at 12 months after filling. Challenger hops have replaced Hersbrucker in some of the brews in the past year.

Organic Blonde

- **ABV 4.5%** ▪ **BOTTLE SIZE 500 ml** ▪ **SERVE cool**
- **INGREDIENTS Pale malt/wheat malt/Challenger and Hallertau hops**

Previous sold as both a cask ale and a filtered bottled ale, this full-bodied beer goes very well with smoked trout, pasta dishes and also raspberries, according to brewer David Gladwin.

Tasting Notes

A golden brew featuring spicy hops and slowly emerging apricot fruit in the aroma. The fruit increases on the palate, with apricot and lemon notes shining through against a backdrop of bittersweet, spicy hops. Dry, bitter fruit features in the aftertaste.

Organic Porter

- **ABV 4.5%** ▪ **BOTTLE SIZE 500 ml** ▪ **SERVE cool**
- **INGREDIENTS Pale malt/crystal malt/pale chocolate malt/wheat malt/oat malt/Challenger and Golding hops**

A Salisbury Beer Festival champion in 2002 under its original cask name of Wagtail, this dark brew is suggested by David as a perfect match for seafood like oysters, crab and smoked salmon, and perhaps a crumbly old cheese like farmhouse Cheddar.

Tasting Notes

A dark ruby porter with a mellow, creamy, coffeeish, chocolatey nose. The taste is also creamy and coffeeish but bittersweet, with a very restrained hoppy fruitiness behind. Bitter, roasted finish.

Organic Scotch Ale

- **ABV 4.5%** ▪ **BOTTLE SIZE 500 ml** ▪ **SERVE cool**
- **INGREDIENTS Pale malt/crystal malt/peat-smoked malt/wheat malt/Challenger and Golding hops/bog myrtle**

A beer – recommends the brewer – to savour with haggis, black pudding or even apple strüdel! Apart from peat-smoked malt (more familiar to whisky drinkers), the unusual ingredient in Scotch Ale is bog myrtle. It may sound like the moaning ghost who hides in a lavatory in the Harry Potter books, but this is an aromatic marshland shrub (also known as sweet gale) that was often used to season beer before the arrival of hops some 500 years ago. First produced in 2002.

Tasting Notes

A red ale with a big malty nose backed up with a hint of mint toffee, spice and smoke. The taste is spicy, smoky and malty with a cool 'peppermint' note. Toasted malt grows in the finish with lingering, cool spice, smoke and bitterness.

Organic Wheat Beer

- **ABV 4.5%** ▪ **BOTTLE SIZE 500 ml** ▪ **SERVE cool**
- **INGREDIENTS Pale malt/wheat malt/Hallertau hops/coriander/orange peel/lemon peel**

Brewed initially in 2001 as a cask beer called Hibernator, this Belgian-style wheat beer was runner-up in 2002's SIBA *Wheat Beer Challenge*. David Gladwin suggests that it should served with fresh Scottish mussels or Black Isle raspberries.

Tasting Notes

A hazy, golden beer with a lemon, orange and spice aroma. The taste is peppery, spicy and full of bitter citrous character; dry, slightly perfumed, bittersweet, orange and lemon finish.

Where to Buy Real Ale in a Bottle

Beers in this book are generally sold locally, through farmers' markets, small grocers, craft shops, delicatessens and some restaurants. Some breweries also sell direct to the public, but this may be by the case only, and some offer a mail order service, which is mentioned in each entry, if relevant. Otherwise beers can be obtained through specialist off-licences or mail order companies, many of which are listed in the Beer Shops section at the back of the book. If a beer has a listing with a major supermarket or off-licence chain, this is indicated at the end of the entry.

BLACKAWTON

Blackawton Brewery, Unit 7, Peninsula Park, Channon Road, Saltash, Cornwall PL12 6LX.
Tel. (01752) 848777 Fax (01752) 848999
E-mail: blackawtonbrewery@talk21.com

Blackawton Brewery was set up in 1977, one of the first of the new wave of microbreweries founded after the early successes of CAMRA. Until 2001 it was the longest established brewery in Devon, but then it was sold and the new owners moved it across the River Tamar to Cornwall. The brewery moved yet again in 2003, but this time just around the corner to larger premises. The beers are bottled for Blackawton by Keltek Brewery. A third bottle, Dragonheart (5%), based on a cask ginger beer, may be introduced in the future.

Winter Fuel

- **ABV 5%** ▪ **BOTTLE SIZE 500 ml** ▪ **SERVE cool**
- **INGREDIENTS Pale malt/crystal malt/chocolate malt/ torrefied wheat/Progress and Golding hops/mace/ ginger/lemons**

The label of this seasonal warmer declares that it conceals a 'secret wintery twist'. Now the secret is out: brewer Steve Brooks adds whole lemons to the copper for a citrous edge and seasons the beer not only with hops but with Christmas spices, too.

Tasting Notes
A tawny ale with an aroma of citrus and Christmas cake spices. The taste is malty but spicy, dry and bitter, with a ginger warmth poking through. Bitter, Christmas spice finish with lingering lemon.

Head Strong

- **ABV 5.2%** ▪ **BOTTLE SIZE 500 ml** ▪ **SERVE cool**
- **INGREDIENTS Pale malt/crystal malt/wheat malt/ Progress, Challenger and Styrian Golding hops**

Head Strong is one of the beers Steve inherited when the company was purchased and it dates right back to the brewery's formative days (first mentioned in the *Good Beer Guide*'s 1979 edition). Steve, however, has personalised the beer a little by adding Challenger hops.

Tasting Notes
A golden beer with a piney, citrous aroma. Spicy, citrous, piney hops dominate the taste until toasted malt emerges. Bitter, toasted malt finish.

BLENCOWE

Blencowe Brewing Co., c/o Exeter Arms, Barrowden, Rutland LE15 8EQ. Tel. (01572) 747247
E-mail: info@exeterarms.com
Website: www.exeterarms.com

Blencowe Brewing was established in 1998 in a barn adjacent to the Exeter Arms pub, initially just to supply that outlet with beers from its tiny, two-barrel kit. Some expansion has taken place since and other pubs now also sell the beer. Bottling began on site in October 2003, with beers matured, filtered, re-seeded and kräusened prior to filling in small batches.

Beach Boys

■ ABV 3.8% ■ BOTTLE SIZE 500 ml ■ SERVE cool
■ INGREDIENTS Maris Otter pale malt/caramalt/wheat malt/Challenger, Fuggle and Styrian Golding hops

Intended merely as a session beer for summer 1999, Beach Boys is now a regular Blencowe cask brew.

Bevin Boys

■ ABV 4.5% ■ BOTTLE SIZE 500 ml ■ SERVE cool
■ INGREDIENTS Maris Otter pale malt/crystal malt/caramalt/wheat malt/Bramling Cross and Cascade hops

An autumn/winter cask beer, first produced in 2002 and recalling in its name the World War II mine workers and their connection with the Minister of Labour of the time, Ernest Bevin.

Danny Boys

■ ABV 4.6% ■ BOTTLE SIZE 500 ml ■ SERVE cool
■ INGREDIENTS Maris Otter pale malt/crystal malt/Munich malt/caramalt/chocolate malt/roasted barley/Bramling Cross and Cascade hops/liquorice/black treacle

Another autumn/winter draught beer, this time described as a porter, with some unusual flavourings.

Tasting Notes

A ruby-coloured beer with a contrasting cream collar of foam. The appealing aroma has a pineapple fruitiness alongside roasted grain and the taste is just as unusual, with nutty, roasted bitterness taking over after a sweet, fruity start. Dry, bitter, roasted grain finish.

Boys with Attitude

■ ABV 6% ■ BOTTLE SIZE 500 ml ■ SERVE cool
■ INGREDIENTS Maris Otter pale malt/crystal malt/ caramalt/wheat malt/Bramling Cross and Cascade hops

A beer that proved difficult when first brewed, leading brewer Peter Blencowe to think it had an attitude problem.

BLUE ANCHOR

Blue Anchor Inn, 50 Coinagehall Street, Helston, Cornwall TR13 8EL. Tel./Fax (01326) 565765
Mail order service

Famous as one of the handful of home-brew houses still in operation when CAMRA accepted the challenge of preserving British brewing heritage in 1971, The Blue Anchor is one of the UK's classic pubs. The thatched building began life as a monks' resting place in the 15th century. Its brewery – famous for its 'Spingo' ales – has been refurbished in recent years. Bottling takes place at Keltek Brewery.

Jubilee Ale

■ ABV 4.5% ■ BOTTLE SIZE 275 ml ■ SERVE cool
■ INGREDIENTS Pipkin pale malt/Golding hops

An IPA first brewed for The Queen's Golden Jubilee in 2002. May also be sold simply as 'IPA'.

Spingo Middle

■ ABV 5% ■ BOTTLE SIZE 275 ml ■ SERVE cool
■ INGREDIENTS Pipkin pale malt/Golding hops

Spingo has been on tap at The Blue Anchor for centuries, the pub claims. The origin of the name is the Old English 'stingo', a term for strong beer.

Tasting Notes

A dark amber, robust ale with an earthy, spicy malt aroma. The distinctive taste merges earthy maltiness and spice, before a dry, thick, bittersweet, spicy finish.

Spingo Bragget

■ ABV 6% ■ BOTTLE SIZE 275 ml ■ SERVE cool
■ INGREDIENTS Pipkin pale malt/honey/apple juice

A hop-less, honey-flavoured brew originally sold as Spingo

800 when introduced in 2001 to commemorate the 800th anniversary of the granting of the royal charter to the town of Helston by King John.

Tasting Notes

A golden drink with a herbal aroma of honey and green apples. The same flavours come through in the sweet taste and aftertaste.

Spingo Special

- **ABV 6.6%** ■ **BOTTLE SIZE 275 ml** ■ **SERVE cool**
- **INGREDIENTS Pipkin pale malt/Golding hops**

This is a stronger version of Spingo Middle and, like its stablemate, may be found in dishes like beef in Spingo and Spingo burgers at the pub.

Tasting Notes

A powerful ruby ale with an earthy, appley, spicy nose. Sweet malt is well to the fore in the mouth, allowing the earthy, bitter spiciness to provide a nice contrast. Bittersweet, fruity, spicy aftertaste.

Christmas Special/Easter Special

- **ABV 7.6%** ■ **BOTTLE SIZE 275 ml** ■ **SERVE cool**
- **INGREDIENTS Pipkin pale malt/crystal malt/Golding hops**

A seasonal draught ale available in bottle for a month either side of the two holidays and labelled up under the appropriate name.

Tasting Notes

A strong ruby ale with a peppery, malt and fruit nose and the distinctive Blue Anchor spiciness in the sweet and malty taste. Red fruit and oranges lurk in the background before a sweetish, fruity finish.

BOGGART

Boggart Hole Clough Brewing Company, Unit 13, Brookside Works, Clough Road, Moston, Manchester M9 4FP. Tel./Fax (0161) 277 9666
E-mail: mark@boggart-brewery.co.uk
Website: www.boggart-brewery.co.uk

The peculiar name of this brewery comes from the peculiar name of the park next door. Mark Dade is the founder. A former brewer at Marble Brewery, he set up on his own in northern Manchester in 2001.

Steaming

- **ABV 9%** ▪ **BOTTLE SIZE 500 ml** ▪ **SERVE cool**
- **INGREDIENTS Pale malt/wheat malt/Galena and Challenger hops**

Both these bottled beers are available in cask form but are not typical of the Boggart selection, which features half-a-dozen or more brews in the 3–5% range. Steaming was first brewed and bottled in late 2001 and is now a regular product.

Rocket Fuel

- **ABV 14%** ▪ **BOTTLE SIZE 330 ml** ▪ **SERVE cool**
- **INGREDIENTS Pale malt/amber malt/wheat malt/ Nugget and Liberty hops**

Brewed every six months or so, this powerful, take-no-prisoners ale was introduced in May 2003.

BRAGDY CEREDIGION

Bragdy Ceredigion, Brynhawk, New Road, Newquay, Ceredigion SA45 9SB.
Tel./Fax (01545) 561417 Brewery tel. (01239) 654888
Mail order service

This brewery was constructed in a converted barn on a working West Wales farm in 1997. The address above is the office address: the brewery itself is in the village of Pentregat. The beers are targeted at the local tourist trade and have bilingual Welsh/English labels, hand-drawn by Julia Tilby, wife of brewer Brian Tilby. Each beer is siphoned into bottles direct from the fermenter, or from a cask, and is primed with raw demerara sugar. Best before dates are 12–18 months after bottling. All the beers are declared suitable for vegetarians.

Gwrach Ddu

- **ABV 4%** ▪ **BOTTLE SIZE 500 ml** ▪ **SERVE cool**
- **INGREDIENTS Maris Otter pale malt/crystal malt/amber malt/First Gold hops**

Translated as 'Black Witch', Gwrach Ddu was first brewed for Hallowe'en, in 1998. The cask version is dry hopped and sold as a 'dark porter', whereas this bottled equivalent – a touch of 'cyfareddol du' (black magic), as the label used to claim – is labelled a 'stout'. Try it with a selection of strong Welsh cheeses, suggests Brian.

Tasting Notes
A ruby-coloured beer with a creamy aroma of dark malt. On the palate it is dry and immediately moreish, with flavours like fruit, bitterness and roasted malt well restrained, before a gently bitter, toasty, dry finish that is also lightly fruity.

Draig Aur

- **ABV 4.2%** ■ **BOTTLE SIZE 500 ml** ■ **SERVE cool**
- **INGREDIENTS Maris Otter pale malt/crystal malt/amber malt/Challenger and Fuggle hops**

Launched in cask at CAMRA's Cardiff Beer Festival in 1998, and in bottle soon after, 'Gold Dragon' is another brew to try with rich cheeses. The strength, originally set at 5%, has now been reduced to a more quaffable 4.2%.

Tasting Notes
An orange-gold ale with a fruit salad aroma. The taste is hoppy and bitter, with blackcurrant and other fruitiness. Dry, bitter finish.

Barcud Coch

- **ABV 4.3%** ■ **BOTTLE SIZE 500 ml** ■ **SERVE cool**
- **INGREDIENTS Maris Otter pale malt/crystal malt/amber malt/Challenger and Golding hops**

The name of this bitter, introduced in summer 1998, means 'Red Kite'. Challenger hops provide the main bitterness in the copper, with Goldings supplying some late variation and also dry hopping the brew in the fermenting vessel. The beer was once described on the label as being 'coch', 'prin' and 'prydferth'– red, rare and beautiful, just like the bird it is named after.

Tasting Notes
A reddish-bronze beer with a fruity hop aroma. The taste is smooth and quite bitter, and features fruity flavours. Dry, gently bitter, fruity-hop finish.

Blodeuwedd

- **ABV 4.5%** ■ **BOTTLE SIZE 500 ml** ■ **SERVE cool**
- **INGREDIENTS Pale malt/Hallertau hops**

Brewed from organic malt and organic hops, and primed with organic sugar, this beer, launched in 2000 and now officially accredited as organic by the Soil Association, takes its name from Welsh legend. Blodeuwedd, it is said, was a beautiful maiden created from flowers by two powerful magicians. Tragedy befell the girl when she plotted with her lover to kill her husband and, for her punishment, was transformed into an owl, 'a creature of the night'. 'Blodeuwedd' is Welsh for owl and literally translates as 'flower face'.

Tasting Notes

A golden ale with a fruity nose. The taste features spicy, peppery hops, bitterness and underlying light fruit, before a very hoppy, bitter finish.

Cwrw 2000

- **ABV 5%** ▪ **BOTTLE SIZE 500 ml** ▪ **SERVE cool**
- **INGREDIENTS Maris Otter pale malt/crystal malt/amber malt/pale chocolate malt/Challenger and Fuggle hops**

Brewed originally for the new millennium celebrations, Cwrw 2000 ('Ale 2000') owes its longevity to the picture of seaside Llangranog on the label, which makes it a good seller among summer visitors to the area.

Tasting Notes

A ruby ale with a full, biscuity malt aroma. The taste is soft and malty with suggestions of dark fruit and a light citrous edge. Bitter, malty finish with a touch of roasted malt and a lingering hint of fruit.

Nadolig

- **ABV 6.2%** ▪ **BOTTLE SIZE 500 ml** ▪ **SERVE cool**
- **INGREDIENTS Maris Otter pale malt/crystal malt/amber malt/pale chocolate malt/Challenger, Fuggle and Golding hops/spices**

Laced with spices – including cinnamon and nutmeg – for a festive feel, Nadolig (literally 'Christmas') is only available from October to January.

Tasting Notes

A red beer with mixed spices in the aroma and a well-rounded combination of malt and perfumed spice in the taste. Bittersweet, scented, increasingly bitter finish.

Yr Hen Darw Du

- **ABV 6.2%** ▪ **BOTTLE SIZE 500 ml** ▪ **SERVE cool**
- **INGREDIENTS Maris Otter pale malt/crystal malt/amber malt/dark chocolate malt/black malt/Challenger hops**

'The Old Black Bull', for those not versed in the language of Heaven. This complex winter warmer takes its name from the brewery's bovine neighbours on the Pentregat farm. It also recalls a Welsh legend of the Green Lady of the Lake, who, it is said, bestowed the Welsh Black cattle on the people as a gift for saving her magical white cow from slaughter.

Tasting Notes

A deep ruby beer with a slightly leathery, fruit cocktail aroma. The taste is smooth, bitter, fruity and a touch warming. Dry, bitter, lightly roasted, fruity finish.

BRAGDY YNYS MÔN

Bragdy Ynys Môn (Isle of Anglesey Brewery),
Cae Cwta Mawr, Lôn Cae Cwta, Talwrn, Llangefni,
Anglesey LL77 7SD. Tel. (01248) 723801
E-mail: martyn@angleseyale.co.uk
Website: www.angleseyale.co.uk
Mail order service

Martyn Lewis founded this brewery in June 1999, installing a five-barrel plant in a former cow shed. The beers listed below were initially bottled by Hanby Ales, but are now filled on site (unfiltered and straight from the cask).

Medra

▪ABV 4% ▪BOTTLE SIZE 500 ml ▪SERVE cool
▪INGREDIENTS Maris Otter pale malt/crystal malt/Fuggle and Cascade hops

Literally translating as 'I can', Medra seems a peculiar name for a beer. Its origins lie in the days of slate quarrying in North Wales, when men seeking employment were asked what jobs they could do. The men of Anglesey were always able to turn their hands to anything, simply replying 'Medra' when asked if they could handle a suggested task. Anglesey, henceforward, became known as 'Gwlad y Medra', the Land of I Can.

Wennol

▪ABV 4.1% ▪BOTTLE SIZE 500 ml ▪SERVE cool
▪INGREDIENTS Maris Otter pale malt/crystal malt/ Cascade hops

Introduced in spring 2000, Wennol ('swallow' in Welsh) was inspired by the nesting of the said bird in a stable opposite the brewery.

Tasting Notes

An amber ale with malt and grassy hops in the aroma. The taste is spicy, lightly fruity and mostly bitter, with some toasted malt flavour. Hoppy, bitter finish.

Sosban Fach

▪ABV 4.3% ▪BOTTLE SIZE 500 ml ▪SERVE cool
▪INGREDIENTS Pale malt/crystal malt/First Gold hops

The Little Saucepan, more associated with South Wales rugby, and Llanelli RFC in particular, than North Wales, is the name Martyn has bestowed on his organic beer.

Tarw Du

▪ABV 4.5% ▪BOTTLE SIZE 500 ml ▪SERVE cool
▪INGREDIENTS Maris Otter pale malt/crystal malt/ chocolate malt/black malt/roasted barley/Cascade and Fuggle hops

The first of the brewery's bottled ales, launched in November 1999, Tarw Du ('Black Bull') recalls the former use of the brewery premises in its name. Bottled beer is now stored in the area where the bull used to be kept.

Tasting Notes

A near-black stout with a slightly leathery aroma of dark malt and roasted barley. Silky malt features on the palate, with roasted grain, a little fruit and a touch of sourness. Strong roasted grain finish.

Amnesia

▪ABV 4.9% ▪BOTTLE SIZE 500 ml ▪SERVE cool
▪INGREDIENTS Maris Otter pale malt/crystal malt/ Cascade and Fuggle hops

A stronger version of Medra, Amnesia was trialled at Christmas 2000 and is now brewed monthly.

Tasting Notes

An amber beer with a flowery, spicy nose. The taste is also spicy and fruity, with good, crisp bitterness and a persistent malty sweetness. Spicy, hoppy, bitter finish.

BRANCASTER

The Brancaster Brewery, The Jolly Sailors, Main Road, Brancaster Staithe, King's Lynn, Norfolk PE31 8BJ.
Tel. (01485) 210314 Fax (01485) 210396
E-mail: enquiries@jollysailors.co.uk
Website: www.jollysailors.co.uk

Brewery established in 2003 at The Jolly Sailors pub in the Norfolk seaside town of Brancaster Staithe. The brewer is Andy Skene, who also brews for Pitfield Brewery.

IPA

- **ABV 3.7%** ▪ **BOTTLE SIZE 500 ml** ▪ **SERVE cool**
- **INGREDIENTS Pale malt/caramalt/roasted barley/ Fuggle and Brewer's Gold hops**

A session bitter, rather than a genuine IPA. As with Old Les, below, the beer is allowed to drop bright and then bottled by hand. Both beers are also sold on draught.

Tasting Notes

A crisp and easy-drinking, golden bitter with a clean, lightly hoppy-fruity aroma. Well-balanced malt and hops follow in the taste, rounded off by a light bitter finish.

Old Les

- **ABV 5%** ▪ **BOTTLE SIZE 500 ml** ▪ **SERVE cool**
- **INGREDIENTS Pale malt/caramalt/roasted barley/ Challenger and Fuggle hops**

This strong ale was named in memory of a Brancaster Staithe character who died a few years ago.

Tasting Notes

An amber ale with a malty aroma and a malty, sweetish, slightly warming taste, with hop bitterness fighting back to lead over dry, grainy malt in the aftertaste.

BRANSCOMBE VALE

Branscombe Vale Brewery, Great Seaside Farm, Branscombe, Devon EX12 3DP. Tel. (01297) 680511

It was in 1992 that Branscombe Vale set up home in an old farm that is now owned by the National Trust. It has dabbled in bottled beers in the past but only in 2002 did it make the move into regular bottle-conditioned beer production, with beer brewed at Branscombe and bottled by Devon neighbour O'Hanlon's, without filtration or re-seeding of yeast. The best before dates are set at 12 months.

Drayman's Best Bitter

- **ABV 4.2%** ▪ **BOTTLE SIZE 500 ml** ▪ **SERVE cool**
- **INGREDIENTS Pipkin pale malt/chocolate malt/Phoenix and Bramling Cross hops**

Brewed with spring water and also sold in cask form.

Tasting Notes

An amber ale with a malty, lightly citrous nose, a bittersweet, citrous, hoppy taste and a dry, bitter finish.

BRECONSHIRE

The Breconshire Brewery, Ffrwdgrech Industrial Estate, Brecon, Powys LD3 8LA.
Tel. (01874) 623731 Fax (01874) 611434
E-mail: sales@breconshirebrewery.com
Website: www.breconshirebrewery.com

The Breconshire Brewery was opened in 2002 to expand the business of CH Marlow, a beer wholesaler which has supplied pubs in South and West Wales for more than 30 years, and which also owns eight pubs of its own. The three bottled beers are bottled off site under contract but are cold conditioned for at least a week prior to filling. The beers are then sterile filtered and re-seeded with fresh yeast. Best before dates stand at 12 months.

Golden Valley

- **ABV 4.2%** ▪ **BOTTLE SIZE 500 ml** ▪ **SERVE cool**
- **INGREDIENTS Optic pale malt/crystal malt/Progress hops**

First bottled in 2003, Golden Valley is an award-winner in its cask form and is an ideal beer to enjoy with a barbecue on a warm evening, according to Breconshire's head brewer Justin Grant.

Tasting Notes

An amber ale with malt and hops in the nose, and bitterness leading sweet malt in the taste, with a light floral character throughout. Bitter, dry, floral finish.

Red Dragon

- **ABV 4.7%** ▪ **BOTTLE SIZE 500 ml** ▪ **SERVE cool**
- **INGREDIENTS Optic pale malt/crystal malt/torrefied wheat/Golding, First Gold, Pioneer and Susan hops**

A red ale suited to washing down game pies or strong Welsh cheeses, says Justin, and also a prize-winner in its draught version.

Ramblers Ruin

- **ABV 5%** ▪ **BOTTLE SIZE 500 ml** ▪ **SERVE cool**
- **INGREDIENTS Optic pale malt/crystal malt/black malt/Golding, Progress and First Gold hops**

Like Red Dragon, Ramblers Ruin – a strong bitter – was first bottled in summer 2004.

BREWSTER'S

Brewster's Brewery, Penn Lane, Stathern, Leicestershire LE14 4JA.
Tel. (01949) 861868 Fax (01949) 861901
E-mail: sara@brewsters.co.uk
Website: www.brewsters.co.uk

In centuries past, brewsters were female brewers and their work was prolific, many brewing beer for consumption at home at a time when water supplies were less than reliable. There is a small core of professional women brewers employed today in breweries across Britain, but the brewster in the name of this Leicestershire business is Sara Barton. Sara used to work for Courage, brewing some of the biggest names in world beer. Leaving it all behind, she returned to her native Vale of Belvoir, setting up this microbrewery in 1998.

Vale Pale Ale

- **ABV 4.5%** ▪ **BOTTLE SIZE 500 ml** ▪ **SERVE cool**
- **INGREDIENTS Maris Otter pale malt/caramalt/ Northdown, Golding and Cascade hops**

Belvoir Castle features on the label of this beer inspired by the vale in which the brewery sits. It was one of Sara's first beers, launched in cask in 1998 but only released in bottle in summer 2003. Drink with white meat and fish dishes is her dining recommendation.

Tasting Notes

A light copper bitter showcasing its Cascade hops right from the juicy grapefruit aroma, through the zesty, bitter, citrous taste to the tangy grapefruit finish.

BRIDGE OF ALLAN

Bridge of Allan Brewery, The Brew House, Queens Lane, Bridge of Allan, Stirlingshire FK9 4NY.
Tel. (01786) 834555 Fax (01786) 833426
E-mail: brewery@bridgeofallan.co.uk
Website: www.bridgeofallan.co.uk
Mail order service

Founded in 1997, this Victorian spa town brewery now serves around 100 pubs. It produces quite a range of bottled beers, but only one is bottle conditioned (although there are plans to install a new bottling line and produce a wider range of bottle-conditioned beers).

Brig O'Allan

■ ABV 4.1% ■ BOTTLE SIZE 500 ml ■ SERVE cool
■ INGREDIENTS Maris Otter pale malt/crystal malt/ chocolate malt/wheat malt/Hallertau and Golding hops

This traditional 80/- style beer was introduced in 2001. The beer is allowed two weeks in conditioning tanks after fermentation, so that it drops bright. No finings are used, making it appealing to vegetarians. The beer is then primed with sugar and re-seeded with fresh yeast.

Tasting Notes

A dark amber ale with a malty nose. The taste is surprisingly crisp and bitter with a toasted malt flavour. Bitter, toasted malt finish.

BROADSTONE

The Broadstone Brewing Company Ltd., The Rum Runner, Wharf Road, Retford, Nottinghamshire DN22 6EN. Tel. (01777) 719797
E-mail: broadstone@btconnect.com
Website: www.broadstonebrewery.com
Mail order service

Alan Gill, founder of Springhead Brewery (see separate entry), moved on to establish The Broadstone Brewing Company in the village of Tuxford in 1999. Since spring 2001, the brewery has been based at The Rum Runner pub in Retford. Alan now supplies around 100 local pubs and brews five regular cask beers, plus seasonals, as well as the three bottled beers mentioned below. These are conditioned in casks, fined and primed, allowed to stand for 24 hours and then bottled. Best before dates are fixed at 12 months.

Two Water Grog

■ ABV 4% ■ BOTTLE SIZE 500 ml ■ SERVE cool
■ INGREDIENTS Pearl pale malt/crystal malt/rye crystal malt/roasted barley/Northdown and Bramling Cross hops

This bottled version of The Rum Runner's own house bitter (it's not sold in its cask version anywhere else) draws on the naval grog tradition for its name (the daily ration for sailors aboard ship was often made up of two parts water to one part rum).

Major stockists Local Tesco and Waitrose

Black Abbot

■ **ABV 5%** ■ **BOTTLE SIZE 500 ml** ■ **SERVE cool**
■ **INGREDIENTS Pearl pale malt/crystal malt/rye crystal malt/roasted barley/Northdown hops**

A dark and mysterious name for a dark and mysterious beer, according to Alan. The label provides a warning not to mess with the Black Abbot or 'oblivion and chaos will be the outcome'.

Major stockist Local Waitrose

Broadstone Gold

■ **ABV 5%** ■ **BOTTLE SIZE 500 ml** ■ **SERVE cool**
■ **INGREDIENTS Pearl pale malt/Northdown hops**

Alan's very first beer at Broadstone, this beer festival award-winner is described as a 'golden pale ale in the Belgian style', which will come as no surprise to readers who sampled the adventurous beers he created when he was brewing at Springhead.

Major stockist Local Waitrose

BURTON BRIDGE

Burton Bridge Brewery, 24 Bridge Street,
Burton upon Trent, Staffordshire DE14 1SY.
Tel. (01283) 510573 Fax (01283) 515594

Burton Bridge Brewery, a microbrewery in the pale ale capital, was established in 1982 by former Allied Breweries employees Bruce Wilkinson and Geoff Mumford. They began bottle conditioning beers in the same year, making them one of the first small breweries to expand into bottling.

Burton Porter

■ **ABV 4.5%** ■ **BOTTLE SIZE 500 ml** ■ **SERVE cool**
■ **INGREDIENTS Pale malt/crystal malt/chocolate malt/ Challenger and Target hops**

The simple yellow paint and rubber stamp label that used to adorn bottles of this popular porter has long given way to a more sophisticated paper badge. However, inside the bottle the beer is just the same as before, following the same recipe as draught Burton Porter. Bottles are filled from one-week-old casks, and the beer is said to be on form at any stage from one- to six-months-old (the period indicated by the best before date). This and all Burton Bridge's bottled beers are warm-conditioned at the brewery for around ten days before dispatch to ensure a good secondary fermentation is underway. Most bottling is still handled within the brewery, but some Burton Porter has been bottled by Integrated Bottling Solutions. The beer is also exported to Canada.

Tasting Notes

A dark red, almost black, porter with an aroma of fruit and chocolate. Dry roast malt in the taste is backed by gentle, sweet malt, with dryness, roast malt and bitterness coming through to dominate the finish.

Major stockist Local Tesco

Bramble Stout

- **ABV 5%** ▪ **BOTTLE SIZE 500 ml** ▪ **SERVE cool**
- **INGREDIENTS Pale malt/chocolate malt/Challenger hops/blackberry juice**

Introduced in 1999, Bramble Stout is an unusual creation, consisting of the brewery's Top Dog Stout with blackberry juice added to the cask before bottling.

Tasting Notes

An almost black beer, with a smoky, biscuity, fruity aroma. In the mouth it is bitter, blackberry-fruity and roasty. Bitter, fruity, strong roast finish.

Derbyshire Estate Ale

- **ABV 5%** ▪ **BOTTLE SIZE 500 ml** ▪ **SERVE cool**
- **INGREDIENTS Maris Otter pale malt/Northdown, Fuggle and Golding hops**

A special bottling for the National Trust, and launched in March 2002 for sale in the organisation's outlets in Derbyshire, Derbyshire Estate Ale is actually one of the brewery's cask beers, Stairway to Heaven, under a new name.

Tasting Notes

Golden in colour, with a deep toffee-malty aroma, a toffee-malty, bitter taste and a bitter, malty finish.

Empire Pale Ale

- **ABV 7.5%** ▪ **BOTTLE SIZE 500 ml** ▪ **SERVE cool**
- **INGREDIENTS Pipkin pale malt/invert sugar/Challenger and Styrian Golding hops**

The Guardian newspaper's *Best Bottle-Conditioned Beer* 1997, and runner-up in the joint *Guardian*/CAMRA competition a year later. As its name suggests, this brew is a re-creation of the classic IPAs which once sailed out to the far corners of the

Empire from Burton upon Trent. Being very strong, bitter and hoppy, it fits the bill admirably. The days of the Raj are recalled on the label, too, which depicts an army officer in full regalia alongside a Victorian cricketer, both patriotically embraced by a Union flag. The first brew arrived in 1996 and now the ale is brewed twice a year. After primary fermentation, it is conditioned in cask for six months and is dry-hopped with Styrian Goldings two weeks before being primed and bottled. The yeast carried over from the cask takes care of the bottle fermentation. B United distributes this beer in the USA.

Tasting Notes

Bitter oranges are the main characteristic of this heady, copper-coloured IPA. They feature, with hops, in the nose; they figure highly in the malty taste, again with powerful hops on the side; and carry right through to the warming, mouth-tingling finish.

Tickle Brain

- **ABV 8%** ▪ **BOTTLE SIZE 500 ml** ▪ **SERVE cool**
- **INGREDIENTS Pale malt/crystal malt/invert sugar/ Northdown hops**

At 8%, this beer – first brewed in 1996, as the intended first of a series of beer style re-creations – more than tickles the brain. However, the brewery gives credit for this euphemism to Shakespeare, from whose writings the name is derived. The ale is an interpretation of an early (16th-century) hopped beer, as might have been produced by brewer monks. To emphasise the era it comes from (at least in spirit), Henry VIII, the king who ordered the dissolution of the monasteries, dominates the label. The result is an Abbey-style beer which is best drunk about two months into its 12-month shelf life.

Tasting Notes

A dark red beer with a sweet, malty, lightly fruity aroma. The taste is sweetish, malty and very fruity (hints of raspberries), with good bitterness to ensure it does not become cloying. Mouth-numbing, fruity and bitter finish.

BUTTS

Butts Brewery Ltd., Northfield Farm, Great Shefford, Hungerford, Berkshire RG17 7BY.
Tel. (01488) 648133 Fax (01488) 648134
E-mail: enquiries@butts.brewery.com
Website: www.buttsbrewery.com

Butts Brewery was established in 1994 in converted farm buildings north of Hungerford and the M4 motorway by Chris Butt. His organic (Soil Association-accredited) beers now find their way into around 80 outlets in West Berkshire and surrounding counties. Two bottled beers, Barbus Barbus and Blackguard, were introduced in 1999, and two more have followed since. Each beer is primed, filtered and then re-seeded with Butts's own yeast prior to bottling on site. The beers are then conditioned in the bottle for at least a month before they are released for sale.

Blackguard

■ **ABV 4.5%** ■ **BOTTLE SIZE 500 ml** ■ **SERVE cool**
■ **INGREDIENTS Not declared**

Blackguard (pronounced 'blaggard') is Butts's popular porter, introduced as a winter brew but now likely to be found on the bar all year round. The label features a variation on the brewery's playing card joker logo, showing a 'jester with attitude', as Chris describes it. Ingredients-wise, the only information the ever-secretive Mr Butt will supply is that he uses British malt and British hops.

Tasting Notes
A deep ruby-coloured beer with a contrasting white head. The appetising aroma features orange hop fruit and a peppery roastiness, while the soft, bittersweet, roasted malt taste has a touch of liquorice and more fruit. Long, dry, bitter, charcoal-like roast finish.

Major stockists Local Somerfield and Waitrose

Barbus Barbus

■ **ABV 4.6%** ■ **BOTTLE SIZE 500 ml** ■ **SERVE cool**
■ **INGREDIENTS Not declared**

Barbus Barbus is the Latin name for the barbel fish and this beer celebrates the sport of coarse fishing. In cask form, it has quickly become the brewery's most popular ale, and the bottled version has also gained itself a fan club. Three hop strains contribute to the flavour, although, yet again, the brewery refuses to say which.

Tasting Notes
An attractive bronze beer with a full hoppy nose backed with juicy orange fruit notes. The orange-citrus theme continues on the palate, but with hop bitterness quickly taking over. Very hoppy, dry fruity finish.

Major stockists Safeway, local Somerfield and Waitrose

Golden Brown

■ ABV 5% ■ BOTTLE SIZE 500 ml ■ SERVE cool
■ INGREDIENTS Not declared

Chris Butt confesses to being a Stranglers fan, hence the use of one of their song titles for this beer's name. In the lyrics there is reference to 'tied to a mast', which explains the girl tied to a mast of a ship on the label. The beer contains three different malts and just one hop strain.

Tasting Notes

A light ruby ale with a toasted malt aroma and a rich, nutty, toasted malt taste. Silky smooth, it also has a pleasant tang of hop before a long, nutty, bitter finish.

Major stockist Local Somerfield

Le Butts

■ ABV 5% ■ BOTTLE SIZE 500 ml ■ SERVE cold
■ INGREDIENTS Pale malt/wheat malt/hops not declared

Why bother with cross-Channel booze runs when you can buy a French lager brewed in Berkshire? Le Butts is produced with lager yeast and a lager hop to parody the efforts of the booze cruisers and, through its name, has a little fun at the expense of the Canadian lager giant Labatt in the process.

Tasting Notes

A golden beer with a spicy, fruity, almost sherbety aroma. Light, tart fruit features in the taste over delicate malt and soft, peppery hops, with the same peppery bitterness and fruit in the finish.

Major stockist Local Somerfield

CHILTERN

The Chiltern Brewery, Nash Lee Road, Terrick, Aylesbury, Buckinghamshire HP17 0TQ.
Tel. (01296) 613647 Fax (01296) 612419
E-mail: info@chilternbrewery.co.uk
Website: www.chilternbrewery.co.uk
Mail order service

Chiltern Brewery was set up in 1980 on an attractively-positioned small farm and is the oldest microbrewery in Buckinghamshire and the Chilterns. The Jenkinson family who run it specialise in beer-related foods (cheeses, sausages, mustards, etc.), as well as traditional ales. On site is a very well-stocked visitors' centre-cum-shop and a small but interesting collection of Buckinghamshire breweriana. Chiltern produces a range of bottled beers but only two, so far, are bottle conditioned.

Glad Tidings

■ ABV 4.6% ■ BOTTLE SIZE 500 ml ■ SERVE cool
■ INGREDIENTS Maris Otter pale malt/chocolate malt/ roasted barley/Bramling Cross hops/nutmeg/ coriander/orange

The name reveals the timing of this Christmas beer, first brewed in 2003 to much acclaim. The brewery describes it as a spiced milk stout, and takes pride in using only authentic ingredients – no extracts, oils, juices or flavourings – to create the seasonal accents of the beer.

Tasting Notes

A ruby ale with dark malt overlaid by spices (nutmeg and a whiff of orange) in the nose. The mildly warming taste is also spicy but soft, with a mellow maltiness and smooth sweetness nicely balanced by a persistent orange-lemon tang. Bittersweet, spicy finish with hops building and gentle roasted grain lingering.

Bodgers Barley Wine

■ ABV 8.5% ■ BOTTLE SIZE 500 ml ■ SERVE cool
■ INGREDIENTS Maris Otter pale malt/Fuggle and Golding hops

Brewed first in 1990, to commemorate the tenth anniversary of the founding of the brewery, Bodgers recalls the tradition of the Chiltern Bodger (a craftsman-chairmaker who worked in the surrounding beechwoods) in its name, and the year of the brewery's birth in its original gravity (1080). It is a fine accompaniment to the Chiltern range of beer-related foods. The brewery particularly recommends it with powerful cheeses, full-flavoured sausages and strong meats, although the Jenkinsons also suggest it could be served lightly chilled as an aperitif or at room temperature instead of a dessert wine. Bottled by hand in house, the beer is conditioned in tank for a month first, then fined rather than filtered. It is not primed with new yeast or sugar. The individually-numbered bottles are kept at the brewery to mature for four weeks and are then released for consumption – if you follow the best before date – sometime within the next 12 months. The brewery's own literature has described it as 'a thunderbolt of a barley wine'. New labels are planned.

Tasting Notes

A golden beer, tasting smooth, sweet, fruity, warming and

dry, with a hop resin note. The nose combines creamy malt with a soft, melony fruitiness and light hop resins. Gum-tingling, bittersweet, hoppy aftertaste.

CHURCH END

Church End Brewery Ltd., Ridge Lane, Nuneaton, Warwickshire CV10 0RD.
Tel. (01827) 713080 Fax (01827) 717328
Church End Brewery was founded in 1994, in an old coffin workshop next to The Griffin Inn in Shustoke, Warwickshire. In 2001 it moved to new premises, five miles away in Ridge Lane, near Atherstone. Church End had already experimented with bottle-conditioned beers on a few occasions before making a major commitment when launching Rugby Ale in the spring of 1998. Since then two further bottles have been added to the range. Beers are bottled outside the brewery under contract and carry a nine–12-month best before date.

Nuns Ale

- **ABV 4.5%** ■ **BOTTLE SIZE 500 ml** ■ **SERVE cool**
- **INGREDIENTS Pale malt/crystal malt/Green Bullet, Cascade and Amarillo hops**

Brewed to raise money for St Mary Abbey in Nuneaton (which once had its own brewery and was responsible in part for the town's name), Nuns Ale first appeared in 2002 and is now produced several times a year. The choice of hops is interesting to say the least, with Green Bullet from New Zealand teamed up with Cascade and the rare Amarillo from America.

Tasting Notes

A yellow-gold ale with an aroma of spicy, fruity hops. The taste is crisp, bitter and fruity, with lemon notes to the fore, building to a dry, bitter, lemony finish.

Rugby Ale

- **ABV 5%** ■ **BOTTLE SIZE 500 ml** ■ **SERVE cool**
- **INGREDIENTS Pale malt/crystal malt/amber malt/ chocolate malt/Northdown hops**

Church End's Warwickshire home is not far from the town of Rugby, the birthplace of the sport of the same name back in 1823. The brewery, therefore, sought to capitalise on the 1999 Rugby World Cup with the launch of this dark beer – a joint venture with Rugby Tourist Board. However, the recipe has now changed, with Hallertau hops giving way to Northdown.

Tasting Notes

A ruby ale with tropical fruit notes, dark malt and a slight smokiness in the nose. Dark malt figures in the mouth, but with a lightening sweet fruitiness. Coffee and chocolate feature in the bitter finish.

Arthur's Wit

- **ABV 6% ▪ BOTTLE SIZE 500 ml ▪ SERVE cool**
- **INGREDIENTS Pale malt/torrefied wheat/Mount Hood and Cascade hops**

Introduced as a cask beer six years ago, Arthur's Wit was bottled for the first time in 2002. Despite its Belgian sounding name, this is not a spiced wheat beer, but a strong golden ale – and a good bread and cheese accompaniment, according to the brewers.

Tasting Notes

A big malty aroma heralds this powerful, bittersweet mix of malt and orangey hops, the hops taking over, along with bitterness, in the finish.

CITY OF CAMBRIDGE

City of Cambridge Brewery Co. Ltd., Ely Road, Chittering, Cambridge CB5 9PH. Tel. (01223) 864864
E-mail: sales@cambridge-brewery.co.uk
Website: www.cambridge-brewery.co.uk

City of Cambridge Brewery was opened by Steve Draper in May 1997 and moved to new premises, on the Ely road (A10), just north of the city, in 2002. All available cask beers are bottled regularly to maintain stocks, and are kräusened with fresh Hobson's Choice wort first.

Jet Black

- **ABV 3.7% ▪ BOTTLE SIZE 500 ml ▪ SERVE cool**
- **INGREDIENTS Maris Otter pale malt/crystal malt/ caramalt/roasted malt/First Gold hops**

A Cambridge Beer Festival champion from 1998.

Tasting Notes

Subtle chocolate features in the aroma of this softly malty, light-bodied beer which has a gentle fruit edge and some roasted malt in the easy finish.

Boathouse Bitter

■ABV 3.8% ■BOTTLE SIZE 500 ml ■SERVE cool
■INGREDIENTS Maris Otter pale malt/crystal malt/First Gold and Cascade hops

Most of the brewery's bottled beers reflect the life and culture of the university city of Cambridge in their names, this one majoring on the rowing heritage.

Tasting Notes

A deep amber beer with a rich, chocolatey nose, supported by a little citrous hoppiness. The taste is malty and fruity (tell-tale pineapple notes from the Cascade hops), with hints of chocolate, but quite dry. Very dry, mostly bitter, malt and fruit aftertaste. Plenty of depth for its modest strength.

Major stockist Local Asda

Hobson's Choice

■ABV 4.1% ■BOTTLE SIZE 500 ml ■SERVE cool
■INGREDIENTS Maris Otter pale malt/caramalt/First Gold hops

This brew, launched in 1997, takes its name from the story of Mr Hobson, a Cambridge horse-merchant who, as legend has it, allowed only the particular horse he specified to be hired – hence 'Hobson's Choice'.

Tasting Notes

A bronze beer with a fresh, fruity, spritzy nose, backed by malt. On the palate, it is crisp and generally bitter but delicately fruity, too, although it is clearly less malty to taste than some of the brewery's other ales. Very dry, bitter finish with lingering fruit.

Major stockists Local Asda and Waitrose

Sunset Square

■ABV 4.4% ■BOTTLE SIZE 500 ml ■SERVE cool
■INGREDIENTS Maris Otter pale malt/crystal malt/caramalt/roasted malt/First Gold hops

Now named after one of Cambridge's squares – a suntrap on summer evenings – this beer was formerly known as Blend 42 and is actually a mix of two of City of Cambridge's other brews – Hobson's Choice and Atomsplitter. The '42' referred to the answer to the Ultimate Question to Life, the Universe and Everything, as posed by the late Douglas Adams in *The Hitch-hiker's Guide to the Galaxy* (Adams was born in Cambridge).

Tasting Notes

An amber ale with a juicy, citrous nose. Juicy, fruity and

peppery hops dominate the taste and also bring a crisp, firm bitterness. Long, dry, bitter and hoppy aftertaste.

Drummer St Stout

- **ABV 4.5%** ▪ **BOTTLE SIZE 500 ml** ▪ **SERVE cool**
- **INGREDIENTS Maris Otter pale malt/crystal malt/roasted malt/torrefied wheat/sea salt/Challenger and Golding hops**

The newest bottled beer, introduced in 2003: a stout named after a street in the city where buses congregate!

Tasting Notes

A near-black stout with fruity notes over dark malt in its aroma. The moderate body makes for easy drinking as the bitter coffee notes of the malt are balanced and sweetened by fruit. Hints of charcoal in the bitter finish.

Atomsplitter

- **ABV 4.7%** ▪ **BOTTLE SIZE 500 ml** ▪ **SERVE cool**
- **INGREDIENTS Maris Otter pale malt/crystal malt/caramalt/roasted malt/First Gold hops**

It was in Cambridge that scientist Ernest Rutherford did much of his research into splitting the atom and this beer, introduced in bottle in 1998, recalls those days. (The working title for the beer was Rutherford's IPA.)

Tasting Notes

An amber beer with a rich, malty, chocolatey nose, backed by a hint of orange. Mouthfilling malt and lemon/orange fruitiness feature in the well-rounded taste which leans towards sweetness but never quite gets there as hop bitterness blends in. Clean, dry, pleasantly bitter finish, with lingering malt and orange notes.

Major stockist Local Asda

Darwin's Downfall

- **ABV 5%** ▪ **BOTTLE SIZE 500 ml** ▪ **SERVE cool**
- **INGREDIENTS Maris Otter pale malt/crystal malt/caramalt/roasted malt/First Gold hops**

Darwin's Downfall is another of City of Cambridge's blends, this time successfully combining Atomsplitter and Parkers Porter. Its name recalls Charles Darwin's links with the university city and the label shows the various stages of human/ape evolution.

Tasting Notes

A flavoursome, ruby-coloured beer with luscious tropical fruit in the aroma. The taste is bitter and fruity, with some roasted grain behind. Dry, roasted, bitter finish.

Parkers Porter

▪ABV 5.3% ▪BOTTLE SIZE 500 ml ▪SERVE cool
▪INGREDIENTS Maris Otter pale malt/crystal malt/caramalt/roasted malt/First Gold hops

The central area of greenbelt in Cambridge is a meadow known as Parkers Piece, as recalled in the name of this complex porter.

Tasting Notes

A dark ruby beer featuring nutty, roasted malt in the aroma. The taste is malty and lightly chocolatey, nodding towards sweetness through the dark malt, rather than roastiness. It is fairly fruity and has a good bitter balance. Dry, fruity, gently bitter finish, with a suggestion of liquorice.

Bramling Traditional

▪ABV 5.5% ▪BOTTLE SIZE 500 ml ▪SERVE cool
▪INGREDIENTS Maris Otter pale malt/crystal malt/caramalt/roasted malt/First Gold and Bramling Cross hops

Distinctive Bramling Cross hops make their presence known in the both the title and the taste.

Tasting Notes

Strong blackcurrant notes fill the aroma of this reddish-amber bitter and emerge again in the fruity taste. Not as sweet as many beers of this strength, it has good balancing bitterness, and a dry, bitter, fruity finish.

CLARKE'S ORGANIC

Clarke's Organic Brewery Ltd., Thornhill Hall Farm, Dewsbury, West Yorkshire WF12 0QL.
Tel. (01924) 489222
Website: www.beersinabox.com

Clarke's Organic Group is a bottling, sales and marketing enterprise that takes beers (not solely organic) from small brewers and makes them available to a wider audience than may otherwise be possible. Such beers from Anglo Dutch, E&S Elland, Halifax and Old Bear feature elsewhere in this book, but the company also has two beers contract brewed under the Clarke's Organic name.

COB No.1

■ ABV 4.2% ■ BOTTLE SIZE 500 ml ■ SERVE cool
■ INGREDIENTS Malts not declared/Cascade hops

An organic beer seasoned with Cascade and one other strain of hop, and featuring horsey imagery on the label. Like Bright Bay (below), this is declared to be 'hand brewed in Yorkshire', although the precise brewery is not named.

Tasting Notes

A pale golden ale with hops in the nose, in the bittersweet taste, and in the aftertaste.

Bright Bay

■ ABV 5% ■ BOTTLE SIZE 500 ml ■ SERVE cool
■ INGREDIENTS Malts not declared/Pacific Gem hops

Another horsey, organic beer, an IPA this time seasoned with New Zealand hops, plus a further, undisclosed, hop strain.

Tasting Notes

A yellow-gold beer, with a lightly fruity aroma. The taste is sweetish and spicy with lightly-scented hop and a hint of almond. Hops and a trace of marzipan in the finish.

CLEARWATER

Clearwater Brewery, 2 and 4 Devon Units, Great Torrington, Devon EX38 7HP. Tel./Fax (01805) 625242

A brewery founded in 1999, Clearwater acknowledges the impact of the English Civil War on Devon in its beer names. Its bottled beers are filled on site from casks conditioned at the brewery for seven–ten days, or are bottled for Clearwater by Keltek Brewery.

Cavalier Ale

■ ABV 4% ■ BOTTLE SIZE 500 ml ■ SERVE cool
■ INGREDIENTS Pipkin pale malt/crystal malt/chocolate malt/Challenger and Golding hops

Remembering the Royalists who supported King Charles I in the Civil War, this beer also marks the defeat of those Cavaliers at the local battle of Torrington in 1646.

Tasting Notes

Malt and figgy hop fruit stand out in the nose of this amber ale. Figgy-orangey fruit continues in the taste, which is mostly malty but bitter, with roasted notes. The bitter finish features the same fruit.

1646

■ ABV 4.8% ■ BOTTLE SIZE 500 ml ■ SERVE cool
■ INGREDIENTS Pipkin pale malt/crystal malt/Golding hops

1646 was the year when Sir Thomas Fairfax took the town of Torrington for the Parliamentarian side, bringing to an end Royalist resistance in the West Country. A re-enacted scene fronts the bottle's label.

Tasting Notes

There's a surprise in the nose of this golden ale, as an Ovaltine maltiness is the main feature and not hops. Malt continues up front in the taste but there's also a light, citrous edge from the hops. The finish is bittersweet and malty, with some hop lingering.

Oliver's Nectar

■ ABV 5.2% ■ BOTTLE SIZE 500 ml ■ SERVE cool
■ INGREDIENTS Pipkin pale malt/crystal malt/roasted barley/Challenger and Golding hops

Another re-enactment features on the label of Oliver's Nectar – obviously a reference to Cromwell, who, after the battle of Torrington, went on to become Lord Protector of the Commonwealth.

Tasting Notes

A dark copper beer with spicy hop overlaying malt in the nose. The taste is tangy and nutty with a lemon fruitiness and a dark malt backdrop. Hops and toasted malt figure in the finish as bitterness takes over.

CONISTON

Coniston Brewing Co. Ltd., Coppermines Road, Coniston, Cumbria LA21 8HL.
Tel. (01539 4) 41133 Fax (01539 4) 41177
E-mail: coniston.brewery@kencomp.net
Website: www.conistonbrewery.com

This little brewery was set up in 1994 behind Coniston's Black Bull pub. The ten-barrel plant achieved a minor miracle in turning out CAMRA's supreme *Champion Beer of Britain* in 1998, in the shape of Bluebird Bitter. With orders flooding in, and capacity way surpassed by demand, Coniston contracted out the brewing of this bottled version to Brakspear, who also produced the bottles of Old Man Ale that were introduced in 2000. Since the demise of the Henley brewery, the contract to brew Coniston beers for the bottle has remained with former Brakspear head brewer Peter Scholey. Through his new business, Beer Counter, he now produces the beers himself, using equipment at Hepworth & Co. in Horsham.

Bluebird Bitter

■ ABV 4.2% ■ BOTTLE SIZE 500 ml ■ SERVE cool
■ INGREDIENTS Maris Otter pale malt/crystal malt/ Challenger hops

Hot on the heels of the success of cask Bluebird (3.6%), this stronger version soon began to win accolades of its own. A gold medal at London's International Food Exhibition in 1999 was soon followed by first prize in the *Beauty of Hops* competition. In 2001, the beer picked up yet another *Beauty of Hops* gold, this time judged by a panel of female experts as *The Ultimate Fem'ale in a Bottle*, and in 2003 it earned a silver in the *International Beer Competition*. Before bottling, the beer is filtered and re-seeded with the same primary yeast. The best before date is set at 12 months after bottling. The beer – which Coniston boss Ian Bradley sees as an ideal pairing for fish and curry dishes, because of the spicy hop character – takes its name from the famous Bluebird land and water speed machines used by Donald Campbell, who was tragically killed on Coniston Water in 1967. The beer is imported into the US by Shelton Brothers of New York.

Tasting Notes

A copper-coloured beer with a peppery, spicy, fruity hop nose. Pepper, spice and the zest of citrus continue in the clean, crisp taste and the dry, bitter finish.

Major stockists Asda, Booths, Co-op, Sainsbury, Unwins, Waitrose

Old Man Ale

■ ABV 4.8% ■ BOTTLE SIZE 500 ml ■ SERVE cool
■ INGREDIENTS Maris Otter pale malt/crystal malt/ roasted barley/Challenger hops

Named after the mountain overlooking Coniston, Old Man – described as 'an old style bitter' – was first produced in cask in 1995, although at a lower ABV (4.4%) than this bottled version. The inclusion of roasted barley helps the beer to nicely complement beef and venison dishes, Ian reckons, and he says Old Man also goes well with black pudding.

Tasting Notes

A ruby-coloured strong ale with a malty aroma featuring a little orange fruit. The crisp taste also features dark malt and

spicy, orangey hops, with a suggestion of creamy toffee behind. Dry, bitter, malty finish with roasted barley notes.
Major stockists Booths, Co-op

CONWY

Conwy Brewery Ltd., Unit 17, Conwy Morfa Business Park, Ffordd Sam Pari, Conwy LL32 8HB. Tel. (01492) 585287
E-mail: enquiries@conwybrewery.co.uk
Website: www.conwybrewery.co.uk
New small brewery set up in autumn 2003 after two years of planning and now serving around 40 pubs in North Wales. The beers are sold under both Welsh and English names.

Celebration Ale/Cwrw Gwledd

- **ABV 4.2%** ▪ **BOTTLE SIZE 500 ml** ▪ **SERVE cool**
- **INGREDIENTS Maris Otter pale malt/crystal malt/ chocolate malt/Cascade hops**

Featuring famous Conwy Castle on the label, this was the first beer off the brewery's production line. The distinctive hoppy aroma comes from American Cascades which are allowed to stand in the copper after the boil has finished to impart their citrous qualities. Bottling is handled by Leek Brewery.

COORS

Coors Brewers Ltd., PO Box 217, High Street, Burton upon Trent, Staffordshire DE14 1BG. Tel. (01283) 511000 Fax (01283) 513873

The White Shield Brewery, Coors Visitor Centre, Horninglow Street, Burton upon Trent, Staffordshire DE14 1YQ.
Tel. (01283) 513507 Fax (01283) 513509
E-mail: steve.wellington@coorsbrewers.com
Website: www.coorsvisitorcentre.com
Proof that large-scale brewing is now an international affair was provided by the sale of Bass. The historic brewing company was purchased in 2000 by Interbrew, which, because it also owned Whitbread, was then forced to sell off part of its new acquisition. In stepped Coors, one of America's major brewers, to purchase most of the Bass breweries and some of its brands, including the Worthington's range. Thus a high-tech Colorado company became owners of the Bass

Museum, a shrine to the halcyon days of traditional ale production, and with it its vibrant Museum Brewing Company. This has now been re-named Coors Visitor Centre.

The Museum Brewery began life as a static display. It is housed in a former engine room, in a corner of what used to be the Bass tradesmen's yard, amidst former cobblers', coppersmiths' and tailors' units. The equipment was recovered from M&B's Cape Hill brewery in Birmingham, with parts of the kit dating from 1850 and 1920. Although pieced together in 1976, the equipment only became fully operational again in 1994 and, with long-term Bass employee Steve Wellington installed as brewer, began to specialise in reviving lost beer brands from the company's archives.

A new bottling line, capable of filling 900 bottles per hour, was introduced to cope with demand for Worthington's White Shield, which was acquired following the closure of King & Barnes in Horsham. The beer had suffered a chequered recent past. At the end of 1997 Bass had announced that the beer, one of the world's classic bottle-conditioned ales, was to be discontinued, with sales down to a mere 1,000 barrels a year. After a wave of protest, Bass relented and sold the brewing and marketing rights to King & Barnes, who made a success of the beer, taking gold in the 2000 *Champion Beer of Britain* competition, but the Horsham brewery was closed shortly after, leaving White Shield looking for another new home. Steve Wellington was keen to accept the challenge. Under Coors, a major rebranding of the Worthington's range has taken place, including for White Shield, which Coors has added to its general portfolio. The Museum Brewing Company has now been re-titled The White Shield Brewery.

Worthington's White Shield

■ ABV 5.6% ■ BOTTLE SIZE 275/500 ml ■ SERVE cool
■ INGREDIENTS Pearl pale malt/crystal malt/Fuggle, Golding and Northdown hops

For years Worthington's White Shield, along with Guinness Extra Stout, was the welcome standby for serious drinkers who found themselves tragically marooned in a keg-only pub. In many ways, it's the archetypal Burton pale ale, so it's wonderful news that it has now returned home, after short stopovers at Bass plants in Sheffield and Birmingham, and most recently at King & Barnes. The beer is now brewed five times a week and has been given a new label, underlining the history of India pale ales. Following primary fermentation, the beer is filtered and re-seeded with new 'sticky' yeast (a different strain to that used earlier in the brewing process).

Bottles should improve with keeping up to the best before date of 12 months. White Shield fans consider that equivalent to drinking green beer: some tuck crates away for a rainy day long into the future. Imported into the US by B United.

Tasting Notes
An amber beer with a malty, fruity nose, including a hint of tropical fruit. The full taste features silky, nutty malt sweetness, solid hop bitterness and a light undercurrent of tropical fruit and almond. Bitter hops dominate the finish.

Major stockists Booths, Majestic, Safeway, Tesco, Unwins, Waitrose,

P2

- **ABV 8%** ■ **BOTTLE SIZE 275 ml** ■ **SERVE cool**
- **INGREDIENTS Halcyon pale malt/crystal malt/black malt/Fuggle and Golding hops**

P2 is a dark, very strong, Russian-style stout, of the sort once shipped to the imperial court of Russia in the 19th century. Unearthed in the Bass archives, the beer is allowed eight or nine days' primary fermentation, then cooled to 10°C in tanks for two weeks. The temperature is then lowered further for another couple of weeks of conditioning before the beer is primed with sucrose and bottled. Although a six-month best before date is applied, the strength of the beer ensures it survives and matures well beyond this period.

Tasting Notes
A very dark brown, almost black, beer with a honey-coloured head and a powerful aroma which combines fruit with the scent of polished leather. In the mouth, it is not as aggressive as expected, but instead smooth and sweetish with good roast malt and fruit flavours. The dry finish features mellow, sweetish roast malt with pleasant hop bitterness to balance.

No.1 Barley Wine

- **ABV 10.5%** ■ **BOTTLE SIZE 275 ml** ■ **SERVE cool**
- **INGREDIENTS Halcyon pale malt/Fuggle and Golding hops**

No.1 is a re-creation of the famous Bass barley wine of the same name which was consigned to the archives a number of years ago. In its latter days, that beer was pasteurised but it had been enjoyed by many drinkers in its natural, bottle-conditioned form for decades. No.1 is an intriguing beer. Its hue is dark red yet the colour is only derived from pale malt that caramelises during the extra-long, 12-hour boil. This evaporates the wort down from an initial five barrels to three.

With three separate hop charges at various stages, however, this is no sweet, cloying mixture. The beer is matured in cask for more than 12 months before bottling.

Tasting Notes

A dark ruby beer with a powerful, sherry-like nose. The taste is mouth-filling, warming and fruity, with some liquorice character and bitterness. Ultra-long, creamy, bitter fruit finish.

CORVEDALE

Corvedale Brewery, The Sun Inn, Corfton, Craven Arms, Shropshire SY7 9DF. Tel. (01584) 861503
E-mail: normanspride@aol.com
Website: www.suninncorfton.co.uk

Publican Norman Pearce is the brewer in the tiny brewery housed behind The Sun Inn in rural Shropshire. His beers are bottled for him by Hanby Ales and special/commemorative brews are also bottled up when available. Small runs of 'own label' beers are often sold to local restaurants.

Teresa's Birthday

- **ABV 4.3%** ▪ **BOTTLE SIZE 500 ml** ▪ **SERVE cool**
- **INGREDIENTS Maris Otter pale malt/crystal malt/wheat malt/Northdown and Susan hops**

A tawny beer devised by Norman for his wife's birthday: the strength is raised by 0.1% every January.

Norman's Pride

- **ABV 4.3%** ▪ **BOTTLE SIZE 500 ml** ▪ **SERVE cool**
- **INGREDIENTS Maris Otter pale malt/crystal malt/wheat malt/Northdown hops**

Norman's own beer, his first commercial brew, introduced in autumn 1999.

Tasting Notes

An amber ale with a soft, fruity, bubblegum-like aroma. The taste is bitter and fruity with a lingering trace of bubblegum, while the finish is bitter.

Secret Hop

- **ABV 4.5%** ▪ **BOTTLE SIZE 500 ml** ▪ **SERVE cool**
- **INGREDIENTS Maris Otter pale malt/crystal malt/wheat malt/Susan hops**

As its name suggests, this premium ale began life using an

undisclosed hop strain. Initially given only a number (93/50), the hop – grown near Ledbury – is now in general circulation under the name of Susan.

Tasting Notes

A crisp, amber bitter with a strong blackcurrant nose. Juicy blackcurrants and bitterness fill the mouth before a slightly toasted, bitter, blackcurrant finish.

Dark and Delicious

- **ABV 4.6%** ▪ **BOTTLE SIZE 500 ml** ▪ **SERVE cool**
- **INGREDIENTS Maris Otter pale malt/crystal malt/chocolate malt/wheat malt/Northdown and Susan hops**

Described by Norman as a 'black bitter', this beer was introduced as a one-off for Christmas 2000 but has proved popular enough to take its place as a regular on the bar of The Sun.

Tasting Notes

A ruby beer with an aroma that is hop-fruity rather than deeply malty, as expected, but with a little chocolate all the same. The taste is fairly bitter and hop-fruity, with roasted malt and another hint of chocolate. Dry, bitter, roasted finish.

COTLEIGH

Cotleigh Brewery, Ford Road, Wiveliscombe, Somerset TA4 2RE. Tel. (01984) 624086 Fax (01984) 624365
E-mail: cotleighbrewery@btopenworld.com
Website: www.cotleighbrewery.co.uk

One of the South-west's most successful microbreweries, Cotleigh was founded way back in 1979 and has moved home a number of times as trade has developed. New owners took over in 2003 and the first bottle-conditioned beer rolled out in the same year.

Red Nose Reinbeer

- **ABV 5%** ▪ **BOTTLE SIZE 500 ml** ▪ **SERVE cool**
- **INGREDIENTS Optic pale malt/crystal malt/chocolate malt/Golding, Fuggle and Northdown hops**

Available from mid-November each year as a draught Christmas beer, this brew is bottled straight from the cask for Cotleigh by Keltek Brewery in Cornwall.

Tasting Notes
Malt, hops and fruit feature in the aroma of this tawny-red ale, while the taste is malty, nutty and hoppy. Chocolate and coffee emerge in the finish.

COTTAGE

The Cottage Brewing Company Ltd., The Old Cheese Dairy, Hornblotton Road, Lovington, Castle Cary, Somerset BA7 7PS. Tel. (01963) 240551 Fax (01963) 240383 Website: www.cottagebrewing.com

It's a welcome return to the *Good Bottled Beer Guide* for Cottage Brewing, which hasn't featured since the 1998 edition. The beer then, as now, was the 1995 CAMRA *Champion Beer of Britain*, Norman's Conquest, that, regrettably, has enjoyed a mixed bottled history since. For the first three years of its life, it was brewed and bottled by Thomas Hardy in Dorchester, and then spent some time being produced and marketed by Hampshire Brewery in Romsey. After a few years out of production, the beer has now been revived, with brewing carried out at Cottage and bottling handled by Integrated Bottling Solutions (formerly Wessex Craft Brewers) in Gloucestershire.

Norman's Conquest

- **ABV 7%** ▪ **BOTTLE SIZE 500 ml** ▪ **SERVE cool**
- **INGREDIENTS Maris Otter pale malt/crystal malt/ chocolate malt/Challenger hops**

After winning CAMRA's supreme accolade in its cask version, Norman's Conquest seemed a particularly appropriate name for this dark old ale/barley wine, not least because the name of the brewery's founder is Chris Norman and the original gravity of the beer is 1066. Prior to bottling, the beer is filtered, re-seeded with the same yeast used for primary fermentation and primed with sugar. The brewers reckon the beer needs at least a couple of months after bottling to come into prime condition, and you can work out whether your bottle meets this criterion by checking the best before date, which is set 12 months post-packaging. Game and cheeses are the recommended food pairings.

Tasting Notes
This garnet-coloured beer has a biscuity, lightly chocolatey, malt nose, with a faint winey fruitiness that builds in the glass. Restrained winey fruit and a suggestion of orange join grainy, sweetish, roasted malt flavours in the mouth, with a

lick of hops on the swallow. Bitter, roasted finish with a lingering trace of fruit.

COUNTRYLIFE

Countrylife Brewery, The Big Sheep, Abbotsham, Devon EX39 5AP. Tel. (01237) 420808
E-mail: countrylifebrewery@tiscali.co.uk
Website: www.countrylifebrewery.co.uk

This small brewery was acquired from Lundy Island in 1999 and set up at the Pig on the Hill pub, near Westward Ho! The plant was then moved in 2002 to The Big Sheep farm attraction, where the beers are offered in daily tastings to visitors and brewery tours are available in summer. The beers are filtered prior to bottling and re-injected with fresh yeast. A 12-month shelf life is predicted. Monthly special cask brews may also find their way into bottles from time to time.

Old Appledore

■ABV 4.2% ■BOTTLE SIZE 500 ml ■SERVE cool
■INGREDIENTS Maris Otter pale malt/crystal malt/ roasted malt/wheat malt/Fuggle and Golding hops

A stronger version of Countrylife's cask beer of the same name (3.7%). A fish and chips/pie and mash sort of beer, suggests brewer Simon Lacey.

Tasting Notes

A big, fruity amber ale with a good smack of bitterness. Very fruity, resin-like aroma; bitter, fruity finish.

Wallop

■ABV 4.4% ■BOTTLE SIZE 500 ml ■SERVE cool
■INGREDIENTS Maris Otter pale malt/wheat malt/Fuggle and Golding hops

A fine match for Chinese or Indian food, says Simon.

Tasting Notes

A golden ale with biscuity malt and hop in the aroma. Full, bittersweet taste with a light fruit acidity, floral notes and a biscuity malt base. Hops charge in for the finish.

Golden Pig

■ABV 4.7% ■BOTTLE SIZE 500 ml ■SERVE cool
■INGREDIENTS Maris Otter pale malt/Challenger and Golding hops

Golden Pig was the first of Countrylife's bottled beers and is good with fish, according to Simon.

Tasting Notes
A golden bitter with malt and grassy hop in the nose, strong hop-fruit, hop-resins and bitterness in the taste and a long, tangy hop finish.

Lacey's Real Lager

- **ABV 5.2–5.4%** ▪ **BOTTLE SIZE 500 ml** ▪ **SERVE cold**
- **INGREDIENTS Lager malt/Mount Hood and Hersbrucker hops**

Brewed in the winter and sold throughout the year, in the old lager tradition, this beer varies in strength from batch to batch, but is brewed with a lager yeast and given three–four weeks' lagering at 3°C. The hopping rate may also vary. 'Only 3000 bottles made a year', declares the label.

Tasting Notes
(*5.2% version*): A golden beer with an aroma of herbs and slightly toasted malt. Fruity and quite sweet for a lager, it has lightly perfumed hop notes in the taste and a gentle acidity, before hops build in the bittersweet finish.

Country Bumpkin

- **ABV 6%** ▪ **BOTTLE SIZE 500 ml** ▪ **SERVE cool**
- **INGREDIENTS Maris Otter pale malt/chocolate malt/ Challenger and Golding hops**

Country Bumpkin, Simon reckons, makes a good match for steak meals.

Tasting Notes
An amber ale, with an aroma that is spicy, malty, resin-like and a little fruity. A blast of strong hops, fruit and sweet malt, with a little chocolate, follows on the palate, rounded off by a hoppy, bitter, fruity finish with lingering chocolate.

CROPTON

Cropton Brewery Co., The New Inn, Cropton, Pickering, North Yorkshire YO18 8HH.
Tel. (01751) 417330 Fax (01751) 417310
E-mail: info@croptonbrewery.co.uk
Website: www.croptonbrewery.co.uk
Mail order service

Cropton Brewery was set up in 1984 in the cellar of the New Inn, just to supply that pub. By 1994 it had outgrown the cellar and a purpose-built brewery was installed behind the pub, which also now has a visitor's centre for brewery tours. The beers all bear logos declaring that they are suitable for both vegetarians and vegans. They are matured in conditioning tanks, filtered and then re-seeded with fresh yeast before bottling, and all carry a 12-month best before stamp. The US importer is Shelton Brothers.

King Billy Bitter

- **ABV 3.6%** ▪ **BOTTLE SIZE 500 ml** ▪ **SERVE cool**
- **INGREDIENTS Pale malt/Challenger and East Kent Golding hops**

King Billy is a rare, bottle-conditioned session ale. Its name was derived from the statue of King William III outside the King William pub in Hull, which Cropton has long supplied with cask beer. In 1993, the landlord of the pub asked for a brew which his regulars could 'drink all day and not become excitable', hence this popular quaffing brew.

Tasting Notes

A golden beer with a surprisingly strong aroma of malt, hops and creamy fruit. Reasonably thin in body, it tastes malty and dry before an even drier, increasingly bitter finish.

Major stockist (all beers) Local Tesco

Endeavour

- **ABV 3.8%** ▪ **BOTTLE SIZE 500 ml** ▪ **SERVE cool**
- **INGREDIENTS Pale malt/Challenger and Golding hops**

Named after Captain Cook's famous ship, that originally sailed from nearby Whitby, Endeavour is a bitter aimed at the tourist market in the seaside resort (a replica of *Endeavour* sails into Whitby every year and draws in the crowds).

Tasting Notes

A dark golden ale with hop fruit and malt in the nose and taste, and a light, bittersweet finish.

Two Pints Bitter

- **ABV 4%** ▪ **BOTTLE SIZE 500 ml** ▪ **SERVE cool**
- **INGREDIENTS Pale malt/crystal malt/Challenger and East Kent Golding hops**

A pint of Two Pints was first served at the New Inn back in 1984, the brewery's first year of operation, but the beer did not find its way into a bottle until 1996. It's now the brewery's biggest selling beer, taking its name from the idea that one pint of Two Pints 'is worth two of any other'. The label shows a landlord handing over two foaming tankards of ale.

Tasting Notes

A dry, amber-coloured bitter with citrous fruitiness, malt and bitterness the key elements in the taste, preceded by a hoppy, malty nose. The dry finish is bitter and hoppy.

Honey Gold

▪ ABV 4.2% ▪ BOTTLE SIZE 500 ml ▪ SERVE cool
▪ INGREDIENTS Pale malt/honey/First Gold hops

This beer (for a time known as Honey Farm Bitter) was introduced in cask-conditioned form for Cropton's own first beer festival, held in March 1998, and is now a summer supplement to the brewery's standard draught range. It is a single-varietal hop brew, using only the popular dwarf hop, First Gold, plus a dose of Yorkshire honey.

Tasting Notes

A golden beer with a honeyed nose. The crisp, bitter taste has a light hop edge, with soft honey evident particularly on the swallow. Bitter, hoppy finish with more than a hint of honey.

Scoresby Stout

▪ ABV 4.2% ▪ BOTTLE SIZE 500 ml ▪ SERVE cool
▪ INGREDIENTS Pale malt/crystal malt/roasted barley/ Challenger and Golding hops

This rich, dark stout takes its name from the late William Scoresby, a whaling captain who hailed from Cropton – which explains the presence of a whaling ship being tossed on the high seas on the label. Among his various achievements, Scoresby is said to have invented the crow's nest. He is now commemorated with a plaque at Whitby harbour. The cask equivalent of this beer made its debut in 1988 and this bottled option was first produced in 1996.

Tasting Notes

This almost black beer (with just a hint of red) has a strong coffee aroma. The taste is soft, malty and coffeeish, enhanced by some burnt grain notes. Bitter coffee features in the finish.

Uncle Sams Bitter

▪ ABV 4.4% ▪ BOTTLE SIZE 500 ml ▪ SERVE cool
▪ INGREDIENTS Pale malt/crystal malt/Cascade hops

Certainly the most distinctive of Cropton's bottled ales, Uncle Sams is a homage to the American microbrewer revolution and is chock-full of the perfumed aroma and taste of

American Cascade hops. Lest there be any doubt about its inspiration, the label has a Wild West image, with a gun-toting Annie Oakley (or some other girl sharp-shooter) as the focal point. Both this and the original cask version were introduced in 1997.

Tasting Notes

A golden beer with an aroma rich in tangy Cascade hops. These spill over into the taste, bringing strong bitter lemon and grapefruit notes. The aftertaste is dry and full of scented hops.

Rudolph's Revenge

- **ABV 4.6%** ■ **BOTTLE SIZE 500 ml** ■ **SERVE cool**
- **INGREDIENTS Pale malt/crystal malt/roasted barley/ Cascade, Styrian Golding and Challenger hops**

This is Cropton's Christmas beer and shares with Uncle Sams an American nuance, thanks to the use of Cascade hops. At 4.6%, it is one of the UK's less potent Christmas ales, and is also sold in cask.

Tasting Notes

A red ale with a malty, lightly citrous aroma. Citrous fruit continues in the malty taste, as the aromatic hops take hold and roasted barley drifts well into the background. The long aftertaste is hoppy, tangy and roasty.

Yorkshire Moors

- **ABV 4.6%** ■ **BOTTLE SIZE 500 ml** ■ **SERVE cool**
- **INGREDIENTS Pale malt/crystal malt/roasted malt/ Challenger and Styrian Golding hops**

Created to help commemorate 50 years of the National Park service in 2002, Yorkshire Moors has now become a permanent part of the Cropton range, replacing Backwoods Bitter (the recipe is basically the same, but this is more quaffable than the 5.1% Backwoods).

Tasting Notes

A light ruby ale with a citrous, malty nose that is also a little peppery. The soft, dark malt taste is balanced by a peppery, fruity bitterness that smacks of cherries. The finish is dry and malty, yet also bitter and hoppy, with some roast character.

Monkman's Slaughter

- **ABV 6%** ■ **BOTTLE SIZE 500 ml** ■ **SERVE cool**
- **INGREDIENTS Pale malt/crystal malt/roasted malt/ Challenger and East Kent Golding hops**

Originally known by the name 'Special Strong', this powerful beer takes its unusual, and rather macabre, title from two quite innocent sources. These are Messrs Colin Monkman and Colin Slaughter, the brewery's barley farmer and head brewer, respectively.

Tasting Notes

A ruby-coloured ale with vinous fruit and dark malts dominant in the nose. The taste is initially sweetish, fruity and malty, with roast grain gradually taking over. Roasty, bitter aftertaste, with hints of liquorice.

DARK STAR

Dark Star Brewing Co. Ltd., Moonhill Farm, Burgess Hill Road, Ansty, Haywards Heath, West Sussex RH17 5AH.
Tel./Fax (01444) 412311
E-mail: sales@darkstarbrewing.co.uk
Website: www.darkstarbrewing.co.uk

Dark Star's history can be traced back to the 1980s, when brewer Rob Jones was a partner in Pitfield Brewery. Pitfield achieved a major coup in 1987 by winning CAMRA's *Champion Beer of Britain* contest with a beer called Dark Star. When Rob left Pitfield, he took Dark Star with him and named his new brewery after it. Brewing began in 1995 at another star, The Evening Star pub in Brighton. Demand grew to the point that extra capacity was needed, so Rob and his colleagues decamped to the country in 2001, taking up residence in a former dairy. Two beers are currently bottled in house, but there are plans to bottle the famous Dark Star itself, although under contract this time.

Porter

- **ABV 5.5%** ▪ **BOTTLE SIZE 500 ml** ▪ **SERVE cool**
- **INGREDIENTS Maris Otter pale malt/crystal malt/brown malt/black malt/caramalt/Target and Styrian Golding hops**

Although a cask brew for winter for several years, Dark Star's Porter was only bottled for the first time for winter 2003–4. As for the Critical Mass overleaf, the beer is dropped bright and re-seeded with fresh yeast (same strain as primary fermentation) and then bottled from the cask, perhaps with some primings to ensure a good secondary fermentation.

Tasting Notes

A dark red porter with creamy coffee and a suggestion of fruit in the aroma. The taste is smooth and sweetish, offering mellow coffee in the malt mix plus light hop. Gentle, hoppy bitterness blends with soft coffee in the drying finish.

Critical Mass

- **ABV 7.4%** ▪ **BOTTLE SIZE 500 ml** ▪ **SERVE cool**
- **INGREDIENTS Maris Otter pale malt/Munich malt/crystal malt/black malt/chocolate malt/roasted barley/Hallertau and Perle hops**

First brewed in 1995 and bottled in short runs ever since, this is Dark Star's potent winter warmer.

Tasting Notes

A ruby ale with a restrained aroma of juicy fruit (including tropical) and creamy dark malt. The taste is a smooth, warming mix of the same juicy fruit and creamy, sweet malt, with a bittersweet, malty, fruity finish to round off.

DARWIN

Darwin Brewery Ltd., 63 Back Tatham Street, Sunderland, Tyne & Wear SR1 3SD.
Tel. (0191) 515 2535 Fax (0191) 515 2531
E-mail: info@darwinbrewery.com
Website: www.darwinbrewery.com

Darwin Brewery was founded in 1994 as a research facility for students at the University of Sunderland's Brewlab. In 1997, its directors took over the nearby Hodge's Brewery and the whole business was relocated to a new site in Sunderland in 2002. One of the brewery's specialities is the re-creation of historic beer styles, such as some of the bottled brews below. A new range of specialist beers (novel and traditional) is planned and these will be bottled in small quantities (150-bottle batches). Darwin also brews beers for High Force Brewery (see separate entry).

Richmond Ale

- **ABV 4.5%** ▪ **BOTTLE SIZE 500 ml** ▪ **SERVE cool**
- **INGREDIENTS Pale malt/crystal malt/brown malt/black malt/Fuggle and Golding hops**

Showing Richmond Castle on its 'stained-glass'-style label, Richmond Ale is described as a 'double brown ale' and is brewed using North Yorkshire malt and a northern yeast strain. A recipe from a Ripon brewery gave Brewlab director Dr Keith Thomas a feeling for the malt character of a beer that might have been available in the late 1800s and records from a maltings near Richmond showed what brewers were ordering at the time. For the yeast, Keith turned to local fruit. He felt that the brewers of the time would have thrown their yeast around without much thought and he considered that yeast living wild on fruit in the area today would have been related to the brewers' yeast of the time. Richmond Ale is also available in cask form and as a filtered bottle, so look carefully for the tastier bottle-conditioned version, which is kräusened prior to filling.

Tasting Notes

A ruby-red/brown beer with an aroma of malt and toffee. The taste is deeply malty, nutty and fruity, with balancing hop bitterness. Dry, bitter, malty finish.

Hammond's Porter

- **ABV 4.7%** ■ **BOTTLE SIZE 500 ml** ■ **SERVE cool**
- **INGREDIENTS Pale malt/crystal malt/black malt/ maize/glucose sugar/Fuggle hops**

Once again Darwin proves that there is life after death. This time the brewers have resurrected the taste of Hammond's Bradford brewery, using 1903 brewery records and authentic yeast from the brewery that became a victim of Bass Charrington consolidation. Small runs mean that the beer is only likely to be found in the North-East.

Tasting Notes

Virtually black in colour, with a beige foam, this porter has a mix of chocolate, coffee and treacly malt in the nose, a smooth, bittersweet, roasted malt taste, with a light hop balance, and a finish of sweet coffee, with hops building.

Extinction Ale

- **ABV 8.2%** ■ **BOTTLE SIZE 500 ml** ■ **SERVE cool**
- **INGREDIENTS Pale malt/crystal malt/Fuggle and Golding hops**

Extinction Ale is based on a bottled beer discovered in a cellar on the North York Moors in 1998. Dating from 1927, the beer – a barley wine bottled from the remains of a cask – was thought to have come from the now defunct Scarborough and Whitby brewery. Thanks to close analysis at Brewlab – which sought to identify hops from the bitterness of the beer and the malt from its colour – plus a trawl through brewing archives, a comparable recipe was produced. Extinction Ale is now brewed using yeast isolated from that original bottle. A cask version has also been sold. One to enjoy with a rich dessert perhaps.

Tasting Notes
A red-brown, powerful ale with a vinous malty and fruity (strawberries) aroma. Clean and well-rounded on the palate, it tastes sweet, malty and fruity (prune?). Mouth-numbing, mostly sweet, fruity finish.

Hammond's Stingo

- **ABV 10%** ▪ **BOTTLE SIZE 500 ml** ▪ **SERVE cool**
- **INGREDIENTS Pale malt/black malt/maize/glucose sugar/Fuggle hops**

Like the aforementioned Hammond's Porter, this powerful barley wine was re-created at Brewlab with the help of the County and Durden Park groups of amateur brewing enthusiasts.

Tasting Notes
A ruby beer with a heady nose of vinous fruit and malt. The gum-tingling taste has lots of malt and bitter orange fruit, with a red berry fruitiness emerging on the swallow. Bitterness fights back in the finish, but sweet fruit lingers.

DOGHOUSE

Doghouse Brewery, Scorrier, Redruth, Cornwall TR16 5BN. Tel./Fax (01209) 822022
E-mail: starhawk@dsl.pipex.com
Why end up in the doghouse by slinking off to the pub when you can now get into the same trouble at home? Doghouse Brewery was set up in 2001 in a former canine rescue centre. Its bottled ales are all treated with priming sugars and filled directly from the cask, with six months allowed in the best before dates.

Biter

- **ABV 4%** ▪ **BOTTLE SIZE 500 ml** ▪ **SERVE cool**
- **INGREDIENTS Optic pale malt/crystal malt/Northdown and Styrian Golding hops**

One of the brewery's original beers, a play on the term 'bitter'.

Dozey Dawg

- **ABV 4.4%** ▪ **BOTTLE SIZE 500 ml** ▪ **SERVE cool**
- **INGREDIENTS Optic pale malt/crystal malt/Pilot and Cascade hops**

First brewed as a summer beer in 2003 and retained as a regular brew.

Tasting Notes

A golden beer with light malt and fruit in the nose, a sharp mix of hops and malt in the mouth and a little toasted grain complementing these same flavours in the finish.

Cornish Corgi

- **ABV 4.5%** ▪ **BOTTLE SIZE 500 ml** ▪ **SERVE cool**
- **INGREDIENTS Optic pale malt/crystal malt/Pilot and Styrian Golding hops**

Originally the Golden Jubilee beer (then called Loyal Corgi), this beer, like other Doghouse brews, employs a new strain of dwarf hops, Pilot, that was named by brewer Steve Willmott in a competition organised by hop merchant Charles Faram.

Dogfight

- **ABV 4.7%** ▪ **BOTTLE SIZE 500 ml** ▪ **SERVE cool**
- **INGREDIENTS Optic pale malt/crystal malt/chocolate malt/roasted barley/Pilot and Cascade hops**

A blend of Dozey Dawg and Bow Wow, creating a ruby-coloured ale.

Tasting Notes

A tawny ale with a malty aroma, a sharp, malty, nutty taste with citrous notes, and roasted grain in the aftertaste.

Staffi Stout

- **ABV 4.7%** ▪ **BOTTLE SIZE 500 ml** ▪ **SERVE cool**
- **INGREDIENTS Optic pale malt/black malt/roasted barley/Fuggle and Golding hops**

'A Staffordshire bull terrier has a strong bite and so does this stout', says brewer Steve Willmott. Usually brewed in springtime.

Tasting Notes

A ruby beer with light fruit and creamy malt in the nose. Nutty, roasted malt in the taste is rounded off by a malty, roasted finish.

Bow Wow

- **ABV 5%** ▪ **BOTTLE SIZE 500 ml** ▪ **SERVE cool**
- **INGREDIENTS Optic pale malt/crystal malt/chocolate malt/roasted barley/torrefied wheat/Challenger hops**

A strong ale continuing the 'doggie' theme.

Tasting Notes
A tawny ale with an estery, pear drop and treacly malt nose. Malty to taste, with a tart fruitiness, it finishes malty and bittersweet.

Dingo Lager

- **ABV 5% ▪ BOTTLE SIZE 500 ml ▪ SERVE cold**
- **INGREDIENTS Lager malt/Hallertau hops**

Brewed with a lager yeast, this is the brewery's wild dog response to ubiquitous Aussie beer brands. The beer is lagered for two–three months prior to bottling.
Tasting Notes
A pale golden beer with a light, malty aroma. Light, sweet malt in the taste is offset by sharp, fruity hops. Bittersweet finish.

Colliewobbles/Christmas Tail

- **ABV 5.8% ▪ BOTTLE SIZE 500 ml ▪ SERVE cool**
- **INGREDIENTS Optic pale malt/crystal malt/chocolate malt/roasted barley/torrefied wheat/Fuggle and Golding hops**

A winter brew called Christmas Tail that is re-branded as Colliewobbles for sale at other times of the year.

DORSET

Dorset Brewing Company Ltd., The Quay Brewery, Hope Square, Weymouth, Dorset DT4 8TR.
Tel./Fax (01305) 777515 (call first to fax)
E-mail: mail@quaybrewery.com
Website: www.fineale.com
Brewery set up by Giles Smeath under the name of Quay Brewery in summer 1996. It is housed in buildings once home to Weymouth's Devenish and Groves breweries and, with its arrival, beer production was re-introduced to the seaside town after a ten-year absence. The brewery's name was changed to Dorset Brewing Company (DBC) in 2004. It can now be visited as part of the Timewalk tourist attraction, which includes two on-site off-licences where Dorset's beers can be purchased. The bottled beers, produced in short runs, are presented in swing-stoppered glassware, which is filled on site from a conditioning tank. There is no filtration and the beers are only primed when required to boost the condition.

Weymouth JD 1742

■ ABV 4.2% ■ BOTTLE SIZE 500 ml ■ SERVE cool
■ INGREDIENTS Maris Otter pale malt/Challenger and Mount Hood hops

Introduced in 2002 to commemorate the founding of the Devenish Brewery in Weymouth by John Devenish in 1742.

Steam Beer

■ ABV 4.5% ■ BOTTLE SIZE 500 ml ■ SERVE cool
■ INGREDIENTS Lager malt/black malt/wheat malt/ Cascade hops

Steam Beer is Quay's homage to the hybrid beers created during the days of California's Gold Rush in the 19th century. These were brewed in the ale style with lager ingredients, and enjoyed high carbonation levels that provided a steamy hiss on dispense. (The style is perpetuated today by San Francisco's Anchor brewery.)

Jurassic

■ ABV 4.7% ■ BOTTLE SIZE 500 ml ■ SERVE cool
■ INGREDIENTS Pale malt/crystal malt/Hallertau and Saaz hops

Reflecting the brewery's position on the Jurassic Coast of Dorset, this is made from mostly organic ingredients, including the malt and the Hallertau hops from New Zealand.

Durdle Door

■ ABV 5% ■ BOTTLE SIZE 500 ml ■ SERVE cool
■ INGREDIENTS Maris Otter pale malt/wheat malt/ Cascade, Brewer's Gold and Fuggle hops

A new, rusty-golden beer named after Dorset's famous coastline landmark.

Silent Knight

■ ABV 5.9% ■ BOTTLE SIZE 500 ml ■ SERVE cool
■ INGREDIENTS Maris Otter pale malt/chocolate malt/ wheat malt/Bramling Cross hops

This dark wheat beer, brewed in the style of a German weizenbock, picked up the supreme accolade at SIBA's *Wheat Beer Challenge* in 1997. At 5.9%, it is just a touch stronger than its cask brother of the same name and, like most wheat beers, is designed to be drunk hazy.

DUNN PLOWMAN

Dunn Plowman Brewery, Unit 1A, Arrow Court Industrial Estate, Hergest Road, Kington, Herefordshire HR5 3DL.
Tel. (01544) 231993 Fax (01544) 231985
E-mail: dunnplowman.brewery@talk21.com
Mail order service

Dunn Plowman was set up in 1987 and moved to a new site, behind The Queen's Head pub in Kington, in 1994. In 2002 it transferred to its present site, relocating brewing equipment acquired with the purchase of the SP Sporting Ales brewery. It remains a family business, with Steve and Gaye Dunn as proprietors. The beers are filtered, then re-seeded with fresh yeast of the same strain and primed with sugar before bottling. Best before dates are fixed at nine months.

Old Jake

- **ABV 4.8%** ■ **BOTTLE SIZE 500 ml** ■ **SERVE cool**
- **INGREDIENTS Maris Otter pale malt/wheat malt/flaked barley/roasted barley/Fuggle and Golding hops**

A stout, first bottled in 2000, and now brewed all year. As the label explains, the name commemorates the passing of the family's beloved black-and-tan crossbreed dog.

Golden Haze

- **ABV 5%** ■ **BOTTLE SIZE 500 ml** ■ **SERVE cool**
- **INGREDIENTS Maris Otter pale malt/wheat malt/First Gold hops/orange peel/coriander**

Dunn Plowman's wheat beer, in the Belgian wit style, with orange peel and coriander added during the copper boil.

Kyneton Ale

- **ABV 5%** ■ **BOTTLE SIZE 500 ml** ■ **SERVE cool**
- **INGREDIENTS Maris Otter pale malt/crystal malt/wheat malt/Fuggle and Golding hops**

A strong bitter brewed first in spring 2000.

Crooked Furrow

- **ABV 6.5%** ■ **BOTTLE SIZE 330/500 ml** ■ **SERVE cool**
- **INGREDIENTS Maris Otter pale malt/crystal malt/black malt/Fuggle and Golding hops**

Strong enough to tempt a ploughman off the straight and narrow, this powerful ale was first produced in draught form in 1997 and then bottled for the first time in 1999.

Tasting Notes

An amber strong ale with a fruity, malty, spicy aroma. Although it is fruity, with cherry notes, in the mouth, it is not too sweet, but the alcohol is obvious. Dry, bitter fruit finish.

DURHAM

The Durham Brewery, Unit 5A, Bowburn North Industrial Estate, Bowburn, Co. Durham DH6 5PF.
Tel. (0191) 377 1991 Fax (0191) 377 0768
E-mail: gibbs@durham-brewery.co.uk
Website: www.durham-brewery.co.uk
Mail order service

Durham Brewery was set up by music teachers Steve and Christine Gibbs who foresaw redundancy heading their way as cuts in their local education budget loomed. That was back in 1994 and the brewery now produces a wide range of cask beers and seven highly-regarded bottle-conditioned beers. All are brewed and bottled on site, with beers passing from fermenters into conditioning tanks, where they are chilled and fined with non-animal finings. This ensures that all the bottled beers are perfectly acceptable to vegetarians and vegans. The yeast count is then adjusted before bottling takes place, and primings are added only if deemed necessary. One month's conditioning is allowed before the beers go on sale.

Cloister

- **ABV 4.5%** ▪ **BOTTLE SIZE 500 ml** ▪ **SERVE cool**
- **INGREDIENTS Maris Otter pale malt/crystal malt/ Challenger, Target, Columbus and Saaz hops**

Like this golden ale, all the brewery's beer names have connections with the spiritual roots of the city of Durham and in particular the spellbinding cathedral.

Tasting Notes

A dark golden bitter with a citrous hop aroma backed by light malt. The taste is crisp, pleasantly bitter, citrously fruity and hoppy, with a very dry bitter and hoppy aftertaste.

Evensong

- **ABV 5%** ▪ **BOTTLE SIZE 500 ml** ▪ **SERVE cool**
- **INGREDIENTS Maris Otter pale malt/crystal malt/ Golding hops**

Introduced in 2001 and based on a recipe dating from 1937.

Tasting Notes
A rich ruby ale with a white head and a soft aroma of citrus and berry fruits along with gentle dark malt. The soft taste features a restrained fruitiness, gentle malt and a rounded bitterness, with toasted malt emerging in the lightly fruity malt finish.

Black Abbot

- **ABV 5.6%** ■ **BOTTLE SIZE 500 ml** ■ **SERVE cool**
- **INGREDIENTS Maris Otter pale malt/lager malt/Munich malt/pale chocolate malt/black malt/wheat malt/rye crystal malt/Saaz and Northdown hops**

Durham used to bottle a beer with the similar name of Black Bishop, but, despite being close in strength and title, Black Abbot is quite a different beer. It's actually a dark lager.

Tasting Notes
A rich ruby beer with a white foam. The aroma is complex: gentle, nutty, roasted malt, mellow coffee and a hint of fruit. The taste is well balanced and clean, with dark malt and a persistent fruity edge continuing into the moreish finish.

St Cuthbert

- **ABV 6.5%** ■ **BOTTLE SIZE 500 ml** ■ **SERVE cool**
- **INGREDIENTS Maris Otter pale malt/crystal malt/Challenger, Target, Columbus, Golding and Saaz hops**

St Cuthbert was Durham's first bottle-conditioned beer and was initially called Millennium City – a reference to the fact that Durham was celebrating its 1,000th year as a city at the turn of the millennium. In 2000 Durham re-christened the beer in honour of the saint whose relics were brought to Durham from Lindisfarne by monks. Inspired by a vision, the monks' decision to settle here heralded the foundation of the city and St Cuthbert still lies in the magnificent cathedral.

Tasting Notes
This strong amber ale has an orange aroma and a smooth, toffeeish malt taste, balanced by citrus fruits. Hints of pear drops expose the strength, but the beer falls on the bitter side of bittersweet. Soft, bitter finish of malt and fruit.

White Magic

- **ABV 7%** ■ **BOTTLE SIZE 500 ml** ■ **SERVE cool**
- **INGREDIENTS Maris Otter pale malt/Golding hops**

A new beer, created in spring 2004 and brewed only for the bottle, to an original recipe for India pale ale.

Benedictus

- **ABV 8.4%** ■ **BOTTLE SIZE 500 ml** ■ **SERVE cool**
- **INGREDIENTS Maris Otter pale malt/crystal malt/ Golding, Target, Saaz and Styrian Golding hops**

Based on St Cuthbert, but with a deeper golden colour, Benedictus was added to the range in 2001.

Tasting Notes

An orange/copper barley wine with orange and pineapple fruits sharing the aroma. Lots of malty body follows in the mouth, but with fruity, spicy hops taking the lead. The bitter, hoppy finish leaves a warming glow. Somewhat reminiscent of Chimay White in its strength and hoppiness.

Temptation

- **ABV 10%** ■ **BOTTLE SIZE 500 ml** ■ **SERVE cool**
- **INGREDIENTS Maris Otter pale malt/lager malt/black malt/roasted barley/wheat malt/Target and Golding hops**

We all know the Biblical perils of succumbing to temptation, but Durham thinks it's worth making an exception for this brew. The name it was first sold under reveals the style: it was simply called Imperial Russian Stout.

Tasting Notes

A beer as black as sin with a beige clerical collar. Traces of mellow coffee, fruit and treacly malt enhance the lightly winey aroma. In the mouth, the beer is light and easy drinking, making a mockery of the declared strength, with sweet malt well to the fore ahead of coffee and fruity hop notes. Soft liquorice emerges in the gum-numbing, sweet coffee finish

E&S ELLAND

Eastwood & Sanders (Fine Ales) Ltd., Units 3–5, Heathfield Industrial Estate, Heathfield Street, Elland, West Yorkshire HX5 9AE.
Tel. (01422) 377677 Fax (01422) 370922
E-mail: EandS@btconnect.com

Brewery formed in 2002 as the result of a merger between the Barge & Barrel and West Yorkshire breweries. Although the company name remains Eastwood & Sanders, E&S Elland is now the preferred name for use in the trade. The beers overleaf, although brewed by E&S, are actually bottled and marketed by Clarke's Organic (see separate entry).

Beyond the Pale

- **ABV 4.2%** ▪ **BOTTLE SIZE 500 ml** ▪ **SERVE cool**
- **INGREDIENTS Maris Otter pale malt/amber malt/ wheat malt/Challenger, Centennial, Cascade and First Gold hops**

Pale in colour, but also inspired by a track of the same name by the band The Mission. Originally a West Yorkshire Brewery beer, Beyond the Pale is now a touch stronger (up from 4%).

Tasting Notes

Orange-gold with a hoppy, fruity nose. Crisp, hoppy, bitter taste with fruit in the background; dry, hoppy, bitter finish.

1872 Porter

- **ABV 6.5%** ▪ **BOTTLE SIZE 500 ml** ▪ **SERVE cool**
- **INGREDIENTS Maris Otter pale malt/amber malt/ chocolate malt/brown malt/Golding, Challenger and First Gold hops/muscovado sugar/molasses**

A multi-award-winning porter (including a 2004 *Brewing Industry International Awards* gold), re-created by brewer Dave Sanders from a 19th-century recipe.

Tasting Notes

A deep, dark red porter with a soft, coffee-roast aroma. The big, coffeeish taste is smooth, sweetish and malty, with a creamy mouthfeel. Dry, bittersweet, roasted finish.

EARL SOHAM

Earl Soham Brewery, The Street, Earl Soham, Suffolk IP13 7RT.
Tel. (01728) 684097 (brewery)/685557 (Tastebuds)
E-mail: malcolmwalker@beeb.net
Website: www.earlsohambrewery.co.uk

Founded behind The Victoria pub in the village of Earl Soham in 1984, this brewery moved along the road to larger premises in a converted garage in 2001. Next door stands Tastebuds, a well-stocked post-office/delicatessen that sells Earl Soham's beers on draught and in bottle.

Gannet Mild

- **ABV 3.3%** ▪ **BOTTLE SIZE 500/750 ml** ▪ **SERVE cool**
- **INGREDIENTS Maris Otter pale malt/crystal malt/black malt/Fuggle and Golding hops**

Like other Earl Soham's beers, Gannet Mild – one of the

brewery's earliest offerings – is allowed 14 days in cask before bottling. The same yeast used in primary fermentation is carried over and the beers are only primed with sugar if it is deemed necessary for optimum carbonation. Bottling takes place in a 'jug and bottle' room next to the brewery.

Tasting Notes

A light ruby mild with a malty, nutty, fruity aroma. The taste is bittersweet and malty yet with a little hop adding dryness. Gently bitter, drying finish with nutty roasted grain behind.

Victoria Bitter

- **ABV 3.6%** ■ **BOTTLE SIZE 500/750 ml** ■ **SERVE cool**
- **INGREDIENTS Maris Otter pale malt/crystal malt/ Whitbread Golding Variety, Fuggle and Golding hops**

First brewed in 1985, Victoria Bitter (described as a 'throat opening session bitter'), takes its name from the pub which was Earl Soham's first home. Brewery owner John Bjornson suggests trying Victoria Bitter with salads. His colleague at Tastebuds, Malcolm Walker, recommends it with all foods, except salads. Each to his own, I suppose.

Tasting Notes

A golden bitter with a good aroma for its strength, fruity, hoppy and malty. Grassy hops overlay a smooth, malty base in the bittersweet taste, before a hoppy finish.

Sir Roger's Porter

- **ABV 4%** ■ **BOTTLE SIZE 500/750 ml** ■ **SERVE cool**
- **INGREDIENTS Maris Otter pale malt/crystal malt/black malt/roasted barley/Fuggle, Styrian Golding and Golding hops**

A dark, malty porter, first brewed for Christmas 1999 and now usually produced about once a year.

Gold

- **ABV 4%** ■ **BOTTLE SIZE 500 ml** ■ **SERVE cool**
- **INGREDIENTS Maris Otter pale malt/crystal malt/ Brewer's Gold hops**

A single-varietal hop beer (exclusive to Tastebuds) brewed every six months and considered a fine accompaniment to summer foods, including salads.

Tasting Notes

Actually more of a copper colour, this beer has a hoppy, orange-zesty nose, a perfumed, bitter orange taste on a base of sweet, smooth malt, and a dry, hoppy aftertaste.

Albert Ale

■ ABV 4.4% ■ BOTTLE SIZE 500/750 ml ■ SERVE cool
■ INGREDIENTS Maris Otter pale malt/crystal malt/black malt/roasted barley/Whitbread Golding Variety and Golding hops

As for most other beers from the brewery, Albert Ale ('an ale for the evening, when there is time to savour its subtleties') is mainly hopped with Whitbread Golding Variety (WGV) but is given a charge of Goldings after the boil for extra aroma. Goldings are also used to dry hop the beers. It was first brewed in 1985.

Tasting Notes

A copper beer with a malty, hoppy aroma. The taste is malty but not sweet, with nutty, roasted grain prominent and a strong hop balance. Nutty, dark malt and hops finish.

Empress India Premium Pale Ale

■ ABV 4.7% ■ BOTTLE SIZE 500/750 ml ■ SERVE cool
■ INGREDIENTS Maris Otter pale malt/crystal malt/Whitbread Golding Variety, Fuggle and Golding hops

Now produced weekly, this IPA (like other Earl Soham brews) is marked with the date of each bottling, so that customers know the precise age of each bottle.

ELVEDEN

Elveden Ales, by Walled Garden, Elveden Courtyard, Elveden, Thetford, Norfolk IP24 3TQ.
Tel. (01842) 878922

This five-barrel brewery was opened in early 2004 by Frances Moore, daughter of Iceni Brewery's Brendan Moore. It is housed on the Elveden estate, the home of the Guinness family, who encourage the production and sale of local crafts and food and drink on the site. As well as brewing, Frances also demonstrates the skill of malting here, and hops are allowed to grow alongside the brewery.

Stout

■ ABV 5% ■ BOTTLE SIZE 500/750 ml ■ SERVE cool
■ INGREDIENTS Maris Otter pale malt/roasted barley/wheat/Boadicea hops/molasses

Aged in oak casks when it is sold on draught, this traditional stout is laced with black strap molasses in the copper.

Tasting Notes
A very dark brown beer with dark malt but also floral, fruity notes in the nose. The taste is bitter, with a light malty sweetness and plenty of roasted grain, plus a hint of peachy fruit. Dry, bitter, roasted finish.

Elveden Ale

- **ABV 5.2%** ■ **BOTTLE SIZE 500/750 ml** ■ **SERVE cool**
- **INGREDIENTS Maris Otter pale malt/wheat/Boadicea hops**

Like the Stout, Elveden Ale incorporates the new strain of Boadicea hops and is bottled in stone-effect jugs, topped with a swing stopper.
Tasting Notes
Orange-gold in colour, this strong ale has a floral, peachy aroma and a predominantly bitter taste with a peachy fruitiness. The finish is hoppy and bitter.

EXE VALLEY

Exe Valley Brewery, Silverton, Exeter, Devon EX5 4HF.
Tel. (01392) 860406 Fax (01392) 861001
E-mail: guysheppard@supanet.com
Website: www.siba-southwest.co.uk/breweries/exevalley
Exe Valley Brewery, formerly known as Barron's Brewery, is now wholly owned by Guy and Sue Sheppard, following the retirement, in June 2003, of Guy's former partner, Richard Barron. The brewery moved into bottled beer production in 2001, using Keltek Brewery in Cornwall for bottling (direct from casks).

Devon Glory

- **ABV 4.7%** ■ **BOTTLE SIZE 500 ml** ■ **SERVE cool**
- **INGREDIENTS Optic pale malt/crystal malt/chocolate malt/Fuggle, Golding and Challenger hops**

A draught beer for many years, Devon Glory was the first of Exe Valley's beers to be regularly bottled (a second beer, Hope – for charity – was available for a while but has been discontinued). Best before dates are fixed at seven months post-bottling.
Tasting Notes
A tawny-coloured, bittersweet, malty beer with tropical fruit notes in the aroma. There are hints of chocolate in the taste, while nutty, roasted malt leads in the finish.

FELSTAR

The Felstar Brewery, Felsted Vineyard, Crix Green, Felsted, Essex CM6 3JT. Tel./Fax (01245) 361504
E-mail: felstarbrewery@supanet.com
Mail order service

Felstar Brewery was built in 2001 in the old bonded stores of Felsted Vineyard, the first commercial vineyard in East Anglia. Production of its own beers neatly filled a space in the site's own shop, between English wines and ciders. The brewery is run by former graphic designer Marcello Davanzo (known to everyone as Franco), who has chosen the rooster as his brewery logo. If you ever call into Franco's shop, you'll know why. Try driving out again without running over one of his free-ranging poultry stock. His beers are bottled on site, being racked bright after conditioning in the cask and primed with the same yeast as used in primary fermentation. Bottom-fermenting beers are kräusened and/or primed with unrefined molasses. Best before dates are generally fixed at 12 months. Franco is one of the most inventive brewers around, cheerfully tearing up the rulebooks and mixing and matching ale recipes with lager production methods. This is a man who, when planning to produce a honey beer, insisted on farming his own honey and learned bee-keeping skills to do so. First, however, he needed to make the hives, and so put his wood-working talents to good use.

Crix Gold

- **ABV 4%** ▪ **BOTTLE SIZE 500 ml** ▪ **SERVE cool**
- **INGREDIENTS Lager malt/caramalt/wheat malt/First Gold, Jenny and Brewer's Gold hops**

The sprawling settlement of Felsted is actually made up of several smaller villages, most ending in 'Green'. Crix Green is where the brewery is located (follow the brown vineyard signs) – hence the name of this and other beers. An unusual selection of hops includes the new dwarf hop named Jenny.

Tasting Notes

A golden ale with a fresh, citrous hop nose backed by biscuity malt. Tart lemon dominates the crisp taste; dry, bitter finish.

Hops & Glory

- **ABV 4%** ▪ **BOTTLE SIZE 500 ml** ▪ **SERVE cool**
- **INGREDIENTS Maris Otter pale malt/crystal malt/chocolate malt/wheat malt/Brewer's Gold and Fuggle hops**

'Fruity when young, complex when mature', is how Franco describes this best bitter, brewed a couple of times a year.

Chick Chat

- **ABV 4.1%** ▪ **BOTTLE SIZE 500 ml** ▪ **SERVE cool**
- **INGREDIENTS Maris Otter and Pearl pale malt/chocolate malt/torrefied wheat/Bramling Cross and Fuggle hops**

Brewed regularly, taking its inspiration from the free-range fowl that wander around the brewery grounds, this beer is described by Franco as an 'easy drinking' bitter, and is also sold in cask form.

Grand Crix

- **ABV 4.1%** ▪ **BOTTLE SIZE 500 ml** ▪ **SERVE cool**
- **INGREDIENTS Maris Otter pale malt/caramalt/crystal malt/unmalted barley/Bramling Cross and Ruth hops**

The use of the new dwarf hop named Ruth is but one idiosyncrasy of this bitter which Franco suggests will go very well with seafood dishes. Maturity is the name of the game here, with the beer given a long conditioning in oak casks that have been seasoned with fresh root ginger and coriander. The beer is brewed just once a year.

Tasting Notes

A light-bodied, copper beer with a perfumed aroma of ginger and other spices. Tangy spice also leads in the bitter taste and continues to feature in the dry, bitter aftertaste.

Lord Kulmbach

- **ABV 4.4%** ▪ **BOTTLE SIZE 500 ml** ▪ **SERVE cold**
- **INGREDIENTS Maris Otter pale malt/lager malt/crystal malt/black malt/wheat malt/Brewer's Gold and Fuggle hops**

Franco describes this as a bottom-fermented stout, in other words a stout that has been brewed like a lager. Primary cold fermentation takes ten days, five more days are permitted to allow diacetyl (unwanted butterscotch notes) to round out and then the beer is cold-matured for eight weeks. It makes a perfect accompaniment for roast beef or meaty sausages, the brewer claims.

Tasting Notes

A near-black beer with light roasted malt and a blackberry fruitiness in the nose. The same fruit emerges in the crisp, clean taste before being passed by roasted malt. The dry aftertaste is also bitter and roasted.

Hoppin' Hen

■ABV 4.5% ■BOTTLE SIZE 500 ml ■SERVE cool
■INGREDIENTS Maris Otter and Pearl pale malt/crystal malt/wheat malt/roasted barley/First Gold, Jenny and Hersbrucker hops

A beer that is best drunk young, according to Franco. This premium ale features dwarf and German hops and is primed with maple syrup.

Tasting Notes

A copper beer with a fruity, malt and hops aroma, underscored by soft melon and pineapple notes. The taste is a crisp mix of malt and fruity hops, with the same tropical fruit notes in evidence. Dry, hoppy, lightly fruity finish.

Old Crix

■ABV 4.5% ■BOTTLE SIZE 500 ml ■SERVE cool
■INGREDIENTS Maris Otter pale malt/crystal malt/chocolate malt/wheat malt/First Gold and Perle hops

When Franco remarks that Old Crix is just perfect with a truffle omelette, he reveals his continental roots once again. Truffles are considerably rarer in the UK than in Italy, so how about a game pie or a mature cheese instead? Again Franco has pulled out all the stops to produce a beer that is different. This time he takes an ale recipe and brews it in the continental fashion, using a double-decoction system (the wort is pumped from vessel to vessel and exposed to varying temperatures to extract the brewing sugars). He then dry hops the beer with more Perle hops.

Tasting Notes

Rich orange notes emerge in the otherwise malty aroma of this robust amber ale. The taste is nutty and malty with a good hop overlay and hints of fruit. The 'mature oak' signposted on the label also comes through. Bitter fruit and hops fill the aftertaste.

Felstar Wheat

■ABV 4.8% ■BOTTLE SIZE 500 ml ■SERVE cold
■INGREDIENTS Pearl pale malt/crystal malt/wheat malt/roasted barley/hops not declared

This seasonal weissbier-styled brew is lightly hopped and typically acidic, making it, according to Franco, a good drink to enjoy with crisp fish and chips.

Tasting Notes

A golden beer with a light orangey aroma spiked with a pinch of pepper. Orangey/lemon notes lead in the mouth, supported by a strong peppery spiciness. Orange and lemon continue in the spicy, warming finish.

Good Knight

■ABV 5% ■BOTTLE SIZE 500 ml ■SERVE cool
■INGREDIENTS Maris Otter pale malt/crystal malt/ caramalt/chocolate malt/roasted barley/Bramling Cross, First Gold and Perle hops

Another double-decoction beer, Good Knight is a strong mild/porter with lager connections. A beer that matures well in the bottle, declares the brewer.

Peckin' Order

■ABV 5% ■BOTTLE SIZE 500 ml ■SERVE cold
■INGREDIENTS Lager malt/crystal malt/wheat malt/ Brewer's Gold and Perle hops

Taking three months from brewing to bottling, Peckin' Order enjoys a primary fermentation with a gradually-reduced temperature and ten days' rest before long cold conditioning. One to try with oriental food, perhaps.

Tasting Notes

Malt, fruit and floral hop notes mark out the aroma of this dark golden brew. Its taste is lightly fruity, with a buttery maltiness plus lemon notes on the swallow. Creamy malt finish with bitterness and hop emerging.

Roosters Rest

■ABV 5% ■BOTTLE SIZE 500 ml ■SERVE cool
■INGREDIENTS Maris Otter pale malt/caramalt/torrefied wheat and barley/Bramling Cross, Jenny and Hersbrucker hops

Roosters Rest is a strong bitter. It is the bottled version of a cask beer that was cheekily called Betty's Best, when it was introduced to commemorate The Queen's Golden Jubilee in 2002.

Dark Wheat

■ABV 5.4% ■BOTTLE SIZE 500 ml ■SERVE cool
■INGREDIENTS Pearl pale malt/black malt/wheat malt/ chocolate wheat malt/hops not declared

A medium-hopped, slowly-fermented wheat beer brewed twice a year. Also available in cask form.

Lord Essex

■ ABV 5.4% ■ BOTTLE SIZE 500 ml ■ SERVE cool
■ INGREDIENTS Maris Otter pale malt/caramalt/chocolate wheat malt/roasted barley/Mount Hood and Phoenix hops

This strong old ale is the result of a long mashing, double decoction and a vigorous lengthy boil. Its conception was a touch accidental, however. Initially, the ever-experimental Franco used American Galena hops in the brew, not appreciating that they would shed a large quantity of seeds. The seeds blocked up the filters on his copper, leading to a long, laborious run-off of wort, which meant that the beer was sitting on the hops for nearly two hours longer than planned. It didn't do the brew any harm. That edition, in cask, was winner of the 2004 Chelmsford Winter Beer Festival competition.

Haunted Hen

■ ABV 6% ■ BOTTLE SIZE 500 ml ■ SERVE cool
■ INGREDIENTS Maris Otter pale malt/caramalt/chocolate malt/chocolate wheat malt/torrefied wheat/Golding, Jenny and Hersbrucker hops

Brewed every October and ripened in heavily toasted oak rum casks, Haunted Hen is a stout brewed for maturity and is claimed to be at its best when over a year old. A Chelmsford Winter Beer Festival award-winner in 2003 in its cask form.

Tasting Notes
A near-black beer with a rich, biscuity, malt and coffee nose. Liquorice notes feature in the bittersweet, nutty, roasted taste, with a suggestion of fruit throughout, though perhaps not as much body as expected. Bittersweet, roasted malt finish.

Howlin' Hen

■ ABV 6.5% ■ BOTTLE SIZE 330 ml ■ SERVE cool
■ INGREDIENTS Maris Otter and Pearl pale malt/wheat malt/roasted barley/Golding, Jenny and Hersbrucker hops

Brewed in September, ideally for drinking at Christmas the following year, this rich beer is conditioned in oak casks for a vanilla accent, making it, says Franco, 'justifiably expensive'. He also claims it goes excellently with fruit cakes and puddings.

Tasting Notes
A very deep ruby stout with a moussey brown foam. Light

fruit notes give way to mellow, creamy, sweet coffee in the aroma, while the creamy, sweetish, coffeeish taste has a warmth that indicates its strength. Strong, bitter coffee finish.

FOX

Fox & Hounds, 22 Station Road, Heacham, Norfolk PE31 7EX. Tel. (01485) 570345 Fax (01485) 579491 Website: www.foxbreweryandphheacham.fsnet.uk

This pub brewery opened in 2002 and brews not just for the pub but other outlets, too. Sales of bottles (added in 2003) have really taken off.

Perfick

- **ABV 3.7%** ▪ **BOTTLE SIZE 500 ml** ▪ **SERVE cool**
- **INGREDIENTS Maris Otter pale malt/pale chocolate malt/First Gold, Bramling Cross and Golding hops/ vanilla extract**

Darling Buds of May-inspired session bitter, flavoured by the addition of vanilla extract as the beer is being run off from the copper.

Branthill Best

- **ABV 3.8%** ▪ **BOTTLE SIZE 500 ml** ▪ **SERVE cool**
- **INGREDIENTS Maris Otter pale malt/amber malt/pale chocolate malt/torrefied wheat/Phoenix, Cascade and First Gold hops**

A beer created in conjunction with Branthill Farm at Wells-next-the-Sea, using the farm's Maris Otter barley.

Tasting Notes

A red-amber brew with a malty, lightly chocolatey, very nutty aroma. The taste and finish are also nutty and malty with reasonable bitterness and hints of roast.

Heacham Gold

- **ABV 3.9%** ▪ **BOTTLE SIZE 500 ml** ▪ **SERVE cool**
- **INGREDIENTS Lager malt/wheat malt/Cascade, Phoenix and First Gold hops**

A fruity bitter named after the brewery's home town.

Tasting Notes

A pale yellow beer with a surprisingly malty nose. The sweetish taste is also malty yet quickly becomes crisp and lightly citrous. Bittersweet, lemony, lingering malt finish.

LJB

- **ABV 4%** ■ **BOTTLE SIZE 500 ml** ■ **SERVE cool**
- **INGREDIENTS Maris Otter pale malt/crystal malt/ chocolate malt/Challenger, Fuggle and Target hops**

LJB stands for Little John Bristow – brewer Mark Bristow's young son (the beer celebrated his birth in 2002).

Tasting Notes

A dark amber ale with a hoppy nose. The taste is hoppy and quenching, with a light, malty sweetness. Dry, hoppy finish.

Red Knocker

- **ABV 4.2%** ■ **BOTTLE SIZE 500 ml** ■ **SERVE cool**
- **INGREDIENTS Maris Otter pale malt/crystal malt/ Cascade, Fuggle and First Gold hops**

A copper-coloured bitter, bottled, like the others featured here, by allowing cask beer to drop bright, transferring it to a new cask and kräusening before filling.

Tasting Notes

Another red-amber beer, this time with a hoppy aroma backed by a little malt. It's a full-flavoured, hoppy, malty best bitter to taste, with a mellow, moreish, pleasantly bitter and hoppy finish.

Branthill Light

- **ABV 4.3%** ■ **BOTTLE SIZE 500 ml** ■ **SERVE cool**
- **INGREDIENTS Maris Otter pale malt/torrefied wheat/ Challenger, Bramling Cross and Cascade hops**

Another beer brewed from Branthill Farm barley.

Tasting Notes

An exceptionally pale golden beer with a light, hoppy nose. The taste is crisp, bittersweet and lemony, with a dry, bitter, hoppy finish.

Cerberus Norfolk Stout

- **ABV 4.5%** ■ **BOTTLE SIZE 500 ml** ■ **SERVE cool**
- **INGREDIENTS Maris Otter pale malt/crystal malt/ torrefied wheat/crushed wheat/roasted barley/ Fuggle hops**

A stout recalling the three-headed guardian dog of Hell from mythology.

Tasting Notes

A dark ruby beer with a mellow, creamy, coffee aroma, plus a hint of blackberry. The taste is creamy, mellow, coffeeish, bittersweet and easy-drinking, with blackberry fruit emerging. Drying, bittersweet, creamy, roasted malt finish.

Peddars Sway

- **ABV 5%** ▪ **BOTTLE SIZE 500 ml** ▪ **SERVE cool**
- **INGREDIENTS Maris Otter pale malt/crystal malt/pale chocolate malt/Challenger, Fuggle and Target hops**

Peddars Way, a very popular East Anglian footpath, passes near The Fox & Hounds.

Tasting Notes

A red-amber beer with malt, hops and spicy fruit in the nose. The taste is a crisply bitter, lightly fruity mix of malt and hop. Nutty, pleasantly bitter, dry finish with a touch of roast.

IPA

- **ABV 5.2%** ▪ **BOTTLE SIZE 500 ml** ▪ **SERVE cool**
- **INGREDIENTS Maris Otter pale malt/crystal malt/Target and First Gold hops**

A traditional India pale ale, re-created by Mark after researching beer recipes from the 19th century.

Tasting Notes

A golden ale with a sharp, fruity hop aroma, a robustly hoppy, pleasantly fruity, drying taste, and a dry, hoppy finish.

Punt Gun

- **ABV 5.9%** ▪ **BOTTLE SIZE 500 ml** ▪ **SERVE cool**
- **INGREDIENTS Maris Otter pale malt/crystal malt/black malt/torrefied wheat/Fuggle and Bramling Cross hops**

A strong old ale in the mould of Theakston's Old Peculier.

Tasting Notes

A very dark ruby beer with a malty, lightly fruity aroma that is a little creamy and grainy. The taste is malty, lightly sweet and alcoholic, with hints of almonds and gentle fruit. Bittersweet, dark malt finish.

FREEMINER

Freeminer Brewery Ltd., Whimsey Road, Steam Mills, Cinderford, Gloucestershire GL14 3JA.
Tel. (01594) 827989 Fax (01594) 829464
Website: www.freeminer.com

Established in 1992, and the only brewery in the Royal Forest of Dean, Freeminer suffered from a fire in a neighbouring industrial unit in 2000, which forced a two-month suspension of production. Up and running again, it eventually moved to new, larger premises in December that year. Bottling on a major scale resumed in 2003, with the launch of the Co-op own label beer, Gold Miner, and continued with the re-launch in stylish new packaging of three old favourites, Trafalgar, Speculation and Waterloo. These beers, like other Freeminer ales, despite suggesting otherwise, recall the Forest's mining heritage in their titles. (For the record, a 'freeminer' is a male born within the hundred of St Briavels who has claimed his birthright to mine the area without charge by reaching the age of 21 and working a year and a day in a local mine.) Bottling is now handled by Marston's. Green beer is trunked from Freeminer to Burton upon Trent, where it is matured, chilled, fined, sterile filtered and then re-pitched with a special bottling yeast before filling. Other standards like Freeminer Bitter (4%) and Deep Shaft Stout (6.2%) hopefully will return in due course.

Waterloo

- **ABV 4.5%** ■ **BOTTLE SIZE 500 ml** ■ **SERVE cool**
- **INGREDIENTS Optic pale malt/crystal malt/Cascade, First Gold and Golding hops**

Based on a Freeminer cask beer called Iron Brew, but with less bitterness, Waterloo has returned after an absence of a couple of years with its strength now raised a touch to 4.5%. A good partner for barbecue food, roast pork and cheeses, according to the brewery.

Tasting Notes

There's plenty of malt in the aroma of this red-amber ale, along with hints of orange and a light milk-chocolate sweetness. The taste is smooth, milky and malty, with traces of bitter orange and a notable hop character that develops strongly without being aggressive. Bitter, hoppy, drying finish.

Speculation

- **ABV 4.8%** ■ **BOTTLE SIZE 500 ml** ■ **SERVE cool**
- **INGREDIENTS Optic pale malt/crystal malt/chocolate malt/Fuggle and Golding hops**

Well-appreciated by *Decanter* magazine, which awarded it five stars in 1997, Speculation is a premium strength bitter with a smoky character. Its name is derived from a long-closed mine which is now used as a popular picnic area.

Tasting Notes

A deep amber beer with a spicy, malty aroma. Robust and

bitter in the mouth, it also features a spicy maltiness for balance and a light fruit tang. Bitter, hoppy, drying finish.

Gold Miner

■ABV 5% ■BOTTLE SIZE 500 ml ■SERVE cool
■INGREDIENTS Optic pale malt/pale crystal malt/First Gold hops

Exclusive to Co-op supermarkets, Gold Miner was launched in summer 2003, although the beer had previously enjoyed success as a cask beer called Gold Standard, winner of a *Beauty of Hops* award for its use of First Gold hops.

Tasting Notes

A golden beer with lots of tangy hop character, but also a fine malty-sweet balance. Hoppy, fruity finish.

Major stockist Co-op

Trafalgar

■ABV 6% ■BOTTLE SIZE 500 ml ■SERVE cool
■INGREDIENTS Optic pale malt/crystal malt/Golding hops

The heavy hop character of this potent brew recalls the days of the British Empire when strong, hoppy IPAs were stashed aboard sailing ships for the long journey to the Indian subcontinent. Trafalgar is reputedly based on a formula for a 9% beer but the restraints of excise duties prohibit the recipe from being followed to the letter. As if there weren't enough hops in the brew to start with, Freeminer also dry hops to embellish the nose and finish. This clearly impressed judges at the 1997 *Beauty of Hops* awards who accorded the beer the title of *Best Bottled Single Varietal*. Trafalgar was a Forest of Dean mine, the first in the world to be electrically lit.

Tasting Notes

A dark golden beer with estery fruits – pineapple, melon and orange – in the nose, with toffee notes emerging. The full-bodied taste is fairly sweet and toffee-malty, with lots of estery fruit and a developing hop presence. The big, long, hoppy finish is dry and lipsmacking.

FROG & PARROT

Frog & Parrot, 64 Division Street, Sheffield, South Yorkshire S1 4SG. Tel. (0114) 272 1280

This brew pub began production in 1982 and uses malt extract rather than whole malt to make its single beer (although this may change in the near future). Roger & Out is generally only on sale at the pub itself.

Roger & Out

- **ABV 12.5%** ■ **BOTTLE SIZE 330 ml**
- **SERVE at room temperature**
- **INGREDIENTS Malt extract/Challenger, Styrian Golding and Golding hops**

This beer once had the privilege of being described in the *Guinness Book of Records* as Britain's strongest ale. That honour has since been claimed by other ridiculously strong brews but Roger & Out will always be known as the original mind-blower. It was first produced in cask form in 1982 and this bottled version followed soon after. It took its name from the brew pub's former manager, Roger Nowill. Today it is brewed about once a month. The cask beer is allowed two months to condition, before being fined. The bottles are then simply hand-filled from the cask. A rather timid six-week best before date is placed on the labels but the pub is in no doubt about the beer's longevity. Special certificates and T-shirts have been issued with purchases, proclaiming the beer's reputation for potency.

Tasting Notes

A dark brown beer with a heady, alcoholic aroma. To taste, it is very sweet and malty but with some hop bitterness and fruit (strawberries) to balance. Sweet fruit and malt feature in the warming finish.

FROG ISLAND

Frog Island Brewery, The Maltings, Westbridge, St James Road, Northampton NN4 8DU.
Tel. (01604) 587772
E-mail: beer@frogislandbrewery.co.uk
Website: www.frogislandbrewery.co.uk
Mail order service

Taking its name from an area of Northampton that is prone to flooding, Frog Island hopped into the brewing world in 1994. It set up shop in an old malthouse once owned by the defunct Thomas Manning brewery. The bottle-conditioned beers listed are also available under 'own labels' for celebrations, fund-raising events and other occasions. They are bottled on site, unprimed, direct from the conditioning tank, without the use of isinglass finings (rendering all three perfectly acceptable to vegetarians).

Natterjack

■ ABV 4.8% ■ BOTTLE SIZE 500 ml ■ SERVE cool
■ INGREDIENTS Maris Otter pale malt/wheat malt/Target and Golding hops

Natterjack – extending the amphibian theme – was only introduced in bottle in 2000, but the cask equivalent had already been around for about five years.

Tasting Notes

A copper ale with a rich, orangey, hoppy aroma. The bittersweet taste is powerfully fruity and hoppy (smoky orange notes), while the finish is bitter and fruity with a strong, lingering hoppiness.

Fire-Bellied Toad

■ ABV 5% ■ BOTTLE SIZE 500 ml ■ SERVE cool
■ INGREDIENTS Pale malt/crystal malt/wheat malt/ Phoenix hops

This single-varietal hop beer was introduced in 1998 and comes wrapped in a dramatic label showing a mythical bird-creature attacking the eponymous toad. The best before date is set at around six months.

Tasting Notes

A dark golden, hoppy ale. The aroma features orangey citrous notes from the hops, whilst the taste is fruity but bitter, again with citrous notes and tangy hop. Long-lasting, dry, bitter, tangy hop-fruit finish.

Croak & Stagger

■ ABV 5.6% ■ BOTTLE SIZE 500 ml ■ SERVE cool
■ INGREDIENTS Pale malt/crystal malt/chocolate malt/ wheat malt/Target and Cascade hops

Croak & Stagger was Frog Island's first foray into the bottled beer world. It is a variation of a cask winter ale of the same name that was first brewed in 1995. Brewers Bruce Littler and Graham Cherry toned down the ABV (to provide a little less Croak and a smaller chance of a Stagger) and began bottling in 1996. Though a dark winter ale by definition, it is now sold all year. The best before date is set at eight months.

Tasting Notes

Dark amber in colour, this robust ale has an aroma of dark, chocolatey malt and hop fruit. The very full, sweet taste is packed with orange and pineapple hop flavours on a smooth, chocolatey malt base, before a dry, bittersweet, chocolatey finish, with tangy hops.

FULLER'S

**Fuller, Smith and Turner PLC, Griffin Brewery, Chiswick Lane South, Chiswick, London W4 2QB.
Tel. (020) 8996 2000 Fax (020) 8995 0230
Website: www.fullers.co.uk**

One of the capital's two major brewers, Fuller's operates on a site linked to beer production for over 325 years. Messrs Fuller, Smith and Turner came together in 1845 and descendants of the founders are still on the board today, running a highly successful and much-acclaimed business. Its beers are imported into the US by Distinguished Brands International. In addition to the beers listed below, Fuller's has also experimented with a bottle-conditioned version of its London Porter, but this has not yet been released to the trade.

1845

- **ABV 6.3%** ▪ **BOTTLE SIZE 500 ml** ▪ **SERVE cool**
- **INGREDIENTS Pale malt/crystal malt/amber malt/ Golding hops**

1845 was first brewed in February 1995, with the Prince of Wales doing the honours and adding the hops to the copper. It was a new ale to commemorate the 150th anniversary of the founding of the Fuller, Smith and Turner company and its conception was precise: it was designed as a beer to reflect the type of brew available during the 1840s, hence the use of only Golding hops, the inclusion of amber malt for some biscuity character and the decision to bottle condition it. Its success (twice CAMRA's *Champion Bottle-conditioned Beer*) has meant that it is now a permanent member of the award-winning Fuller's range of traditional ales, with brews taking place monthly. In winter, the brew is sometimes available in cask form. After primary fermentation, 1845 enjoys two weeks in conditioning tanks and is then filtered, re-seeded with fresh primary fermentation yeast and bottled, with no primings. Two weeks of conditioning follow before the bottles are released. Once this two-week period has been observed, Fuller's reckons that the beer is at its best and will remain so at least up to the 12-month best before date.

Tasting Notes

A rich, dark amber beer with a glorious, fruity, malty nose, balanced by hints of sherry and Golding hop. The very full, smooth, malty and fruity taste is quickly tempered by hop bitterness. Hops and bitter fruit feature in the lingering finish.

Major stockists Asda, Budgens, Co-op, Morrisons, Safeway, Sainsbury, Tesco, Unwins, Waitrose

Vintage Ale

■ **ABV 8.5%** ■ **BOTTLE SIZE 550 ml** ■ **SERVE cool**
■ **INGREDIENTS (*2003 vintage*) Optic pale malt/Target, Challenger and Northdown hops**

Fuller's Vintage Ale is usually brewed in a one-off batch (initially 85,000 bottles, now 50,000) in September each year. The packaging is high quality, allowing the brewery to charge around £3.50 per bottle. For that, you get an individually numbered item in a presentation box, with a best before date set three years on. More importantly, you get a rather special beer. Fuller's aficionados will probably gather that the ale is in fact a version of the brewery's excellent Golden Pride, a rich barley wine which is parti-gyled (brewed from the same mash) with ESB and London Pride. But, by giving this beer the bottle conditioning treatment (including four weeks in conditioning tanks before filtering and re-seeding with fresh Fuller's yeast), the result is a noticeably lighter, fresher beer, quite different to the original Golden Pride, which is supplied in pasteurised bottles. Some brews have used annual champion strains of barley and hops, although now there has been a return to standard floor-malted barley and regular hops. The 2002 edition, timed to coincide with The Queen's Golden Jubilee, had a golden theme, using only Golden Promise pale malt and Golding hops. In March 2003, Fuller's organised a fascinating 'vertical tasting' of all six Vintage Ales produced to date, showcasing how the beers had matured and the flavours ripened over the years.

Tasting Notes

Vintage Ale 1997 (tasted after six years): Red in colour, with a raisin aroma and a silky, warming, fruity taste.

Vintage Ale 1998 (tasted young): Chestnut-coloured, with pronounced orangey, hop-resin notes in the aroma, alongside thick, treacly malt and a little sherry. Very full on the palate, it is rather sweet but also tangy and hop-fruity. Sugary sweet notes just win over fresh, fruity hops in the finish. Soft, creamy raisin notes emerge with time as the sugary notes fade.

Vintage Ale 1999 (tasted after 18 months): Amber, with a slightly savoury aroma of bitter, orangey hops. The taste is malty, sweet, fruity and warming, with a hint of almond. Malt, hops and bittersweet fruit fill the aftertaste. Becomes winey with maturity.

Vintage Ale 2000 (tasted young): Bright amber, with a luscious Seville orange aroma. The taste bursts with orange fruit and thick, malty sweetness, countered by zesty, orange peel bitterness. Bitter orange finish. Still sweetish when

tasted two years on but with a Cointreau-like quality and a lipsmacking hop dryness in the aftertaste.
Vintage Ale 2001 (tasted young): Deep amber, with raspberryish fruit notes in the nose before a tangy, bittersweet, warming taste of orange fruit and a liquorice-like bitterness. Fruit, bitter hops and lingering sweetness run into the finish. Cherry and marzipan notes come through with age, along with more bitterness in the aftertaste.
Vintage Ale 2002 (tasted young): Dark copper, with an orangey, hoppy, tobacco-fragranced aroma, and cherries and marzipan in the sweet, peppery taste.
Vintage Ale 2003 (tasted young): Red-amber in colour, with light hop aromas, backed with orange fruit and malt. The rich, malty taste is sweetish but excellently balanced by tangy hop notes, bitter fruit and hints of cherry and marzipan. Bitter, hoppy finish with lingering malt and fruit.
Major stockists Safeway, Sainsbury, Waitrose

GALE'S

George Gale & Co. Ltd., The Hampshire Brewery, London Road, Horndean, Hampshire PO8 0DA.
Tel. (023) 9257 1212 Fax (023) 9259 8641
Website: www.gales.co.uk

Hampshire's major brewery, Gale's was founded in 1847 and is still family owned. Its commitment to bottle-conditioned beers, in evidence since the 1920s through its production of the classic Prize Old Ale, was reinforced in 1997 with the installation of a new bottling line. The line does not handle carbonated beer, but it allows Gale's to produce a wider range of naturally-conditioned bottled beers (which are filtered and then re-seeded with a fresh batch of the same yeast), including limited edition commemorative brews (such as Golden Century at 10% for the Queen Mother's 100th birthday in 2000) and 'own label' beers for companies. Gale's beers are distributed in the USA by B United, Regal Wines and Mannekin-Brussels.

GB Export Strength

- **ABV 4.5%** ▪ **BOTTLE SIZE 500 ml** ▪ **SERVE cool**
- **INGREDIENTS Maris Otter pale malt/pale crystal malt/ Fuggle and Challenger hops**

In 1998, Gale's introduced a new cask ale at 4%, designed to compete with the likes of Fuller's London Pride and Draught Bass in the guest ale market. It was called GB and, among the accolades it gathered was the title of *Ultimate Ploughman's Lunch Beer* in the 2003 *Beauty of Hops* competition. The beer was discontinued in 2004 but a bottled version does still exist, albeit 'Export Strength' at 4.5%.

Tasting Notes

A copper-coloured ale with lemon and a hint of pear drop in the nose. The taste is a soft, well-rounded mix of malt and hop, with sweet fruitiness ever present, a hint of almond behind and bitterness building as you drink. Moreishly bitter, hoppy and dry finish.

Major stockist Safeway

Festival Mild Ale

- **ABV 4.8%** ▪ **BOTTLE SIZE 500 ml** ▪ **SERVE cool**
- **INGREDIENTS Maris Otter pale malt/crystal malt/black malt/Fuggle, Golding and Challenger hops**

Gale's used to produce two milds – one light, one dark – both below 3% alcohol. They were phased out in the early 1990s but, in response to a request from the CAMRA Farnham Beer Festival in 1994, the brewery created this strong mild as a replacement. (Apart from the use of much more black malt, it is the same beer as HSB, mentioned below.) Festival Mild proved so popular that it was added to the Gale's cask portfolio soon after and went on to collect the accolade of *The People's Pint* at CAMRA's Winter Beer Festival in 1997. It was also overall runner-up in CAMRA's *Champion Winter Beer of Britain* contest in 2003 and 2004. This bottled version first appeared in 1999, but sales are largely confined to the export market, primarily the USA. Drink with chocolate puddings.

Tasting Notes

A very dark ruby beer with a roasted grain nose backed by malt and fruit. The mainly roasted taste has a delicate malty sweetness, some bitterness and a little fruit throughout. Bittersweet, malty finish.

Major stockist Safeway (winter)

HSB

- **ABV 4.8%** ▪ **BOTTLE SIZE 500 ml** ▪ **SERVE cool**
- **INGREDIENTS Maris Otter pale malt/crystal malt/black malt/Fuggle, Golding and Challenger hops**

HSB (Horndean Special Bitter) was introduced in cask form in 1959 to expand a Gale's portfolio that was big on mild and had only one bitter, BBB. It was devised by the then head brewer, Ted Argylle, who pitched the beer at an OG of 1055, the average gravity of a standard bitter in the pre-war years.

The OG is a little lower these days (1050) but the beer is still the brewery's major strong bitter. It has been available, pasteurised, in cans since the early 1980s, but only in 1999 did HSB finally receive bottle conditioning. The best before date is set much shorter than for Gale's stronger beers, at up to 24 weeks. Together with Festival Mild and GB Export, it also differs in being crown capped, rather than corked.

Tasting Notes

A dark amber bitter with an aroma of estery fruit (bananas) and toffee-malt. Fruit continues in the taste, which has a trace of pear drops. Bitterness overcomes a little cloying sweetness and toffee-malt lurks in the background. Dry, hoppy, fruity, bitter finish.

Major stockist Local Co-op

Christmas Ale

- **ABV 8.5%** ▪ **BOTTLE SIZE 275 ml** ▪ **SERVE cool**
- **INGREDIENTS Maris Otter pale malt/crystal malt/Fuggle hops/raisins/cinnamon/mace**

Largely brewed for export to countries like the USA, Sweden and Denmark, Christmas Ale is produced once a year for bottling in late September. The beer is conditioned in tank for a couple of months before being rough filtered. Fresh yeast is then added along with a raisin and spice mix which is introduced as an extract prepared at the brewery from the base ingredients. The spices ensure the beer never achieves perfect clarity but this shouldn't impair the enjoyment. Pour it gently into a wide-brimmed glass to appreciate the rich seasonal aroma. Gale's has produced various Christmas Ales over the years, but seems to have settled on this recipe (although don't rule out the addition of vanilla and/or cloves in the future!).

Tasting Notes

A ruby ale with a spicy, fruity, vinous aroma. The taste is mostly sweet but with a vinous edge, cake spices and tart fruit. This fruit mellows out in the finish as sweetness finally takes over.

Prize Old Ale

- **ABV 9%** ▪ **BOTTLE SIZE 275 ml**
- **SERVE at room temperature**
- **INGREDIENTS Maris Otter pale malt/black malt/Fuggle and Golding hops**

Famous for its corked bottle, Prize Old Ale is fundamental to the traditional, family image of Gale's. It was introduced in the 1920s, when a new head brewer brought the recipe with him from Yorkshire. The recipe has remained largely unchanged in the subsequent 80 years, except for the use of pelletised hops instead of whole and the loss of wooden hogsheads which were used for conditioning the beer. The replacement metal tanks may not be as charming or quaint but, according to head brewer Derek Lowe, they produce more reliable beer, and it is in these containers that the beer is aged for six–12 months. Before being bottled, more of the same original yeast may be added, but, as the beer is not fined, it is acceptable to vegetarians. Being corked, the bottle should be stored lying down, to keep the cork moist. Prize Old Ale is aged for three months at the brewery. Once bottled, it will continue to improve for up to at least five years (although the best before date is set at two years). Some 20-year-old bottles have been known to be excellent, but this doesn't mean that all beers of such an age will prove as fulfilling. All bottles are now individually numbered. Better with cheese than any port, claim the brewers.

Tasting Notes

(*Based on young samples*) A dark ruby beer with a deep, vinous, fruity aroma with hints of vanilla. The taste is a powerful, mouth-filling combination of fruit (dates and raisins), bitterness and alcohol. The finish is dry, with bitter fruit and hops shading out sweetness.

Major stockist Local Tesco

Trafalgar Ale

- **ABV 10%** ▪ **BOTTLE SIZE 275 ml**
- **SERVE at room temperature**
- **INGREDIENTS Maris Otter pale malt/crystal malt/ Golding and Admiral hops**

This powerful ale has been brewed on and off over the past eight years to celebrate Trafalgar Day (October 21) and has proved particularly popular in the naval wardrooms of the nearby city of Portsmouth, home of Nelson's flagship, *HMS Victory*. With the 200th anniversary of the Battle of Trafalgar looming in the year 2005, Gale's intends to increase the strength from 9 to 10%, employing Admiral hops to match the concept. Like Prize Old Ale, it will present no fears for vegetarians.

Tasting Notes

(*Based on 9% version*) A ruby ale with a subdued fruity, malty, hoppy nose for its strength. To taste, it is sweetish, very malty and fairly sharp, but very well-balanced and easy to drink. Decent fruit character. Bitter, fruit and malt finish.

GRAINSTORE

Davis'es Brewing Co. Ltd., The Grainstore Brewery, Station Approach, Oakham, Rutland LE15 6RE.
Tel. (01572) 770065 Fax (01572) 770068
E-mail: grainstorebry@aol.com
Website: www.grainstorebrewery.com

Rutland beers were once famous, thanks to the presence of Ruddles Brewery, now sadly defunct. Rutland beers live on, however, chiefly through Grainstore. The company name is actually Davis'es Brewing, after the names of its founders, Mike Davies and Tony Davis, the latter a former Ruddles employee. Their brewery was established in an old railway grainstore, but is rapidly outgrowing the site and new premises are under inspection. When the move is eventually completed, an automatic bottling line will be installed. In the meantime, just one bottled beer is produced, and this is filled by hand.

Ten Fifty

- **ABV 5%** ▪ **BOTTLE SIZE 500 ml** ▪ **SERVE cool**
- **INGREDIENTS Maris Otter pale malt/Fuggle and Northdown hops**

The brewery's second ever draught beer, taking its name from its original gravity (1050), this brew is filtered and re-seeded with fresh yeast (the same used in primary fermentation) prior to bottling.

Tasting Notes

An amber-red beer with a malty, fruity aroma. Citrous-sharp at first, the taste is generally malty, however, with a hint of almonds. The dry, bitter and hoppy aftertaste features lingering malt.

GREAT GABLE

Great Gable Brewing Co. Ltd., Wasdale Head Inn, Wasdale, Gosforth, Cumbria CA20 1EX.
Tel. (01946 7) 26229 Fax (01946 7) 26334
E-mail: wasdaleheadinn@msn.com
Website: www.greatgablebrewing.com

The Wasdale Head Inn stands remote and welcoming at the heart of Lakeland climbing and walking country. Since 2002, it has been home to Great Gable Brewing, a microbrewery set up by two long-serving employees of the inn, Giles Holiday and Howard Christie. Spring water from the fellside is used in each brew. The first bottled beer arrived in 2004, filled from casks – after three months' conditioning – by Brewlab at the University of Sunderland, without filtration, re-pitching of yeast or kräusening.

Yewbarrow

▪ABV 5.5% ▪BOTTLE SIZE 500 ml ▪SERVE cool
▪INGREDIENTS Pale malt/crystal malt/amber malt/chocolate malt/oat malt/Northdown hops/honey/fruit syrup

First brewed at Christmas 2002 under the name of Yulebarrow – a pun on Yewbarrow, the fell on which the brewery's spring is located – this honey-laced strong mild proved so popular that it was kept on and is now sold under the simpler Yewbarrow name (except in December). The brewers suggest it is good with local lamb, Wasdale cheese and traditional Cumberland sausages.

Tasting Notes

A ruby beer with coffee and plain-chocolate biscuits in the aroma. The taste is a beautifully balanced, quite grainy combination of biscuity malt, coffee and bittersweetness, while the aftertaste is dry and bitter with mellow roasted malt.

GREEN DRAGON

The Green Dragon, 29 Broad Street, Bungay, Suffolk NR35 1EE. Tel./Fax (01986) 892681

This former Brent Walker pub in the sleepy Suffolk town of Bungay was purchased in 1991 and soon boosted by the installation of a small brewery. The brewery expanded into a converted barn across the car park in 1994.

Wynnter Warmer

▪ABV 6% ▪BOTTLE SIZE 500 ml ▪SERVE cool
▪INGREDIENTS Pale malt/chocolate malt/black malt/wheat malt/Fuggle hops

An occasional bottling of a draught winter beer that's been around for four years. The unusual spelling of the title is derived from the name of The Green Dragon's former brewer, Malcolm Wynn. The beer is racked from the fermentation vessel straight into bottles, with primings sometimes added to ensure good conditioning.

GREEN TYE

Green Tye Brewery, Green Tye, Much Hadham, Hertfordshire SG10 6JP. Tel./Fax (01279) 841041
E-mail: bottled@gtbrewery.co.uk
Website: www.gtbrewery.co.uk
Mail order service

Established in 1999, Green Tye is a small brewery in the village of Green Tye. Brewer William Compton turns out a wide range of cask ales, many of which find their way into bottle. He has bottled since late 2002, allowing the beer to drop bright in the cask and then kräusening. Twelve-month best before dates are applied.

Shot in the Dark

- **ABV 3.6%** ▪ **BOTTLE SIZE 500 ml** ▪ **SERVE cool**
- **INGREDIENTS Maris Otter pale malt/crystal malt/dark chocolate malt/wheat malt/Challenger and Golding hops**

This red-coloured quaffing ale was the first beer to be brewed by Green Tye and was very much a trial – hence the name. It is now regularly brewed in the winter months.

Union Jack

- **ABV 3.6%** ▪ **BOTTLE SIZE 500 ml** ▪ **SERVE cool**
- **INGREDIENTS Maris Otter pale malt/crystal malt/amber malt/flaked maize/Challenger and Bramling Cross hops**

In its cask form, Union Jack replaced Green Tye's IPA in 2002. This bottled version arrived later the same year and is now a regular brew.

Tasting Notes

A dark golden session ale with plenty of hops and floral notes in the aroma. The taste is mostly bitter and dry, with hop character but also some background sweetness. Light, dry and hoppy finish.

Mustang Mild

- **ABV 3.7%** ▪ **BOTTLE SIZE 500 ml** ▪ **SERVE cool**
- **INGREDIENTS Maris Otter pale malt/crystal malt/chocolate malt/brown malt/flaked maize/Fuggle hops**

First brewed in 2000, Mustang Mild takes its name from the P-51 Mustang aircraft that flew, under British colours, from a World War II airfield not far from Green Tye Brewery. The beer is usually only brewed between the months of April and June.

Tasting Notes

A light ruby ale with an aroma of fruit and toffeeish malt. The same flavours continue in the taste and the dry finish.

Uncle John's Ferret

- **ABV 3.8%** ■ **BOTTLE SIZE 500 ml** ■ **SERVE cool**
- **INGREDIENTS Maris Otter pale malt/crystal malt/ chocolate malt/flaked maize/Jenny hops**

A ruby/brown mild seasoned with a new hedgerow hop called simply Jenny. It was first brewed in August 2002 to mark the re-opening of The Queen's Head at nearby Allen's Green, which had been closed for six years. One local related a story about his Uncle John, a landlord of the pub some 50 years before, whose pet ferret drowned in the natural spring that runs through the pub's cellar. Asked what his ferret was doing in the cellar, the answer apparently came back: 'backstroke ... for a while'.

Snowdrop

- **ABV 3.9%** ■ **BOTTLE SIZE 500 ml** ■ **SERVE cool**
- **INGREDIENTS Maris Otter pale malt/crystal malt/ Golding hops**

A golden, winter beer, as its name implies, first bottled in 2002 after being introduced in its cask version in 2000.

Smile for the Camera!

- **ABV 4%** ■ **BOTTLE SIZE 500/750 ml** ■ **SERVE cool**
- **INGREDIENTS Maris Otter pale malt/wheat malt/flaked maize/Susan hops/honey/elderflowers**

This summer brew features another new hop, Susan, and was conceived as an entry for the *Beauty of Hops* competition to find the *Ultimate Wedding Beer* in 2002. It has since, reportedly, been drunk in place of Champagne at two weddings known to William, including one in France. To complete the sparkling wine concept, the larger, 750 ml bottles are stoppered with a cork and caged.

XBF

- **ABV 4%** ■ **BOTTLE SIZE 500 ml** ■ **SERVE cool**
- **INGREDIENTS Maris Otter pale malt/crystal malt/amber malt/flaked barley/Pilgrim hops**

First brewed and bottled in April 2003 to celebrate the tenth annual beer festival (hence XBF) at the adjacent Prince of Wales pub.

Tasting Notes

A copper-hued ale with blackcurrant and a little spice in the nose. The same spicy fruitiness runs into the taste and the dry, bitter aftertaste.

St Margaret's

- **ABV 4.1% ▪ BOTTLE SIZE 500 ml ▪ SERVE cool/cold**
- **INGREDIENTS Maris Otter pale malt/Caragold malt/ flaked maize/Willamette hops**

St Margaret's, introduced in May 2003, was the first of a series of beers commemorating the now closed, Buntingford railway branch line. The beer features Caragold malt, a creation of local maltsters French & Jupps.

Tasting Notes

A golden beer with a floral, fruity nose. The taste is moreishly malty with a balancing light hop note. Bittersweet, dry malt and hop finish.

Autumn Rose

- **ABV 4.2% ▪ BOTTLE SIZE 500 ml ▪ SERVE cool**
- **INGREDIENTS Maris Otter pale malt/crystal malt/ chocolate malt/wheat malt/flaked maize/Ros hops**

Now showcasing another new hop, this time called Ros, this tawny/brown seasonal beer was added to the range in 2000 and is usually sold until November in cask.

Ditch Diver

- **ABV 4.2% ▪ BOTTLE SIZE 500 ml ▪ SERVE cool**
- **INGREDIENTS Maris Otter pale malt/dark crystal malt/ amber malt/Challenger and Bramling Cross hops**

A best bitter introduced in cask form in April 2001.

Tasting Notes

An unusual deep amber beer with a malty, nutty aroma. The taste is also malty and nutty but with an over-riding sharp lime fruitiness. Malty, nutty, toasted aftertaste.

Green Tiger

- **ABV 4.2% ▪ BOTTLE SIZE 500 ml ▪ SERVE cool**
- **INGREDIENTS Maris Otter pale malt/crystal malt/flaked maize/Golding hops/ginger**

Designed as a summer quencher when created in 2000, this

light amber ale includes fresh root ginger for a touch of subtle spiciness.

Mad Morris

- **ABV 4.2%** ▪ **BOTTLE SIZE 500 ml** ▪ **SERVE cool**
- **INGREDIENTS Maris Otter pale malt/wheat malt/Susan hops**

A straw-coloured May Day beer (usually available for three months thereafter).

Wheelbarrow

- **ABV 4.3%** ▪ **BOTTLE SIZE 500 ml** ▪ **SERVE cool**
- **INGREDIENTS Maris Otter pale malt/crystal malt/wheat malt/Challenger hops**

This amber beer takes its name from the brewery partners: 'Will' Compton and Gary 'Barra' Whelan.

Tasting Notes

An orange-gold beer with fruity, grassy hops in the nose. The taste is sharp and fruity, with a dry, fruity finish.

Bowled Over!

- **ABV 4.5%** ▪ **BOTTLE SIZE 500 ml** ▪ **SERVE cool**
- **INGREDIENTS Maris Otter pale malt/crystal malt/wheat malt/Ruth hops**

A new beer to the bottle, introduced in spring 2004, although available on draught since 2001. The label shows the game of bowls, rather than cricket.

Tasting Notes

A copper-coloured brew with a nice mix of malt and hops in the nose. Nutty malt and sharpish, fruity hops feature in the taste, rounded off by a modest, nutty, gently bitter, toasted malt finish.

Coal Porter

- **ABV 4.5%** ▪ **BOTTLE SIZE 500 ml** ▪ **SERVE cool**
- **INGREDIENTS Maris Otter pale malt/dark chocolate malt/wheat malt/Bramling Cross hops**

This porter – a winner of several beer festival awards since it arrived in cask in 2000 – is a treat with a hearty winter pie or a stew, according to William. Check the label closely to avoid confusion with Coal Ported, featured overleaf.

Tasting Notes

Deep, deep ruby (almost black) in colour, this porter has a

biscuity aroma of roasted malt and coffee, a nicely balanced taste of sweet malt, bitterness and mellow coffee, and a coffeeish finish.

Merry Maker

- **ABV 4.6%** ■ **BOTTLE SIZE 500 ml** ■ **SERVE cool**
- **INGREDIENTS Maris Otter pale malt/dark crystal malt/ wheat malt/flaked maize/Challenger and Jenny hops**

An amber-coloured Christmas ale introduced in November 2001.

Coal Ported

- **ABV 4.7%** ■ **BOTTLE SIZE 500 ml** ■ **SERVE cool**
- **INGREDIENTS Maris Otter pale malt/dark chocolate malt/wheat malt/Bramling Cross hops/port**

Brewed to the same recipe as Coal Porter, this brew is given the added benefit of a whole bottle of port per firkin (nine gallons) and allowed to mature for two or three months before bottling. This obviously raises the strength slightly. Recommended by the brewers as a fine match for mature cheese and biscuits.

Tasting Notes

Near-black, this dark ruby-coloured brew has a soft fruitiness alongside roasted malt in the nose. The same fruit and roast features continue in the mouth and in the finish.

Conkerer

- **ABV 4.7%** ■ **BOTTLE SIZE 500 ml** ■ **SERVE cool**
- **INGREDIENTS Maris Otter pale malt/crystal malt/wheat malt/Hilary hops**

The name of this robust autumn ale reflects the horse chestnut debris that covers the brewery car park at this time of year.

Citrus Sin

- **ABV 4.8%** ■ **BOTTLE SIZE 500 ml** ■ **SERVE cool**
- **INGREDIENTS Maris Otter pale malt/crystal malt/wheat malt/Hilary hops/orange oil/cinnamon**

Featuring, like Conkerer, the new Hilary hops, this dark copper-coloured winter ale also includes orange oil for extra citrous zest and cinnamon for a seasonal spice flavour (hence the contrived name). It was first brewed in 2001.

Tumbledown Dick

▪ABV 5.3% ▪BOTTLE SIZE 500 ml ▪SERVE cool
▪INGREDIENTS Maris Otter pale malt/crystal malt/wheat malt/Fuggle hops

First brewed in 2000, this strong bitter takes its name from the 17th-century cottage next door to the brewery. Originally home to Richard Cromwell, after whom it was named, it later became the residence of Dick Fuggle, grandson of Richard Fuggle, who, in 1875, propagated the Fuggle hop.

Tasting Notes

This copper-coloured ale has a rich, floral, orange-fruity, hoppy aroma, followed in the mouth by floral hops and gentle bitterness. There's a touch of toasted malt in the hoppy, softly bitter, dry finish.

GREENE KING

Greene King PLC, Westgate Brewery, Bury St Edmunds, Suffolk IP33 1QT.
Tel. (01284) 763222 Fax (01284) 706502
Website: www.greeneking.co.uk

Founded in 1799, Greene King is now one of Britain's 'super-regional' breweries, having expanded by acquiring pub groups and Morland brewery in recent years. From Morland (now closed) Greene King acquired its only bottle-conditioned ale (although it does produce a range of pasteurised beers, including the notable Strong Suffolk, a complex blend of matured and young ales). Greene King has also been at the forefront of the movement to encourage beer drinking with food.

Hen's Tooth

▪ABV 6.5% ▪BOTTLE SIZE 500 ml ▪SERVE cool
▪INGREDIENTS Pipkin pale malt/crystal malt/maltose syrup/Challenger and Golding hops

Hen's Tooth was launched in 1998. The fact that this name was chosen more than suggests that the beer closely resembles the popular Old Speckled Hen in its make up. The other relevance of the name is to convey how rare it is to find a beer of this strength which is not too heavy or chewy – as rare, as Morland put it at the time, 'as a hen's tooth'. The beer is now brewed at Bury St Edmunds to the same Morland recipe, and cool conditioned for a week before being tankered down to Hepworth & Co. in Horsham for bottling. There the yeast count and fermentability of the remaining sugars are checked and, if required, these are corrected with new yeast and primings. The yeast used throughout is the Morland yeast, which is over 100 years old. The best before date is set at 12 months.

Tasting Notes
A dark amber beer with a fruity, estery nose. Sweet and a little nutty in the mouth, it features ripe malt and plenty of hop, with just a hint of pear drops. Dry, hoppy, bittersweet finish.

Major stockists Asda, Booths, Morrisons, Sainsbury, Tesco Waitrose

HAGGARDS

Haggards Brewery Ltd., 577 King's Road, London SW6 2EH.
Tel. (020) 7731 3845 Fax (020) 7731 3874
E-mail: andrewhaggard@haggardsbrewery.fsnet.co.uk
Mail order service

Haggards is a small brewery established in 1998 by two brothers opting out of a life in the City. The main outlet is The Imperial pub on King's Road, after which the bottled beer below was named.

Imp Ale

- **ABV 4.7%** ▪ **BOTTLE SIZE 500 ml** ▪ **SERVE cool**
- **INGREDIENTS Pale malt/crystal malt/Vienna malt/ Golding and Cascade hops/sugar**

The cask version of this intriguing brew is a recent SIBA (Society of Independent Brewers) national champion. What adds to the interest is the choice of Vienna malt (a toasted malt normally used to give a red-amber colour to dark lagers) and Cascade hops, for enhanced citrous character. Bottles are filled direct from the fermenter after cooling and are primed with a little sugar to achieve the right carbonation. A best before date is set at nine months and the Haggard brothers reckon the beer improves for about six of those months.

HALIFAX

Halifax Steam Brewing Co. Ltd., The Conclave, Southedge, Hipperholme, Halifax, West Yorkshire HX3 8EL.
Tel. (01484) 715074
E-mail: davidearnshaw@blueyonder.co.uk

Brewery founded in 2001 by former Barge & Barrel brewer David Earnshaw, with the purchase of a former Firkin brew pub brewery. A number of David's beers are modelled on the brews of the now-defunct Whittaker's Brewery of Halifax. The beers listed below are actually bottled and marketed by Clarke's Organic (see separate entry).

Rhode Island Red

■ ABV 4.5% ■ BOTTLE SIZE 500 ml ■ SERVE cool
■ INGREDIENTS Not declared

A ruby-red, strong mild-type beer. The ingredients, as for all David's brews, remain a closely-guarded secret.

Tasting Notes

A red-orange beer with a malty aroma, a fruity, malty, nutty taste and a bitter, malty, nutty and roasted finish.

Hope & Glory

■ ABV 4.6% ■ BOTTLE SIZE 500 ml ■ SERVE cool
■ INGREDIENTS Not declared

Originally marketed as a football beer, this premium ale incorporates both European and American hops, according to the label.

Tasting Notes

A golden ale with an aroma of fruity, floral hops, plus a hint of toffee-malt. The taste is malty, yet sharply hoppy, with floral notes. Hoppy aftertaste.

HAMPSHIRE

Hampshire Brewery Ltd., 6–8 Romsey Industrial Estate, Greatbridge Road, Romsey, Hampshire SO51 0HR.
Tel. (01794) 830529 Fax (01794) 830528
E-mail: online@hampshirebrewery.com
Website: www.hampshirebrewery.com

Founded in Andover in 1992, Hampshire moved to Romsey in 1997, filling a void left in the town by the closure of Strong's Brewery by Whitbread in 1981. The brewery has now built up a core range of eight bottle-conditioned beers, which are supplemented by short runs in bottle of seasonal cask beers. These have included: Grim Reaper (4.4%, an old ale); Heaven Can Wait (4.8%, a dark wheat beer); Not Tonight Josephine (5%, a German helles); Hampshire Hare (5%, a golden ale); T'ale of the Dragon (4.2%, a lighter golden ale); Ploughmans Punch (4.5%, a summer ale); Wild Thing (4.2%, another IPA);

Porky & Best (4.5%, a best bitter); Bohemian Rhapsody (5%, a pilsner-style beer); Merlins Magic (5%, a ruby ale); Penny Black Porter (4.5%); Good King Censlas (5%, a winter ale); Laughing Leprechaun (4.5%, an Irish stout) and Thunderbolt (4.5%, a hoppy bitter). The beers are both warm- and cold-conditioned after fermentation, then filtered and re-seeded with new bottling yeast. A 12-month best before date is stamped on each bottle.

King Alfred's

■ABV 3.8% ■BOTTLE SIZE 500 ml ■SERVE cool
■INGREDIENTS Maris Otter pale malt/crystal malt/ Challenger, First Gold and Golding hops

Building on the county's association with King Alfred, this bitter was the brewery's first regular cask beer.

Tasting Notes

A copper ale with light fruit and malt in the nose. The taste is hoppy, but not without malt or sweetness, and gentle fruit persists throughout. Hoppy, dry finish.

Strongs Best Bitter

■ABV 3.8% ■BOTTLE SIZE 500 ml ■SERVE cool
■INGREDIENTS Maris Otter pale malt/crystal malt/black malt/Challenger, Progress and Golding hops

Once, billboards advertising Strong's beers were commonplace in the South. Now Hampshire has revived the lost brewery's popular bitter and in doing so has underlined its own position and identity as the Romsey brewery of today.

Tasting Notes

A dark copper bitter with malt leading in the aroma but with plenty of hop fruitiness. On the palate, fruity spritziness lightens a rich, malty base. Hops take over in the initially bittersweet finish.

Ironside Best

■ABV 4.2% ■BOTTLE SIZE 500 ml ■SERVE cool
■INGREDIENTS Maris Otter pale malt/crystal malt/ Progress, Golding and Styrian Golding hops

A premium ale named after Edmund II, 11th-century king of England. Part of Hampshire's ancient kings range.

Tasting Notes

A dark golden ale dominated by citrous hops (orange and grapefruit) in the nose. Mouthfilling grapefruit and orange peel in the taste winds up with a dry, bitter, citrous finish.

Lionheart

- **ABV 4.5%** ■ **BOTTLE SIZE 500 ml** ■ **SERVE cool**
- **INGREDIENTS Maris Otter pale malt/lager malt/ Northdown, First Gold and Perle hops**

A well-established golden ale with King Richard I connections.

Tasting Notes

Toffeeish malt and floral hop notes lead in the nose, while the same maltiness is crisped up by sharp hop in the mouth for an almost 'lemon toffee' taste. Dry, hoppy finish with lingering malt.

King's Ransom

- **ABV 4.8%** ■ **BOTTLE SIZE 500 ml** ■ **SERVE cool**
- **INGREDIENTS Lager malt/caramalt/First Gold, Golding and Styrian Golding hops**

Formerly known as Gold Reserve, a name that reflected its brilliant colour.

Tasting Notes

Lemon fruitiness in the aroma is enhanced by a suggestion of tropical fruit. The crisp, fruity, slightly perfumed, hop-spicy taste has a clean, moreish, light malt base. Hop dryness emerges in the finish.

Pendragon

- **ABV 4.8%** ■ **BOTTLE SIZE 500 ml** ■ **SERVE cool**
- **INGREDIENTS Maris Otter pale malt/crystal malt/black malt/Challenger, Progress and Golding hops**

Named after the father of King Arthur, this strong ale was first produced in cask form in 1993.

Tasting Notes

An appealing reddish beer with light banana notes in the malty aroma. On the palate, it is complex but well balanced, with light banana, malt and hops competing for attention. Dry, bitter, malt and hops finish, with still a little banana character.

Pride of Romsey

- **ABV 5%** ■ **BOTTLE SIZE 500 ml** ■ **SERVE cool**
- **INGREDIENTS Maris Otter pale malt/crystal malt/ Challenger, Golding and Cascade hops**

Pride of Romsey – declared on the label to be an IPA – is a sort of 'thank you' beer, brewed in appreciation of the welcome the people of Romsey have given to the arrival of the brewery, and also to commemorate the revival of brewing in the town. It first appeared in cask form and instantly scooped a bronze medal at the 1998 *Brewing Industry International Awards*. This bottled version followed in the same year.

Tasting Notes

A copper-coloured beer with a slightly spicy, malty nose with hints of citrus fruits (grapefruit). The taste is a strong, bitter, mouth-filling combination of the same fruit, malt and hop, which carries on to dominate the dry finish.

Major stockists Local Asda, Sainsbury and Waitrose

1066

- **ABV 6%** ▪ **BOTTLE SIZE 500 ml** ▪ **SERVE cool**
- **INGREDIENTS Maris Otter pale malt/lager malt/caramalt/Northdown, First Gold and Perle hops**

1066 – William the Conqueror 1066, to give it the full name shown on the label – was first brewed as a cask beer in 1994, although the recipe has been modified since.

Tasting Notes

A dark golden ale with lemon-citrous notes and a touch of pear drop in the malty aroma. Light-textured for its gravity, it is sweet and lemony to taste, with malt, hops and an alcoholic warmth in the background. Citrous hops feature in the dry, bittersweet finish.

HANBY

Hanby Ales Ltd., New Brewery, Aston Park,
Soulton Road, Wem, Shropshire SY4 5SD.
Tel./Fax (01939) 232432
E-mail: jack@hanbyales.co.uk
Website: www.hanbyales.co.uk
Mail order service

Following the closure of Wem Brewery by Greenalls in 1988, its head brewer, Jack Hanby, set up his own business in the same Shropshire town. His base is a unit on an industrial park that, during World War II, was employed as a prisoner of war camp. The Nissen huts are still in evidence.

Rainbow Chaser

- **ABV 4.3%** ▪ **BOTTLE SIZE 500 ml** ▪ **SERVE cool**
- **INGREDIENTS Maris Otter pale malt/Fuggle and Pioneer hops**

Only introduced in bottle in 2001, Rainbow Chaser has been around in cask form for a number of years and is the house beer in a number of Shropshire pubs. Like the other beers, it is brewed and bottled on site, and matured in conditioning tanks. There is no filtration or re-seeding of yeast before bottling and no finings are used, which ensures that all beers are safe for vegetarians (although vegans may have problems with the honey-infused Golden Honey).

Tasting Notes

A pale golden ale with a malty nose and a bitter mix of smooth malt and fruity hop in the taste. Bitter, hoppy finish.

Shropshire Stout

- **ABV 4.4%** ▪ **BOTTLE SIZE 500 ml** ▪ **SERVE cool**
- **INGREDIENTS Maris Otter pale malt/crystal malt/chocolate malt/Fuggle and Golding hops**

New to bottle in 1999, Shropshire Stout had already won several prizes as a cask beer first brewed in 1993.

Tasting Notes

A very dark brown beer with a full coffee/roast grain aroma. There is plenty of roast malt character in the mouth, along with citrous hop notes, good bitterness and just a touch of sourness. Dry, roasty, bitter finish.

Golden Honey

- **ABV 4.5%** ▪ **BOTTLE SIZE 500 ml** ▪ **SERVE cool**
- **INGREDIENTS Maris Otter pale malt/Fuggle and Cascade hops/honey**

Australian honey is the leading feature of this premium ale, added late to the copper boil.

Premium Bitter

- **ABV 4.6%** ▪ **BOTTLE SIZE 500 ml** ▪ **SERVE cool**
- **INGREDIENTS Maris Otter pale malt/crystal malt/Fuggle and Golding hops**

Hanby's Premium was the brewery's first bottled beer, launched in 1997. It's also available as a cask ale and was formerly known as Treacleminer (the name was changed to ensure that buyers are not misled into thinking it is an overly sweet ale).

Tasting Notes

A copper-coloured ale with fruity hops in the nose. Clean and refreshing to taste, it has a nicely sharp, fruity hoppiness, with sweet malt behind. Hoppy and bitter, dry finish.

Cherry Bomb

- **ABV 6%** ■ **BOTTLE SIZE 500 ml** ■ **SERVE cool**
- **INGREDIENTS Maris Otter pale malt/crystal malt/Fuggle and Golding hops/cherry essence**

Winner of a couple of CAMRA's *Beer of the Festival* awards in its well-established cask version, this fruit-flavoured ale was introduced in bottled form in 1999. Cherry essence is added after fermentation.

Tasting Notes

An orange-gold beer with a clean white head. The aroma is very fruity, with estery pear drop notes and cherries. Cherry flavour leads on the palate, but this is a smooth, fairly sweet ale, not sour like many Belgian cherry beers. Dry, bitter cherry finish.

HARVEYS

Harvey and Son (Lewes) Ltd., The Bridge Wharf Brewery, 6 Cliffe High Street, Lewes, East Sussex BN7 2AH.
Tel. (01273) 480209 Fax (01273) 483706
E-mail: maj@harveys.org.uk
Website: www.harveys.org.uk

This popular, family-run brewery, established in the 18th century, has an excellent reputation for its bottle-conditioned 1859 Porter (4.8%). The only problem is that the beer is now only bottle conditioned in small runs on special request (usually around March, when the cask version is available), and most bottles of the porter are pasteurised. However, Harveys did take the bold step of introducing the intriguing, award-winning bottled beer mentioned below in 1999.

Imperial Extra Double Stout

- **ABV 9%** ■ **BOTTLE SIZE 330 ml** ■ **SERVE cool**
- **INGREDIENTS Maris Otter pale malt/amber malt/brown malt/black malt/Fuggle and East Kent Golding hops**

A tribute to Albert Le Coq, a Belgian who successfully marketed Courage's renowned Imperial Russian Stout to the Baltic region and particularly the Russian Empire in the early 1800s. This beer's label re-tells the Le Coq story, including how the brewery his company set up to brew his own powerful beer in Estonia was nationalised by the Bolsheviks in 1917. This beer is inspired by Le Coq's original recipe and the first vintage was sold exclusively in the USA – where such beers are widely revered – but later batches have also been made available in the UK. The beer is bottled with a cork stopper for Harveys by Gale's and is stored for 12 months before release. Full credit goes to Harveys for its faith in this fascinating beer style, when Scottish Courage, regrettably, has allowed the original Imperial Russian Stout to wither on the hop bine. B United are the US importers.

Tasting Notes

A deep, deep ruby beer with a smoky, fruity, vinous aroma with hints of polished leather. This complex brew is vinously fruity, creamy, bittersweet, spicy, roasty and warming in the mouth, with a lingering, bitter, coffee-roast finish and a touch of winey fruit to the end.

HIGH FORCE

High Force Hotel Brewery, Forest-in-Teesdale, Barnard Castle, Co. Durham DL12 0XH.
Tel. (01833) 622222 Fax (01833) 622264

The High Force Hotel is a whitewashed, 19th-century building situated by the 70-foot High Force waterfall in a designated area of outstanding natural beauty, close to the Pennine Way. A small brewery opened here in 1995 and claims to be the highest in Britain, at 1,060 feet above sea level. However, since April 2001, all beer production has been handled for High Force by Darwin Brewery.

Forest XB

- **ABV 4.2%** ▪ **BOTTLE SIZE 500 ml** ▪ **SERVE cool**
- **INGREDIENTS Pale malt/crystal malt/chocolate malt/ torrefied wheat/Willamette hops**

The newer of the two High Force bottled beers, Forest XB was introduced in 1999 and reflects the brewery's setting at Forest-in-Teesdale in its name.

Tasting Notes

An interesting dark amber beer with a fruity, malty, lightly chocolatey aroma. A little salty on the palate, it has good bitterness and fruity hop notes over a rich malty base. Dry, bitter hop finish.

Cauldron Snout

- **ABV 5.6%** ▪ **BOTTLE SIZE 500 ml** ▪ **SERVE cool**
- **INGREDIENTS Pale malt/crystal malt/black malt/ Challenger hops**

Cauldron Snout is named after a waterfall five miles from the hotel in Upper Teesdale. The label depicts a prehistoric water stone, used to indicate sources of water on the Pennine moors. If you make the effort to collect a bottle from the pub, you can also pay a visit to the local butcher's where they occasionally make Cauldron Snout sausages.

Tasting Notes

A very dark ruby beer with a clean, leathery aroma of dark malt. Full and bittersweet in the mouth, it has decent hop character, pruney fruit and smooth, mellow malt on the swallow. Bitter, dry, roasted malt finish.

HILDEN

Hilden Brewing Co., Hilden House, Grand Street, Lisburn, Co. Antrim BT27 4TY.
Tel. (028) 9266 3863 Fax (028) 9260 3511
E-mail: hilden.brewery@ukgateway.net
Mail order service

Hilden, founded in 1981, was, for some years, the only cask ale brewery in Northern Ireland, albeit a very small one with limited outlets. Access to the beers is still difficult, but the installation of a bottling line in 1999 now allows more people to sample Hilden's ales. Four-pack 'Hilden Ale Sacks' form part of the marketing exercise. The beers are bottled at the brewery, with a three-month best before date.

Hilden Original Ale

- **ABV 4.6%** ▪ **BOTTLE SIZE 500 ml** ▪ **SERVE cool**
- **INGREDIENTS Halcyon pale malt/crystal malt/chocolate malt/black malt/First Gold, Northdown and Golding hops**

The big brother of the popular cask beer Hilden Ale (4%), Hilden Original was introduced in 1998. A filtered and pasteurised version of the same beer was sold at the same time as Scullion's Irish Ale. Now, to make the beers more individual, Hilden uses Golding hops in the bottle-conditioned beer and Hersbrucker in the pasteurised. The brewery reckons Hilden Original is worth trying with a stir fry or perhaps a pasta dish.

Tasting Notes

A copper beer with a fruity, malty nose. Smooth, slightly sweet and very fruity to taste, it has plenty of malt flavour and a light bitter edge. Bitterness builds to overshadow malt and fruit in the dry finish.

Molly Malone Single X

- **ABV 4.6%** ▪ **BOTTLE SIZE 500 ml** ▪ **SERVE cool**
- **INGREDIENTS Halcyon pale malt/chocolate malt/black malt/Northdown, Golding and Hallertau hops**

A porter introduced in 2000 and now bottled in small quantities. It incorporates three strains of hops, including Hallertau from New Zealand.

Tasting Notes

A ruby-red porter with a slightly vinous, fruity aroma supported by roasted malt. The dry, vinous taste mostly features gentle roasted malt which continues on into the dry, bitter aftertaste.

HOBSONS

Hobsons Brewery & Co. Ltd., Newhouse Farm, Tenbury Road, Cleobury Mortimer, Kidderminster, Worcester DY14 8RD. Tel. (01299) 270837
E-mail: beer@hobsons-brewery.co.uk
Website: www.hobsons-brewery.co.uk
Mail order service

This family-run brewery was set up in 1993 but moved to its current premises (an attractive old farm building) in 1996. An extension to the property in 2001 provided space for the addition of a bottling plant. All the bottles are very nicely presented, but remember to remove the plastic cowls before trying to open the bottles – it's very tricky to get the caps off if you don't!

Manor Ale

- **ABV 4.2%** ▪ **BOTTLE SIZE 500 ml** ▪ **SERVE cool**
- **INGREDIENTS Maris Otter pale malt/Cascade, Challenger and Golding hops**

Brewed and bottled on behalf of Severn Valley Railway, Manor Ale is also sold in cask form under the name of Steam No.9. As for other Hobsons beers, it is filtered and re-seeded with fresh yeast prior to bottling. Best before dates are fixed at 12 months.

Tasting Notes

An unusual golden beer, surprisingly nutty and malty in the aroma at first, with floral/fruity notes then emerging. A nutty bitterness comes to the fore in the mouth, backed by light citrous notes. Dry, bitter, nutty finish.

Town Crier

■ ABV 4.5% ■ BOTTLE SIZE 500 ml ■ SERVE cold
■ INGREDIENTS Maris Otter pale malt/Progress and Golding hops

Intriguingly described by the brewers as a 'pale Bavarian ale', Town Crier is recommended for drinking younger and cooler than their other bottled offerings. Try it with smoked salmon.

Tasting Notes
A pale golden beer with light floral/lemon notes in the nose. Sweet, gentle malt is overlaid by a lemony, bitter hops in the mouth, leaving a hoppy, bitter finish.

Major stockists Local Spar

Old Henry

■ ABV 5.2% ■ BOTTLE SIZE 500 ml ■ SERVE cool
■ INGREDIENTS Maris Otter pale malt/crystal malt/ Challenger and Golding hops

Old Henry – described in the *Good Beer Guide* as 'an authentic winter ale' – is a touch more heavily hopped for the bottle, to compensate for the absence of dry hops in the cask. The label says this is a beer 'best served with mature Shropshire Blue cheese'.

Tasting Notes
A dark copper ale with a malty nose featuring a light 'boiled sweet' fruitiness and a little burst of lemon. Estery flavours emerge in the mouth, with suggestions of pear drop and almond against a backdrop of sweet, nutty malt and bitterness. Bittersweet, slightly roasted finish, with hops and a squeeze of lemon.

Major stockists Local Spar

HOGS BACK

Hogs Back Brewery Ltd., Manor Farm, The Street, Tongham, Surrey GU10 1DE.
Tel. (01252) 783000 Fax (01252) 782328
E-mail: info@hogsback.co.uk
Website: www.hogsback.co.uk
Mail order service

This purpose-built brewery was set up in restored farm buildings (circa 1768) in 1992, providing a traditional rural setting for ale brewing. All the brewery's bottled beers are handled in house. The brews are filtered and then injected with fresh yeast prior to filling with, occasionally, priming sugars added to ensure a good fermentation in the bottle. Best before dates are set at 14 months. The elaborate, gold-embossed labels are the work of brewery partner Tony Stanton-Precious, a former draughtsman. Hogs Back also has a well-stocked shop/off-licence on site, offering a wide range of bottled beers from other breweries as well as their own. It is well worth a detour if you're in the area.

TEA (Traditional English Ale)

■ ABV 4.2% ■ BOTTLE SIZE 500 ml ■ SERVE cool
■ INGREDIENTS Maris Otter pale malt/crystal malt/Fuggle and Golding hops

TEA is one of Hogs Back's longest established brews but was one of the last of the current crop to find its way into a bottle, when it was launched in October 1997. The beer is now brewed weekly. The cask version claimed the *Best Bitter* title at the 2000 *Champion Beer of Britain* contest.

Tasting Notes
An amber-coloured beer with a malty, fruity nose. Malt and fruit feature in the dry, bittersweet taste, wrapped up by a pleasantly bitter, citrous finish.

Major stockists Safeway, Sainsbury, Tesco, Waitrose

BSA (Burma Star Ale)

■ ABV 4.5% ■ BOTTLE SIZE 500 ml ■ SERVE cool
■ INGREDIENTS Maris Otter pale malt/crystal malt/chocolate malt/Fuggle and Golding hops

Introduced in 1995 to commemorate the 50th anniversary of VJ Day, and as a tribute to members of the Burma Star Association and prisoners of war in the Far East, BSA was re-labelled to mark the 50th anniversary of the founding of the Association in 1951. The beer is available in cask form as well as in this bottle-conditioned version and is now produced every month. The label depicts servicemen of the day (actually the partners' parents – one of whom served in the Burma Star movement) and recalls the famous and poignant quotation:

'When you go home tell them of us and say –
For your tomorrow we gave our today'.

The Imperial War Museum has taken stocks for sale to its visitors and, for every bottle sold, Hogs Back pledges a donation to the BSA's welfare fund. Good to drink with roast lamb, say the brewers.

Tasting Notes
A red ale with a spicy malt aroma, supported by fruity hop.

The taste is hoppy, fruity and quite earthy, and the finish is dry, lightly roasted and notably hoppy, with hints of orange. **Major stockist** Local Sainsbury

OTT (Old Tongham Tasty or Over the Top)

- **ABV 6%** ■ **BOTTLE SIZE 500 ml** ■ **SERVE cool**
- **INGREDIENTS Maris Otter pale malt/crystal malt/chocolate malt/Fuggle and Golding hops**

A cask beer introduced in bottle in 2000, and a fine accompaniment to game dishes, it is claimed. The label features pigs flying 'over the top' of the brewery.

Tasting Notes

A very dark ruby beer with biscuity roasted malt and a touch of liquorice in the nose. The taste is sweet, lightly fruity and filled with dark malt, but with roasted bitterness in the background. Thick, sweet finish with a little roasted bitterness.

Brewster's Bundle

- **ABV 7.4%** ■ **BOTTLE SIZE 275 ml** ■ **SERVE cool**
- **INGREDIENTS Maris Otter pale malt/crystal malt/Fuggle and Golding hops**

Another commemorative brew, this ale was initially produced each February, but is now bottled every two months. The 'Bundle' in question is Charley, the first baby daughter of Hogs Back's lady brewster, Maureen Zieher. Charley was born in February 1994 at the weight of 7lb 4oz (hence the 7.4% ABV). The beer is good with white meats, pork pies and fish dishes, claim the brewers.

Tasting Notes

A copper-coloured beer with a malty, fruity aroma (hints of raspberry). The taste is smooth, sweetish, malty and fruity (with some tropical notes), before a mellow, warming finish of bittersweet fruit.

Wobble in a Bottle/Santa's Wobble

- **ABV 7.5%** ■ **BOTTLE SIZE 275 ml** ■ **SERVE cool**
- **INGREDIENTS Maris Otter pale malt/crystal malt/chocolate malt/Fuggle and East Kent Golding hops**

Wobble in a Bottle is the bottled version of Hogs Back's Christmas beer, Santa's Wobble (a Christmas edition is still released as Santa's Wobble, showing Santa on the label and topped with a white cap to represent snow). It was first produced in 1996 and is now brewed twice a year. Serve, perhaps, instead of a port at the end of a dinner, but go easy or you might end up like the befuddled old chap on the label. The cask version is also made available in summer months, under the alternative name of 'Still Wobbling'.

Tasting Notes

A red-brown beer with a rich, malty, raspberry-ish aroma. The taste is full, malty and fruity, with almond/marzipan notes and a refreshingly sharp edge, but without much of the alcoholic heaviness or cloying sweetness you'd expect. Bitterness dominates fruit in the gum-tingling finish.

A over T (Aromas over Tongham)

▪ABV 9% ▪BOTTLE SIZE 275 ml ▪SERVE cool
▪INGREDIENTS Maris Otter pale malt/crystal malt/ chocolate malt/Fuggle and Golding hops

One of Hogs Back's earliest brews, A Over T (named after its unfortunate side-effect but diplomatically explained as standing for 'Aromas Over Tongham') first tempted drinkers in 1993, when it appeared in cask form. The bottled version – the brewery's first ever bottled beer – conforms to the same recipe, except for the nuances of the bottling procedure. Runner-up in 2003's *Beauty of Hops* contest to find the *Ultimate Beer for an After Dinner Cheese.*

Tasting Notes

A red-brown beer with a malty, sherry-like aroma. Full-flavoured, it is sweet, creamy and a little woody to taste, featuring fruit and hop before a warming aftertaste that is both fruity and bitter.

HOP BACK

Hop Back Brewery PLC, Units 22–24, Downton Business Centre, Downton, Salisbury, Wiltshire SP5 3HU.
Tel. (01725) 510986 Fax (01725) 513116
E-mail: info@hopback.co.uk
Website: www.hopback.co.uk

Originally based at a Salisbury brew pub, The Wyndham Arms, Hop Back was set up in 1986. It moved to a unit on an industrial area at Downton in 1992 and continues to expand. It stepped up its bottled beer production in 1997 with the installation of a new bottling line. All bottled beers are cold-conditioned at 3°C, filtered and kräusened prior to bottling. Best before dates are set at 12 months after bottling. Regrettably, the easy-drinking wheat beer, Thunderstorm, has now been discontinued.

Crop Circle

- **ABV 4.2%** ■ **BOTTLE SIZE 500 ml** ■ **SERVE cool**
- **INGREDIENTS Optic pale malt/flaked maize/wheat malt/East Kent Golding, Pioneer and Tettnang hops/coriander**

Winner of the small brewer category in the Spring/Summer 2000 *Tesco Beer Challenge*, Crop Circle was designed as a light beer for the warmer months, with bitterness playing second fiddle to aroma when it came to the choice of hops. Goldings and Pioneer do most of the hop work, with German Tettnangs added late in the copper. Coriander is added at this stage, too, to enhance the summery fruitiness.

Tasting Notes

A light-bodied, watery-golden-coloured beer with an aroma full of zesty, lemon and orange notes and an earthy coriander spiciness. The taste is rich in fresh, lightly perfumed and spicy, summery flavours – orange, lemon juice and a growing hoppy bitterness. Dry, hoppy, bitter, orange-lemon finish.

Major stockist Local Waitrose

Taiphoon

- **ABV 4.2%** ■ **BOTTLE SIZE 500 ml** ■ **SERVE cool**
- **INGREDIENTS Optic pale malt/East Kent Golding and Pioneer hops/lemongrass/coriander**

Introduced in spring 1999, Taiphoon is designed as a perfect accompaniment for Oriental cuisine. The key ingredient, lemongrass, imparts a distinctive exotic spiciness.

Tasting Notes

A pale golden beer with a malty, yet peppery, spicy and perfumed nose. It is also peppery and scented in the mouth, with enough malt sweetness in the background for balance. The finish is spicy, bitter and scented.

Major stockist Local Waitrose

Entire Stout

- **ABV 4.5%** ■ **BOTTLE SIZE 500 ml** ■ **SERVE cool**
- **INGREDIENTS Optic pale malt/chocolate malt/roasted barley/wheat crystal malt/Challenger and Golding hops**

A cask beer for over ten years, Entire Stout finally made it into bottle in December 2001 and went into regular production a year or so later. Produced without isinglass finings, the beer is good news for vegetarians and vegans (the beer is simply transferred from the fermenting vessel to the tank from which it is bottled). Great to drink with a ploughman's, the brewers say. Winner of the *Tucker's Maltings Bottled Beer Competition* in 2004.

Tasting Notes

A dark red beer with a coffee and caramel aroma preceding a crisp, bitter, dark malt taste with a light, teasing, caramel-like sweetness and a dry, bitter, coffeeish roasted finish.

Major stockists Waitrose

Summer Lightning

▪ ABV 5% ▪ BOTTLE SIZE 500 ml ▪ SERVE cool
▪ INGREDIENTS Optic pale malt/East Kent Golding hops

The story of Summer Lightning goes back to the late 1980s. Managing director and brewery founder John Gilbert came up with the recipe for this pale, crisp and hoppy, yet strong, beer to contrast with the other 5% beers of the time which were nearly all dark, sweet and sickly. For a name, he opted to steal the title of a PG Wodehouse play. In cask form the beer has been a trend-setter. Since winning the *Best New Brewery Beer* award at the *Champion Beer of Britain* contest in 1989, it has inspired brewers up and down the land to create strong but pale beers which have appeal beyond the traditional ale drinker. The bottle-conditioned version is now a single-varietal hop brew, dropping the Challenger hops it used to include in favour of East Kent Goldings only. The draught version is not single-varietal and differs in a number of other respects. Probably the most notable difference is in the carbonation level, with the bottled beer performing more briskly on the tongue. Interestingly, the brewery recommends serving this and the other bottled beers on the cold side of cool. CAMRA's *Best Bottle-Conditioned Beer* in 1997.

Tasting Notes

A pale, easy-drinking, strong bitter, quenching but dry. The citrous, hoppy and malty nose leads to a lightly fruity taste with crisp, clean hoppiness and a dry, hoppy, bitter finish.

Major stockists Asda, Booths, Morrisons, Oddbins, Safeway, Tesco, Thresher, Waitrose

HOPDAEMON

Hopdaemon Brewery Co. Ltd., 18A/B Canterbury Hill, Canterbury, Kent CT2 9LS. Tel. (01227) 784962
E-mail: hopdaemon@supanet.com

New Zealander Tonie Prins founded Hopdaemon in 2001 after working at Swale Brewery. The equipment is housed in two outbuildings – a former plumbing company and an ex-children's nursery – behind his cottage on the fringe of Canterbury. He describes his beers as 'traditional ales with a slight New World twist' and, to market them, has combined the medieval traditions of Canterbury and its cathedral with a sprinkling of legend and a touch of home-spun folklore based around the local hopgardens. He bottles the beers by hand himself, chilling them for up to a week before filling to allow proteins to drop out and then re-seeding with dried bottling yeast. He also supplies 'own label' beers for Southwark Cathedral and the British Museum.

Skrimshander IPA

- **ABV 4.5%** ■ **BOTTLE SIZE 500 ml** ■ **SERVE cool**
- **INGREDIENTS Pale malt/crystal malt/caramalt/Fuggle, Golding and Bramling Cross hops**

Inspired by Herman Melville's classic novel, *Moby Dick*, and its references to skrimshander (the craft of carving whale ivory), this beer, like the other bottled beers, is also sold in cask form.

Tasting Notes
Fruit salad and spicy hop aromas emerge from this copper ale. The taste is wonderfully fruity but delicate, with orange blossom fragrance alongside clean hops. The dry, hoppy finish has more lingering fruit as bitterness grows.

Green Daemon

- **ABV 5%** ■ **BOTTLE SIZE 330 ml** ■ **SERVE cold**
- **INGREDIENTS Pale malt/lager malt/New Zealand hops**

Tonie has yet to apply for accreditation for this organic beer, so he has to settle for calling it 'Natural' instead. However, the ingredients are all organic, including hops from back home which are not, Tonie is quick to point out, the organic Hallertau hops for which New Zealand has become known. Green Daemon is lagered for three weeks before bottling.

Tasting Notes
A golden beer with luscious tropical fruit in the nose. More juicy Caribbean fruits emerge in the mouth, with a whiff of perfume. Mildly bitter, fruity finish.

Leviathan

- **ABV 6%** ■ **BOTTLE SIZE 500 ml** ■ **SERVE cool**
- **INGREDIENTS Pale malt/crystal malt/chocolate malt/caramalt/wheat malt/Fuggle and Bramling Cross hops**

'A beast of a beer', laughs Tonie, referring to the giant sea monster from the pages of the Bible that gives its name to his strong, but subtle, ale.

Tasting Notes

A red-brown beer with hints of pineapple and lemon in the hoppy nose. Easy-drinking for its strength, its taste is full of juicy, fruity hops plus a dash of pepper. The dry, fruity and hoppy finish lasts well.

HUGHES

Sarah Hughes Brewery, Beacon Hotel, 129 Bilston Street, Sedgley, Dudley, West Midlands DY3 1JE.
Tel. (01902) 883381

This old, Black Country brewhouse stands behind the gloriously unspoilt, multi-room Beacon Hotel, a Victorian delight that flash brewery architects would give their eye-teeth to vandalise. The business was purchased by Sarah Hughes in 1920 and she took up the reins of brewing that had commenced back in the 1880s, or even earlier. She produced just one beer, the revered Dark Ruby, and continued to do so until her death in 1951. After lying idle for 30 years, the tower brewery was re-opened in 1987 by her grandson. With his brewer, Guy Perry, John Hughes has expanded the beer range a little, but only the classic strong mild is bottle conditioned.

Dark Ruby

- **ABV 6%** ■ **BOTTLE SIZE 500 ml** ■ **SERVE cool**
- **INGREDIENTS Maris Otter pale malt/crystal malt/Fuggle and Golding hops**

Originally brewed by Sarah Hughes back in 1921, the bottled version of this beer was first made available in 1995. It is identical to the award-winning draught beer, and is simply filled from the cask by contract bottlers with no primings or finings, making it acceptable to vegans. The founder herself is depicted on the label. This bottled version has been out of production for a while but is due to return once new bottlers have been found.

Tasting Notes

As expected, dark ruby in colour. The vinous aroma of fruit gives way to a smooth, fruity, rather sweet taste. Fruity, malty, sweetish finish with a little hop. Older samples become winey.

HUMPTY DUMPTY

Humpty Dumpty Brewery, Church Road, Reedham, Norfolk NR13 3TZ.
Tel. (01493) 701818 Fax (01493) 700727
Mail order service

Opened by brewer Mick Cottrell in 1998 next to The Railway Tavern pub in Reedham, Humpty Dumpty moved in 2001 to a new site. Its new home is a large building handily situated alongside Pettitts Animal Park (a popular family attraction) in the same village. The new premises not only has allowed brewery expansion but also offers a spacious gift shop/off-licence, where Humpty Dumpty's bottled beers (in gift packs and individually), plus other local souvenirs, can be purchased. Reedham itself has an attractive riverside and an old chain ferry, connecting Norfolk to Suffolk.

Little Sharpie

- **ABV 3.8%** ■ **BOTTLE SIZE 500 ml** ■ **SERVE cool**
- **INGREDIENTS Pearl pale malt/caramalt/wheat malt/ Fuggle and Cascade hops**

Humpty Dumpty's beer names either reflect its Broadland setting or recall the names of famous steam engines. Little Sharpie is an engine-driven beer. Like the other bottled beers, this is brewed and bottled on site after conditioning in cask. Each beer is kräusened to ensure a good secondary fermentation. Six months are allowed in the best before date.

Tasting Notes

A golden ale with fruity, spicy hops in the nose, a crisp, spicy, lemony, bitter taste, and a dry, bitter, lemon-hop finish.

Lemon & Ginger

- **ABV 4%** ■ **BOTTLE SIZE 500 ml** ■ **SERVE cool**
- **INGREDIENTS Pearl pale malt/caramalt/wheat malt/ Bramling Cross and Cascade hops/lemons/stem ginger**

It's taken Mick a couple of years to perfect this beer and the 'secret' way in which he incorporates fresh lemons and stem ginger into the brew.

Claud Hamilton

- **ABV 4.1%** ■ **BOTTLE SIZE 500 ml** ■ **SERVE cool**
- **INGREDIENTS Pearl pale malt/chocolate malt/ caramalt/roasted barley/Challenger hops**

Inspired by another famous locomotive, this single-varietal

hop ale showcases dark malts and just the seasoning of Challenger hops.

Humpty Dumpty

▪ ABV 4.1% ▪ BOTTLE SIZE 500 ml ▪ SERVE cool
▪ INGREDIENTS Pearl pale malt/crystal malt/caramalt/ wheat malt/Challenger and Fuggle hops

The beer that shares its name with the brewery is named after a locomotive from the 1920s.

Tasting Notes

A dark golden beer with spicy, light fruit in the nose. Bold flavours hog the palate – hops, bitterness and fruit primarily, over a sweet base – before a bitter, hoppy aftertaste.

Golden Gorse

▪ ABV 4.4% ▪ BOTTLE SIZE 500 ml ▪ SERVE cool
▪ INGREDIENTS Lager malt/wheat malt/Fuggle and First Gold hops

Although it seems to owe more to Broadland than Brunel, Golden Gorse is also named after a famous loco.

Tasting Notes

Pale gold in colour, this ale has fruit and hops in the aroma and a bittersweet, malt-and-lemon taste. Bitterness takes over in the finish, but fruit lingers.

Reed Cutter

▪ ABV 4.4% ▪ BOTTLE SIZE 500 ml ▪ SERVE cool
▪ INGREDIENTS Pearl pale malt/wheat malt/Fuggle and First Gold hops

A pale ale named after local reed beds and in turn giving its name to the brewery's first pub, four miles away at Cantley.

Cheltenham Flyer

▪ ABV 4.6% ▪ BOTTLE SIZE 500 ml ▪ SERVE cool
▪ INGREDIENTS Pearl pale malt/crystal malt/wheat malt/Challenger and Mount Hood hops

Another railway beer, this time incorporating some American Mount Hood hops.

Tasting Notes

A dark golden ale with orange among the fruit and malt in the nose. Orange fruitiness continues in the mouth, alongside bitterness and hops, before a long, hoppy, bitter finish. A robust, full-bodied beer.

Peto's Porter

■ABV 5% ■BOTTLE SIZE 500 ml ■SERVE cool
■INGREDIENTS Pearl pale malt/crystal malt/amber malt/chocolate malt/wheat malt/First Gold hops

A new porter named in honour of one Samuel Peto, 19th-century Lord Mayor of Lowestoft. Peto was a pioneer of railways in East Anglia and his statue can be seen at Norwich station.

Railway Sleeper

■ABV 5% ■BOTTLE SIZE 500 ml ■SERVE cool
■INGREDIENTS Pearl pale malt/crystal malt/amber malt/wheat malt/First Gold hops

A single-varietal hop beer using the popular dwarf hop, First Gold.

Tasting Notes

Fruit leads in the aroma of this dark golden ale, with lots of malt overlaid by a surprisingly light, fruity hoppiness in the taste. Hop eventually wins through over malt in the finish, but lemon notes linger on.

Broadland Gold

■ABV 6% ■BOTTLE SIZE 500 ml ■SERVE cool
■INGREDIENTS Pearl pale malt/amber malt/wheat malt/Challenger hops

Unlike the other beers, which are also sold in cask form, Broadland Gold is mostly brewed only for the bottle and is just available in winter months.

ICENI

The Iceni Brewery, 3 Foulden Road, Ickburgh, Mundford, Norfolk IP26 5BJ.
Tel. (01842) 878922 Fax (01842) 879216

Iceni was founded by Ulsterman Brendan Moore in 1995 and some of his beers are named after Celtic queens and/or the Iceni tribe, which once inhabited this part of England. The beers, left to drop bright, are kräusened with a wort and yeast mixture before bottling from casks. Best before dates are set at one year. Brendan – a driving force in the local microbrewing movement – also bottles for a number of other small producers and is a partner with his daughter, Frances, in Elveden Ales (see separate entry).

Honey Mild

- **ABV 3.6%** ■ **BOTTLE SIZE 500 ml** ■ **SERVE cool**
- **INGREDIENTS Maris Otter pale malt/crystal malt/ roasted barley/flaked barley/Fuggle and Challenger hops/honey**

This ruby beer is the same brew as Thetford Forest Mild (see below), except for the addition of honey. It was first produced in November 2000.

Tasting Notes

A complex beer for its strength, with a honey-caramel nose with roasted bits – like liquid Crunchie bars. The taste begins malty sweet and honeyish but turns dry and gently bitter. Dry, honeyed finish with dark malt.

Thetford Forest Mild

- **ABV 3.6%** ■ **BOTTLE SIZE 500 ml** ■ **SERVE cool**
- **INGREDIENTS Maris Otter pale malt/crystal malt/ roasted barley/flaked barley/Fuggle and Challenger hops**

Introduced in spring 2000, this mild is named after the large tract of forest that runs up to the brewery's home.

Tasting Notes

A very dark ruby mild with a pleasant coffee and biscuity malt aroma. On the palate, it is sweetish and malty, but well balanced. Bittersweet, malty finish.

Boadicea Chariot Ale

- **ABV 3.8%** ■ **BOTTLE SIZE 500 ml** ■ **SERVE cool**
- **INGREDIENTS Maris Otter pale malt/Fuggle and Challenger hops**

Iceni's original beer, Boadicea first tempted Norfolk drinkers back in 1995. It was re-introduced in 2000, replacing Boadicea Strong Ale (4.2%).

Tasting Notes

An amber ale with a slightly piney, nutty, fruity nose. Piney, spicy, perfumed hops lead in the mouth. The finish is bitter and increasingly hoppy.

Brewer's Light

- **ABV 3.9%** ■ **BOTTLE SIZE 500 ml** ■ **SERVE cool**
- **INGREDIENTS Lager malt/wheat/Brewer's Gold hops**

A new ale introduced in 2003 and named after its straw colour and its choice of hops.

Elveden Forest Gold

- **ABV 3.9% ■ BOTTLE SIZE 500 ml ■ SERVE cool**
- **INGREDIENTS Maris Otter pale malt/caramalt/Fuggle, Challenger and Brewer's Gold hops**

Elveden Forest, close to the brewery's home, is probably best known as the site of one of the Centre Parks holiday villages.

Tasting Notes

A golden ale with a floral hop nose, a crisp, fruity, spicy and hoppy taste, and a light, hoppy finish with lingering fruit.

Celtic Queen

- **ABV 4% ■ BOTTLE SIZE 500 ml ■ SERVE cool**
- **INGREDIENTS Maris Otter pale malt/caramalt/Fuggle and Challenger hops**

Most of Iceni's labels are designed to look like the open pages of a book, displaying the name of the beer on the left side of the spread and a picture, plus a legend or quotation about the beer's name, on the right. This beer's image is of the Celtic Queen herself, pondering her duty 'to be a fierce warrior, leader of her people'.

Tasting Notes

An amber beer with a mixed fruit aroma. On the palate, there is full fruitiness and malt, but the beer is dry, not too sweet and nicely restrained, with a gentle, clean hop bitterness. Dry, fruity, moreish, bitter aftertaste.

Fine Soft Day

- **ABV 4% ■ BOTTLE SIZE 500 ml ■ SERVE cool**
- **INGREDIENTS Maris Otter pale malt/caramalt/Fuggle and Challenger hops/maple syrup**

Maple syrup is the unusual ingredient. It is added when the beer is racked into casks after primary fermentation.

Tasting Notes

An attractive bronze beer with an aroma of ripe, sweet malt and citrus fruit. The full, bittersweet taste is grainy, malty, dry and very fruity (citrus and melon), while the aftertaste is particularly dry and increasingly bitter.

Red, White & Blueberry

- **ABV 4% ■ BOTTLE SIZE 500 ml ■ SERVE cool**
- **INGREDIENTS Maris Otter pale malt/caramalt/Cascade hops/blueberries**

As suggested by the US flag on the label, this is a beer

devised to catch the eye of American servicemen on duty at East Anglia's airbases. Originally blueberries fresh from a local farm were used, but these are not always available. The fruit is crushed and added as a priming in a cask prior to bottling.

Swaffham Pride

- **ABV 4%** - **BOTTLE SIZE 500 ml** - **SERVE cool**
- **INGREDIENTS Maris Otter pale malt/caramalt/fruit sugar/Fuggle and Challenger hops**

Swaffham Pride was first brewed in autumn 1999 to commemorate the opening of the Ecotech Centre (shown on the label) in nearby Swaffham. Its fruity character makes it good with desserts, says Brendan.

Tasting Notes

A lovely fruit cocktail – tinned pears and peaches – aroma introduces this amber ale. Juicy fruit also dominates crisp bitterness and a light background sweetness in the taste, before a dry, bitter, nicely hoppy finish.

Cranberry Wheat

- **ABV 4.1%** - **BOTTLE SIZE 500 ml** - **SERVE cool**
- **INGREDIENTS Lager malt/caramalt/wheat malt/ Cascade hops/cranberries**

Cranberries offer brewers a different angle when considering fruit beers. Being rather bitter, they provide fruit character without too much sweetness, as Fuller's discovered when introducing its Organic Honey Dew with Cranberry. Iceni's cranberry beer dates from 2000, arriving first in cask.

Tasting Notes

A peachey-golden beer with a fruity, hoppy nose. The taste is a mostly bitter mix of hop, malt and light cranberry, with bitterness gradually taking over. Dry, bitter cranberry finish.

Snowdrop

- **ABV 4.1%** - **BOTTLE SIZE 500 ml** - **SERVE cool**
- **INGREDIENTS Lager malt/crushed wheat/Fuggle, Challenger and Cascade hops**

An annual brew, Snowdrop appears in spring, and is another beer to try with puddings, according to Iceni.

Tasting Notes

A pale golden beer with a crisp, fruity (peaches and oranges) nose. The clean taste is a pleasant mix of peachy fruit and crisp, lightly-scented hop bitterness. The finish has a gentle smack of bitter, peachy fruit.

Fen Tiger

- **ABV 4.2%** ▪ **BOTTLE SIZE 500 ml** ▪ **SERVE cool**
- **INGREDIENTS Maris Otter pale malt/caramalt/Fuggle and Challenger hops/coriander**

Coriander, one of the many herbs and spices used to flavour beer before hops were imported into the UK, is recalled in this novel bitter. The ancient practice was revived initially by Nethergate Brewery in Suffolk, with its Umbel Ale and Umbel Magna, in the early 1990s. The label depicts a poacher.

Tasting Notes

An amber ale with a balanced aroma of light orange fruit and sweet malt. The taste is a crisp, clean mix of lightly spicy, gently bitter fruits, while the finish is dry, moreish and slightly perfumed, with bitter fruit and emerging hop character.

On Target

- **ABV 4.2%** ▪ **BOTTLE SIZE 500 ml** ▪ **SERVE cool**
- **INGREDIENTS Maris Otter pale malt/caramalt/Target, Fuggle and Challenger hops**

Target hops provide the inspiration for the name of this best bitter. It 'always hits the mark', if you believe the label.

Tasting Notes

Amber in colour, this best bitter has toffeeish malt and an earthy hop fruitiness in the aroma. The taste is predominantly bitter and hoppy, but with good malt support. Plenty of body for its strength. Very dry, bitter and hoppy finish.

Thomas Paine Porter

- **ABV 4.2%** ▪ **BOTTLE SIZE 500 ml** ▪ **SERVE cool**
- **INGREDIENTS Maris Otter pale malt/crystal malt/flaked wheat/torrefied wheat/roasted barley/Fuggle and Challenger hops**

Named after local hero Thomas Paine, a philosopher, theologian and activist in the American War of Independence – 'Born in Thetford in 1737: a noted author, revolutionary and man of reason', according to the label – this ruby porter was added in 1999.

Honey Stout

- **ABV 4.3%** ▪ **BOTTLE SIZE 500 ml** ▪ **SERVE cool**
- **INGREDIENTS Maris Otter pale malt/crystal malt/caramalt/roasted barley/Fuggle and Challenger hops/honey**

A near-black beer, based on the brewery's cask Celtic Stout, with Irish honey added for a new dimension.

Phoenix

■ **ABV 4.3%** ■ **BOTTLE SIZE 500 ml** ■ **SERVE cool**
■ **INGREDIENTS Lager malt/crushed wheat/Phoenix hops**
A single-varietal beer introduced in 2002, showcasing the not-widely-used Phoenix hops, with the fire-regenerated, mythological bird of the same name depicted on the label.

Tasting Notes
A golden ale with a sharp, hoppy, lemon aroma. Piney hops dominate, leaving light lemon in the hoppy, bitter finish.

Deirdre of the Sorrows

■ **ABV 4.4%** ■ **BOTTLE SIZE 500 ml** ■ **SERVE cool**
■ **INGREDIENTS Maris Otter pale malt/roasted barley/ Fuggle and Challenger hops**
A beer dedicated to 'the fairest and most beautiful of all the daughters of Ulster', destined to 'bring sorrow and pain to all the heroes of Ulster', according to the label.

Tasting Notes
Orange-gold, with a malty nose. Fruit, malt and hops combine in the gently bitter taste; dry, fruity, pleasantly bitter finish.

Ported Porter

■ **ABV 4.4%** ■ **BOTTLE SIZE 500 ml** ■ **SERVE cool**
■ **INGREDIENTS Maris Otter pale malt/torrefied wheat/ flaked barley/roasted barley/Fuggle and Challenger hops/port**
Brendan Moore grew up with the Irish tradition of adding fortified wines to stout and in 2000 created his own all-in-one equivalent, adding a bottle of port to each firkin.

Tasting Notes
A dark ruby porter with soft roasted grain, a little fruit and some caramel in the aroma. The taste is also soft, nutty, gently roasted and bittersweet, with a hint of winey fruit. Dry, bitter finish, with a little sweet fruit.

Roísín Dubh

■ **ABV 4.4%** ■ **BOTTLE SIZE 500 ml** ■ **SERVE cool**
■ **INGREDIENTS Maris Otter pale malt/torrefied wheat/ roasted barley/Fuggle and Challenger hops**
Inspired by a sweet, dark beer from the Midlands, Roísín

Dubh is Gaelic for 'dark rose'. The beer first appeared back in 1996.

Tasting Notes

A deep red ale with a fruity, floral nose. Smooth, clean fruity flavours fill the mouth, with a solid balancing bitterness and a little nut. The aftertaste is dry, very moreish, soft and fruity, yet bitter, with a hint of toffee.

Good Night Out

- **ABV 4.5%** ▪ **BOTTLE SIZE 500 ml** ▪ **SERVE cool**
- **INGREDIENTS Maris Otter pale malt/roasted barley/ Fuggle and Challenger hops/port**

First brewed for a brewers' get-together in 1998, this beer takes its name from the fact that the assembled throng considered the event a 'good night out'. The beer is based on Iceni's Deirdre of the Sorrows, but with a bottle of port added per firkin. 'Just the ticket', says the label.

Tasting Notes

Another amber beer with a mellow fruity nose, but this time the added port provides a 'crushed raspberry' aroma. The taste is remarkably fruity – raspberries and melons – but fairly dry and not sweet. Dry, bitter finish.

It's a Grand Day

- **ABV 4.5%** ▪ **BOTTLE SIZE 500 ml** ▪ **SERVE cool**
- **INGREDIENTS Maris Otter pale malt/Fuggle and Challenger hops/ginger**

Designed as a refreshing summer ale, It's a Grand Day ('for a great ale') is a stronger version of Iceni's Fen Tiger, but with the addition of stem ginger instead of coriander.

Tasting Notes

An amber beer with an aroma of fruit and ginger spice. The crisp, refreshing taste features plenty of ginger, but without the accustomed 'burn', and is well balanced to allow malt and hop flavour through. Ginger and hops compete in the finish.

Norfolk Lager

- **ABV 5%** ▪ **BOTTLE SIZE 500 ml** ▪ **SERVE cold**
- **INGREDIENTS Lager malt/wheat malt/Hersbrucker hops**

This lager was initially brewed in 1998 for a subsidiary company of Iceni Brewery called Lager UK Ltd. At the time, the beer was known as L.A.D. Lager. The first batch was a keg product (chilled and filtered but not pasteurised), the initials L.A.D. conveniently standing – apparently – for 'Lager

Awareness Day'. Laddish marketing, complete with poses by a blonde model, helped the beer get off the ground and attracted the attentions of the tabloid press. The beer has since been sold in cask form and this bottle-conditioned version first arrived in 1999. The laddish image has been quietly dropped in recent years as the new name of Norfolk Lager has been adopted.

Tasting Notes

A pale golden beer with a floral hop nose. It is malty and sweet to taste, with clean, lightly perfumed hop notes. Dry, bittersweet, malt and hops finish. Tasty and well rounded.

Norfolk Gold

- **ABV 5%** ▪ **BOTTLE SIZE 500 ml** ▪ **SERVE cool**
- **INGREDIENTS Maris Otter pale malt/caramalt/Fuggle and Challenger hops**

Aimed at the tourist trade on the popular Norfolk coast, this beer is worth sampling with fish, according to brewer Brendan. It was first bottled in 1998.

Tasting Notes

A golden beer with a slightly toffeeish, spicy, fruity nose. There are distinct pineapple notes in the taste, a little spice and a hint of tartness. Dry, fruity, spicy finish.

Raspberry Wheat

- **ABV 5%** ▪ **BOTTLE SIZE 500 ml** ▪ **SERVE cool**
- **INGREDIENTS Maris Otter pale malt/lager malt/wheat malt/Hersbrucker hops/raspberries**

Although pulped raspberries are added after primary fermentation in the Belgian style, this is not a sour framboise-like fruit beer. It is more of a summer quencher, brought to Norfolk from the USA by an itinerant brewer who worked at Iceni for a while.

Tasting Notes

A pale golden beer with raspberries and bubblegum in the aroma. Delicate and bittersweet on the palate, it is refreshingly understated, with gentle raspberries edging out light hops. Moreish, hop and raspberry finish.

Swaffham Gold

- **ABV 5%** ▪ **BOTTLE SIZE 500 ml** ▪ **SERVE cool**
- **INGREDIENTS Maris Otter pale malt/caramalt/Fuggle and Challenger hops/maple syrup**

Another tourist-orientated beer, Swaffham Gold is the

brewery's cask Iceni Gold with added maple syrup, making it popular with sweet dishes.

Tasting Notes

A smooth and tasty, dark golden beer with fruit, spice and butterscotch in the nose. Butterscotch, malt and fruit linger in the mouth, alongside a crisp, but mellow bitterness. Dry malty, gently bitter aftertaste.

Winter Lightning

- **ABV 5%** ▪ **BOTTLE SIZE 500 ml** ▪ **SERVE cool**
- **INGREDIENTS Lager malt/wheat malt/Hersbrucker hops**

Hersbrucker hops add a continental touch to this winter beer which is surprisingly blonde in colour.

Tasting Notes

A pale golden ale with a fruit cocktail aroma. The very fruity, bittersweet taste is full and well rounded. Nicely bitter, very fruity, gently warming finish.

Men of Norfolk

- **ABV 6.2%** ▪ **BOTTLE SIZE 500/750 ml** ▪ **SERVE cool**
- **INGREDIENTS Maris Otter pale malt/crystal malt/ torrefied wheat/flaked barley/roasted barley/Fuggle and Challenger hops**

Aimed at the hardy winter tourists to this lovely part of the world, this strong, rich stout is only brewed for bottling, with a sepia label to encourage gift purchases.

Tasting Notes

This near-black, very dark brown beer features dark malt and a little pineapple and pear drop in the aroma. The taste is smooth, malty and sweetish, but nicely balanced and not cloying. Liquorice notes, roasted grain and estery fruit play in the background, before a lingering, roasted, liquorice finish.

ISLE OF SKYE

The Isle of Skye Brewing Co. (Leann an Eilein) Ltd.,
The Pier, Uig, Isle of Skye IV51 9XY.
Tel. (01470) 542477 Fax (01470) 542488
E-mail: info@skyebrewery.co.uk
Website: www.skyebrewery.co.uk

Founded in 1995, to bring real ale relief to an otherwise discerning drinkers' desert, Isle of Skye has now expanded its brewing capacity and added a bottle-conditioned beer to its range. Shelton Brothers import into the US.

Misty Isle

▪**ABV 4.3%** ▪**BOTTLE SIZE 660 ml** ▪**SERVE cold**
▪**INGREDIENTS Maris Otter pale malt/carapils malt/ wheat malt/Hersbrucker hops/organic lemon juice**

Delivered in outsize, clear-glass bottles, this hazy orange beer is a striking discovery. It's brewed as a summer quencher (also in cask), taking its lead from Belgian wit beers, and is recommended by the brewery as an ideal accompaniment for salads and cold foods. The beer is conditioned in tank and then filled on site without finings or filtration, making it acceptable to vegetarians. As for the name, the Isle of Skye is often called the Misty Isle and, given the cloudy appearance of this brew, it seemed just the right title for the beer too.

Tasting Notes

A cloudy orange beer with a tart, spicy nose. The taste is also tart, spicy and fruity (hints of orange and lemon), before a drying, tart, spicy, increasingly bitter finish.

ITCHEN VALLEY

Itchen Valley Brewery Ltd., Unit 4, Shelf House, New Farm Road, Alresford, Hampshire SO24 9QE.
Tel. (01962) 735111 Fax (01962) 735678
E-mail: info@itchenvalley.com
Website: www.itchenvalley.com

Itchen Valley Brewery was founded in 1997 but changed hands a year later. The new owners launched into bottle-conditioned beers in a big way and bottling now accounts for around 15% of the business. All the beers now are bottled under contract by Gale's at Horndean, having been filtered at the brewery first. Gale's then adds back yeast prior to bottling. Itchen Valley's parent company specialises in pub signage, hence the colourful bottle labels. Many bottles are sold at farmers' markets.

Godfathers

▪**ABV 3.8%** ▪**BOTTLE SIZE 500 ml** ▪**SERVE cool**
▪**INGREDIENTS Maris Otter pale malt/crystal malt/ Whitbread Golding Variety, Progress, Golding and Fuggle hops**

An original Itchen Valley beer, taking its name from the fact that the founders of the brewery first discussed the project while acting as godfathers at a christening. A *Champion Beer of Britain* bronze medallist in cask form.

Tasting Notes
A dark golden, easy-drinking beer with plenty of fruity hop character in the aroma, alongside a hint of toffee from the malt. The taste is also slightly toffeeish, balanced by a gentle, fruity hoppiness. Dry, nicely bitter, fruity and hoppy finish.

Fagins

- **ABV 4.1%** ▪ **BOTTLE SIZE 500 ml** ▪ **SERVE cool**
- **INGREDIENTS Maris Otter pale malt/crystal malt/wheat malt/First Gold, Golding and Fuggle hops**

Depicting the Dickensian villain on the label, Fagins is another early Itchen Valley brew that has been retained by the current ownership.

Tasting Notes
A dark amber ale with malt and grapefruit dominant in the nose. Grapefruit hoppiness and pleasant bitterness feature in the taste, on a silky malt bed. Dry, bitter, lightly fruity finish.

Wykehams Glory

- **ABV 4.3%** ▪ **BOTTLE SIZE 500 ml** ▪ **SERVE cool**
- **INGREDIENTS Maris Otter pale malt/crystal malt/chocolate malt/First Gold hops**

Wykehams Glory, with its striking green label, is named after William of Wykeham, who founded nearby Winchester College in the 14th century.

Tasting Notes
Red-brown in colour, this best bitter has a fruity aroma (both tropical and citrous notes), a mostly bitter, fruity-hop taste, and a dry, bitter finish with lingering fruit.

Treacle Stout

- **ABV 4.4%** ▪ **BOTTLE SIZE 500 ml** ▪ **SERVE cool**
- **INGREDIENTS Maris Otter pale malt/crystal malt/chocolate malt/roasted barley/Progress hops/treacle/liquorice**

The first of two new beers, this time unusually flavoured with liquorice and treacle. The liquorice is added to the copper boil, while the treacle primes the finished beer before it is shipped to Gale's for bottling.

Tasting Notes
A ruby beer with a creamy collar. Coffeeish dark malt and treacle feature in the aroma before more dark malts and treacle combine in the smooth taste. The same flavours lead in the mostly bitter finish.

Hambledon Bitter

- **ABV 4.5%** ▪ **BOTTLE SIZE 500 ml** ▪ **SERVE cool**
- **INGREDIENTS Maris Otter pale malt/Cascade hops/ honey/elderflower**

A new beer celebrating the village that is widely recognised as the home of cricket. Hambledon, with its famous Bat & Ball pub, and cricket club established in 1760, is just 15 miles away from the brewery. Honey and elderflower spice up the finished beer before it heads for bottling.

Tasting Notes

A dark golden ale with a big fruity aroma (elderflower and grapefruit). The same fruitiness dominates the taste, with hops emerging to lead elderflower in the finish.

Major stockist Local Tesco

Pure Gold

- **ABV 4.8%** ▪ **BOTTLE SIZE 500 ml** ▪ **SERVE cool**
- **INGREDIENTS Maris Otter pale malt/lager malt/Saaz and Cascade hops**

Pure Gold is an ale/lager cross, bursting with hop flavour. The secret is the addition of American Cascade hops in the fermenter, to complement the gentler Saaz hops which make their presence known in the copper.

Tasting Notes

A bright golden beer with a stunning aroma of pineapple, grapefruit and resin-like hop. The hop flavours are full and juicy, with pineapple, grapefruit and a rounded bitterness drowning out an initial sweetish note. The finish is dry, strongly hoppy and fruity.

Father Christmas

- **ABV 5%** ▪ **BOTTLE SIZE 500 ml** ▪ **SERVE cool**
- **INGREDIENTS Maris Otter pale malt/crystal malt/ Challenger hops**

Despite its seasonal name, Father Christmas is actually sold all year round. The black and gold label declares, like all the other labels, that the beer is 'Brewed in the heart of Hampshire'.

Tasting Notes

A bright brown brew with a pleasantly fruity nose. The taste is well balanced and has a restrained sweetness, gentle fruit, a hint of spice and a mild bitterness. Moreish malt and hops linger in the dry finish.

Wat Tyler

- **ABV 5%** ■ **BOTTLE SIZE 500 ml** ■ **SERVE cool**
- **INGREDIENTS Maris Otter pale malt/crystal malt/ Progress hops**

Recalling, in its name, the famous leader of the Peasants' Revolt of 1381, Wat Tyler is described on the dark red label as 'a rebel of a beer' and 'a strong real ale winter warmer'.

Tasting Notes

This red-brown premium ale has a fruity, slightly estery, malty nose, a surprisingly bitter but well-balanced taste of smooth malt and hops, and a dry, bitter, hoppy finish.

JOHN O'GAUNT

John O'Gaunt Brewing Co. Ltd., Unit 2, Rural Industries, John O'Gaunt, Melton Mowbray, Leicestershire LE14 2RE
Tel. (07812) 161439 Fax (01664) 820103
E-mail: brewery@john-o-gaunt-brewery.co.uk

Brewery set up in the late 1990s by Celia Frew, in premises rented from Parish Brewery. John O'Gaunt has since moved into its own site and added bottle-conditioned beers to its range. Each beer is allowed to drop bright then transferred to a new cask, from which the beer is bottled after kräusening.

Robin a Tiptoe

- **ABV 3.9%** ■ **BOTTLE SIZE 500 ml** ■ **SERVE cool**
- **INGREDIENTS Maris Otter pale malt/crystal malt/ Willamette and Fuggle hops**

The brewery's first ever beer was named after a local hill where, legend has it, a tall man once escaped execution. The said Robin proved to have such long legs that his tiptoes still reached the ground after he was hanged, thereby allowing him to make good his escape.

Duke of Lancaster

- **ABV 4.3%** ■ **BOTTLE SIZE 500 ml** ■ **SERVE cool**
- **INGREDIENTS Maris Otter pale malt/Willamette and Fuggle hops**

Brewed to celebrate the brewery's arrival at its own home, and named after John O'Gaunt (1340–99), the Duke of Lancaster and fourth son of King Edward III.

Tasting Notes

A golden beer with a soft, melon-fruity, hoppy aroma. The

taste is nicely balanced and bittersweet, with soft, hoppy fruitiness throughout (hint of tropical fruit). Dry, bittersweet, fruity finish.

Coat o'Red

- **ABV 5% ▪ BOTTLE SIZE 500 ml ▪ SERVE cool**
- **INGREDIENTS Maris Otter pale malt/crystal malt/ Willamette and Fuggle hops**

Melton Mowbray may have been the source of the saying 'to paint the town red', thanks to an alleged incident on 6 April 1837. The Marquis of Waterford, it is said, having partaken of too much wine at the races, headed for Melton with his coterie and daubed red paint on the walls of a number of buildings. Evidence of this early act of vandalism was apparently uncovered during refurbishment of The White Swan pub in the 1980s.

Tasting Notes

An amber ale with toffee-malt and hop resins in the nose. Malt and toffee also feature in the mouth, with a lemon-hoppy overlay, and there are hints of roasted grain in the malty, hoppy finish.

JOLLYBOAT

The Jollyboat Brewery Ltd., The Coach House, Buttgarden Street, Bideford, Devon EX39 2AU. Tel. (01237) 424343

This North Devon brewery was established in 1995 and turned to bottling in summer 1998. Packaging is now handled by Keltek Brewery and the beers are filled direct from the cask, without filtration or re-seeding of yeast. All the brewery's beers have a nautical connection and the name 'Jollyboat' itself refers to the smaller vessel used by ships' crews in the days of sail, when they decided to pop over to dry land for a few beers. In addition to the beers listed here, Mainbrace (4.2%) has also been trialled as a bottle-conditioned ale and may join the range.

Plunder

- **ABV 4.8% ▪ BOTTLE SIZE 500 ml ▪ SERVE cool**
- **INGREDIENTS Maris Otter pale malt/crystal malt/ chocolate malt/black malt/wheat malt/Fuggle and two other hops**

The second of Jollyboat's beers into bottle. Like the other bottled beers, Plunder is a version of the cask beer of the same name. Although two 'secret' hops complete the recipe, the beer is predominantly hopped with Fuggles.

Tasting Notes

A red-brown ale with lemon notes and hints of chocolate in the malty nose. The taste is hoppy, with a light, chocolatey malt base and a persistent background fruitiness. Hoppy, bitter finish.

Privateer

- **ABV 4.8%** ▪ **BOTTLE SIZE 500 ml** ▪ **SERVE cool**
- **INGREDIENTS Maris Otter pale malt/crystal malt/ chocolate malt/wheat malt/Fuggle and Cascade hops**

Under the name of Show of Strength, this beer is also sold at the Show of Strength Theatre Company in Bristol.

Tasting Notes

A dark amber beer with a malty, chocolatey aroma supported by citrus fruit. Dark malts lead in the nutty, bittersweet taste, with hints of orange and other citrus fruits emerging. Dry, bitter, fruit and nuts finish.

Contraband

- **ABV 5.8%** ▪ **BOTTLE SIZE 500 ml** ▪ **SERVE cool**
- **INGREDIENTS Maris Otter pale malt/amber malt/black malt/Cascade and Fuggle hops**

Described by brewer Hugh Parry as a 'Victorian porter', this beer is certainly inspired by the 19th century as evidenced in its use of amber malt, common then, not so now. American Cascade hops provide a more modern twist, however. The beer has been brewed for cask sales at Christmas for around nine years, but only in spring 2004 did it reach the bottle.

Tasting Notes

A ruby ale with rich chocolate toffee in the nose. Chocolate toffee continues in abundance in the mouth, with bitter roasted notes on the swallow. Toffee and plain chocolate feature in the bitter finish.

KELTEK

Keltek Brewery, Unit 3A, Restormel Industrial Estate, Lostwithiel, Cornwall PL22 0HG.
Tel./Fax (01208) 871199
E-mail: keltekbrewery@aol.com

Founded in Tregony in 1997, to supply beers to the Roseland peninsula of Cornwall, Keltek was taken over by local wholesaler Andy White in 1998 and moved to Lostwithiel. Andy is very much a one-man band, brewing, bottling, selling and delivering the beers himself. All the beers are bottled (200–300 at a time) direct from the fermenter, without filtration or re-seeding of fresh yeast. A best before date of six months post-bottling is applied. Keltek also bottles for other small brewers in the South West.

King

- **ABV 5.1%** ▪ **BOTTLE SIZE 500 ml** ▪ **SERVE cool**
- **INGREDIENTS Pale malt/crystal malt/Cascade and Hallertau hops**

Featuring the mythical 'sword in the stone' on its colourful label, there's no difficulty guessing to which king this beer alludes. It was first produced in 1998 and is good to drink with curries, according to Andy. Twice winner of the *Tucker's Maltings Bottled Beer Competition*, and winner of the SIBA (Society of Independent Brewers) *National Brewing Competition*'s bottled beer category in 2001.

Tasting Notes

A golden ale with a juicy, orange-fruit aroma. The taste is a delightfully balanced blend of powerful, zesty orange-hop flavour, ripe, sweetish malt and good bitterness. Dry, bitter fruit finish.

Revenge/Lostwithiale

- **ABV 7%** ▪ **BOTTLE SIZE 500 ml** ▪ **SERVE cool**
- **INGREDIENTS Pale malt/crystal malt/chocolate malt/ Cascade and Hallertau hops**

Revenge is a dark red strong ale to be enjoyed – suggests Andy – with a meat pie. Note the spooky skull-tankard on the label. The beer is sold as Lostwithiale in the town of Lostwithiel itself, with a label bearing the town's crest.

Tasting Notes

A strong, ruby ale with an aroma rich in roasted grain and toffee. A soft, sweet, malty, creamy, fruity taste follows, before a thick, creamy, sweet malt finish with a hint of roast. There's a clear alcoholic kick throughout.

Kripple Dick

- **ABV 8.5%** ▪ **BOTTLE SIZE 275 ml** ▪ **SERVE cool**
- **INGREDIENTS Pale malt/crystal malt/chocolate malt/ amber malt/First Gold and Hallertau hops**

At 8.5%, there must be a warning in the title. There are

echoes of a beer once produced by St Austell Brewery in the name and style of this powerful ale, which was introduced by Andy in spring 2001.

Tasting Notes

A dark ruby barley wine with soft, creamy malt and pear drops in the nose. The taste is well balanced and surprisingly understated: fruit, malt sweetness and a liquorice-like bitterness are evident but are not overpowering. Pleasant, sweet, malty finish with a trace of the same liquorice bitterness.

Beheaded

- **ABV 10%** ▪ **BOTTLE SIZE 275/500 ml** ▪ **SERVE cool**
- **INGREDIENTS Pale malt/crystal malt/chocolate malt/ wheat malt/First Gold and Cluster hops**

The label says 'Castle Brewery' but this is a brew Andy developed alongside his activities at Keltek in early 2003. He now brews it about three times a year and conditions it in the bottle at the brewery for two months before it goes on sale. He then recommends drinking it after a further three months. Such is the strength, however, this may well improve over a much longer period.

Tasting Notes

Red in colour, this potent brew has an aroma combining melon and light toffee, with strawberry notes emerging after a while. Smooth and malty-sweet to taste, it has lots of fruit and an underlying creaminess and warmth. The finish is surprisingly thin, but sweetish, fruity and warming. A beer that should really benefit from more time to mature in the bottle.

KHEAN

The Khean Brewing Company, Unit 4, Royle Park, Congleton, Cheshire CW12 1JJ. Tel./Fax (01260) 272144

The Khean Brewing Company is a family venture, run by brewer Ken Newsome and his eldest daughter, Alison Sutch (the brewery's name is an acronym based on Ken and his wife's Christian names). Production started in an industrial unit in 2002 and the first bottles rolled out just before Christmas 2003. All beers have a cricketing theme and, although brewed at Congleton, are bottled for Khean by Leek Brewery, where they are kräusened prior to filling. Safety-first, six-month best before dates are applied.

Caught Behind

- **ABV 4.2%** ■ **BOTTLE SIZE 500 ml** ■ **SERVE cool**
- **INGREDIENTS Maris Otter pale malt/chocolate malt/ roasted barley/Fuggle and Golding hops**

Caught Behind was Khean's first bottled beer and, like all the brewery's beers, owes its cricketing theme to the fact that Ken, a Yorkshireman, is a big fan of the summer game.

Tasting Notes

A deep ruby stout with an aroma that combines coffee, caramel, biscuity malt and a hint of polished leather. The clean, if light, taste features drying, roasted barley bitterness, rounded off by a long, dry, bitter, roasted grain finish.

Fine Leg

- **ABV 4.2%** ■ **BOTTLE SIZE 500 ml** ■ **SERVE cool**
- **INGREDIENTS Maris Otter pale malt/crystal malt/Fuggle and Golding hops**

You have to look carefully at the colourful labels on Khean's beers, as, while they are certainly attractive, there's very little to differentiate between each brew apart from the name and a brief description.

Tasting Notes

A dark golden ale with a lightly fruity aroma. A gentle, orange-fruity acidity leads in the mouth, nicely balanced by malt and a hoppy bitterness that catches up quickly, leaving a dry, hoppy and bitter finish.

Leg Spinner

- **ABV 4.4%** ■ **BOTTLE SIZE 500 ml** ■ **SERVE cool**
- **INGREDIENTS Maris Otter pale malt/pale crystal malt/ Challenger hops**

Like the previous two beers listed, Leg Spinner was first produced as a cask ale in summer 2002.

Tasting Notes

This golden beer has pear fruit in the nose and a fruity, but quite dry taste (orange and pear countered by bitter hop flavour). Hoppy, dry finish.

Jingle Bails

- **ABV 5.2%** ■ **BOTTLE SIZE 500 ml** ■ **SERVE cool**
- **INGREDIENTS Maris Otter pale malt/crystal malt/ Challenger, Golding and Fuggle hops**

Not surprisingly, the Christmas beer.

KING

WJ King & Co. (Brewers), 3–5 Jubilee Estate,
Foundry Lane, Horsham, West Sussex RH13 5UE.
Tel. (01403) 272102 Fax (01403) 754455
E-mail: sales@kingfamilybrewers.co.uk
Website: www.kingfamilybrewers.co.uk
Mail order service

Bill King, latterly managing director of King & Barnes, which was closed following its sale to fellow regional brewer Hall & Woodhouse, returned to brewing on a much smaller scale in 2001. Setting up this microbrewery in the same town of Horsham, Bill was swiftly brewing up to capacity and bottled beers were soon added to the cask range. All beers are filled directly from the fermenter, without filtering or the use of isinglass finings, making them acceptable to vegetarians.

King's Old Ale

- **ABV 4.5%** ▪ **BOTTLE SIZE 500 ml** ▪ **SERVE cool**
- **INGREDIENTS Pale malt/crystal malt/chocolate malt/ wheat malt/Golding, Whitbread Golding Variety and Challenger hops**

A bottled version of the brewery's beer festival award-winning dark winter ale.

Tasting Notes

A deep ruby ale with rich chocolate in the nose. The taste is a silky smooth, mild mix of burnt malt, chocolate, coffee and a little winey fruit, rounded off by a pleasant burnt/roasted flavour and a light toffee-malt edge.

Red River Ale

- **ABV 5%** ▪ **BOTTLE SIZE 500 ml** ▪ **SERVE cool**
- **INGREDIENTS Pale malt/crystal malt/chocolate malt/ Golding, Whitbread Golding Variety and Challenger hops**

This strong beer takes its name from a tributary that runs from a mill pond in Horsham and is one of a few such 'Red Rivers' coloured by rust from the region's old iron workings.

Tasting Notes

A light ruby beer with a white head. There is plenty of fruit on the rich malt in the nose, with a hint of chocolate behind. The smooth taste is nutty and has sweet, fruity notes, plus bits of roasted malt poking through. Nutty, roasty, bitter and slightly estery finish.

Cereal Thriller

▪ ABV 6.3% ▪ BOTTLE SIZE 500 ml ▪ SERVE cool
▪ INGREDIENTS Pale malt/enzymic malt/flaked maize/ Whitbread Golding Variety hops

When Bill was at King & Barnes, they produced a beer with a high percentage of maize called Cornucopia (it was later continued for a while in bottle-conditioned form by Hall & Woodhouse, but now has been discontinued). This is Bill's latest variation on the theme, the name chosen through a local competition.

Tasting Notes

A hazy orange beer with light pear drop, subtle malt and grain in the nose. The taste is sweet, rich and lightly fruity, with a burnt grain edge. Toasted grain and hop bitterness gradually take over from sweetness in the finish.

Merry Ale

▪ ABV 6.5% ▪ BOTTLE SIZE 500 ml ▪ SERVE cool
▪ INGREDIENTS Pale malt/crystal malt/chocolate malt/ Golding, Whitbread Golding Variety and Challenger hops

A stronger version of Red River, this is King's Christmas ale in bottle, introduced in 2003.

Tasting Notes

A red-amber ale with a deeply malty, treacle-toffee aroma. The sweet, full-bodied taste is also rich and full of toffee-malt, with a touch of warmth. A bittersweet, toffeeish aftertaste rounds off.

LEATHERBRITCHES

Leatherbritches Brewery, The Bentley Brook Inn,
Fenny Bentley, Ashbourne, Derbyshire DE6 1LF.
Tel. (01335) 350278 Fax (01335) 350422
E-mail: all@bentleybrookinn.co.uk
Website: www.bentleybrookinn.co.uk

The Bentley Brook Inn is a successful country pub in the Derbyshire Peak District, run by the Allingham family since 1977. The small brewery at the rear has been experimenting with bottled beers for a number of years and now has a regular range of three, all bottled on site direct from a conditioning tank. A fourth beer, Blue (8.2%), to be sold in 330 ml bottles, is planned.

Ale Conner's Tipple

▪ ABV 4.9% ▪ BOTTLE SIZE 500 ml ▪ SERVE cool
▪ INGREDIENTS Maris Otter pale malt/Progress and Styrian Golding hops

The name of the brewery is derived from the garments worn by ale conners in centuries past. The job of these erstwhile Customs and Excise men was to test the quality and strength of the beers in their patch. They did so – it is said – by sitting on a small pool of beer and their assessment of it was based on how sticky their leather britches became. Now the ale conner is remembered in each of the bottled beers' names, starting with this strong ale.

Tasting Notes

A very pale, yellow-gold beer with a big grapefruit aroma. The taste is sweetish, with more grapefruit and scented floral notes. Floral hops persist in the finish, but bitterness just takes over.

Ale Conner's Bespoke

▪ ABV 5.2% ▪ BOTTLE SIZE 500 ml ▪ SERVE cool
▪ INGREDIENTS Maris Otter pale malt/crystal malt/ Progress and Styrian Golding hops

Bespoke was Leatherbritches' first ever cask beer.

Tasting Notes

A dark golden ale with citrous hops in the nose. Floral, fruity notes lead in the mouth, including a hint of pear drop and a waft of orange blossom. Dry, floral-fruity, gently bitter aftertaste.

Ale Conner's Porter

▪ ABV 5.4% ▪ BOTTLE SIZE 500 ml ▪ SERVE cool
▪ INGREDIENTS Maris Otter pale malt/crystal malt/dark chocolate malt/Progress hops

The label of this and the other beers depicts two ale conners 'sitting down on the job', having lunch while their leather pants do their stuff. It is reported that only leather britches were tough enough to stand the wear and tear of the profession.

Tasting Notes

A ruby beer with a dense, creamy head. A lightly roasted, biscuity malt aroma leads to a sweetish, biscuity taste, with a gentle creaminess and soft roasted malt. Bittersweet, malty finish with roasted flavours.

LEEK

Staffordshire Brewery Ltd. (t/a Leek Brewing Company), Units 11 and 12, Churnet Side, Cheddleton, Leek, Staffordshire ST13 7EF. Tel./Fax (01538) 361919
E-mail: leekbrewery@hotmail.com

Brewery established in 2002 that moved to a new home in summer 2004. In addition to being part of a business that also produces hand-made cheeses, Leek now contract bottles for a number of other smaller brewers, as well as turning out a wide range of its own bottled products.

Staffordshire Gold

- **ABV 3.8%** ▪ **BOTTLE SIZE 500 ml** ▪ **SERVE cool**
- **INGREDIENTS Maris Otter pale malt/lager malt/wheat malt/Cascade hops**

A pale beer that, like the other ales, is mostly sold in local off-licences and at farmers' markets.

Danebridge IPA

- **ABV 4.1%** ▪ **BOTTLE SIZE 500 ml** ▪ **SERVE cool**
- **INGREDIENTS Maris Otter pale malt/Fuggle and Cascade hops**

A golden ale named after a bridge in the Peak District National Park, near the village of Winkle.

Tasting Notes

A pale golden beer with a sherbety, hoppy aroma laced with tropical fruit notes. The taste is sharp, hoppy and fruity, while the finish is also hoppy, but dry.

Staffordshire Bitter

- **ABV 4.2%** ▪ **BOTTLE SIZE 500 ml** ▪ **SERVE cool**
- **INGREDIENTS Maris Otter pale malt/crystal malt/ Challenger hops**

An amber best bitter. It's possible that all Leek beers will in future be sold under the Staffordshire name (the new name for the business).

Black Grouse

- **ABV 4.4%** ▪ **BOTTLE SIZE 500 ml** ▪ **SERVE cool**
- **INGREDIENTS Maris Otter pale malt/crystal malt/ chocolate malt/wheat malt/roasted barley/Fuggle and Bramling Cross hops**

A porter named after a rare bird that has been re-introduced recently to the local moorland.

Tasting Notes

A very dark ruby/brown porter with a mellow coffee aroma. There's plenty of roasted grain bitterness in the taste but also a nice balance from a surprising amount of hops. Moderate, bitter, roasted finish.

Hen Cloud

- **ABV 4.5%** ▪ **BOTTLE SIZE 500 ml** ▪ **SERVE cool**
- **INGREDIENTS Maris Otter pale malt/lager malt/wheat malt/Golding hops**

A new beer for summer 2004, named after a local hill.

St Edward's

- **ABV 4.7%** ▪ **BOTTLE SIZE 500 ml** ▪ **SERVE cool**
- **INGREDIENTS Maris Otter pale malt/crystal malt/wheat malt/Target and First Gold hops**

St Edward Street in Leek is home to the brewery tap, The Bull's Head.

Tasting Notes

A red-amber ale with fruity hops and a hint of nut in the nose. The taste is bittersweet, nutty and fruity, and the finish is hoppy and bitter with some dark malt flavour persisting.

Rudyard Ruby

- **ABV 4.8%** ▪ **BOTTLE SIZE 500 ml** ▪ **SERVE cool**
- **INGREDIENTS Maris Otter pale malt/crystal malt/chocolate malt/Fuggle and First Gold hops**

Inspired by Sarah Hughes's Dark Ruby Mild, this brew takes its name from a local lake that is used as a top-up for the region's canals and which, apparently, gave its name to author Rudyard Kipling, too.

Blackcurrant/Cherry/Raspberry/Strawberry Sunset

- **ABV 5%** ▪ **BOTTLE SIZE 500 ml** ▪ **SERVE cool**
- **INGREDIENTS Maris Otter pale malt/wheat malt/Fuggle hops/blackcurrants/cherries/raspberries/strawberries**

Four golden, fruit-flavoured beers with the fruit added between the copper boil and fermentation.

Double Sunset

■ **ABV 5.2%** ■ **BOTTLE SIZE 500 ml** ■ **SERVE cool**
■ **INGREDIENTS Maris Otter pale malt/wheat malt/Fuggle and First Gold hops**

In summer, you can see two sunsets from Leek, as the sun disappears, and re-appears, behind the Bosley Cloud hills.

Leek Abbey Ale

■ **ABV 5.8%** ■ **BOTTLE SIZE 500 ml** ■ **SERVE cool**
■ **INGREDIENTS Maris Otter pale malt/chocolate malt/wheat malt/Fuggle and Challenger hops**

A dark ruby beer for winter, named after the now long-gone local abbey.

Tittesworth Tipple

■ **ABV 6.5%** ■ **BOTTLE SIZE 500 ml** ■ **SERVE cool**
■ **INGREDIENTS Maris Otter pale malt/wheat malt/Fuggle and Cascade hops**

A wheat beer inspired by a local reservoir that is popular for recreational activities.

MARSTON MOOR

Marston Moor Brewery, Crown House, Kirk Hammerton, York YO26 8DD. Tel./Fax (01423) 330341
E-mail: marston.moor.brewery@ic24.net

Marston Moor – taking its name from the famous Civil War battle of 1644 – was set up in 1983. It now makes such a good living providing a consultancy service to new microbreweries that its own beers are being brewed by Rudgate Brewery at Tockwith. The beers are bottled, however, at Marston Moor, straight from the cask, with six-month best before dates applied. However, some versions may be filtered, so check for sediment. Slight changes may also be made to the beer recipes from time to time.

Brewers Droop

■ **ABV 5%** ■ **BOTTLE SIZE 500 ml** ■ **SERVE cool**
■ **INGREDIENTS Maris Otter pale malt/wheat malt/crystal malt/Challenger and Styrian Golding hops**

One of the brewery's earliest cask ales, Brewers Droop was introduced to the bottle in 2000. The label carries a tongue-in-cheek warning about the consequences of drinking this strong ale on 'your most resolute anatomical appendages'.

Tasting Notes

An orange-golden ale with a lightly fruity nose (orange and pear notes). The taste mixes gentle fruit notes, malt smoothness and crisp bitterness. Bitter, lightly fruity finish.

Brewers Pride

- **ABV 5%** ▪ **BOTTLE SIZE 500 ml** ▪ **SERVE cool**
- **INGREDIENTS Maris Otter pale malt/wheat malt/crystal malt/Challenger and Styrian Golding hops**

If you try Brewers Pride on draught, you'll find it is notably less strong (only 4.2%) than this bottled version. 'It's a reet luvely sup', according to the label.

Tasting Notes

Copper in colour, this strong ale has a fruity, spicy aroma with hints of banana toffee. The taste is also toffeeishly malty, with suggestions of banana and other fruit, although more bitter than sweet. Hops are more apparent in the bitter finish.

MAULDONS

Mauldons Ltd., The Black Adder Brewery,
7 Addison Road, Chilton Industrial Estate, Sudbury,
Suffolk CO10 2YW. Tel./Fax (01787) 311055
E-mail: sims@mauldons.co.uk
Website: www.mauldons.co.uk

Founded in 1982, Mauldons was set up by former Watney's brewer Peter Mauldon, who was keen to re-establish the family brewing name. Mauldons had brewed in Suffolk since the 1790s when the Sudbury premises was closed by its new owners, Greene King, at the turn of the 1960s. Peter's story is one of success, his most famous beer, Black Adder, winning CAMRA's *Champion Beer of Britain* contest in 1991. He retired in 2000, selling the business to former Adnams salesman Steve Sims. Steve has sought to capitalise on the fame of Black Adder, adding the subtitle 'The Black Adder Brewery' to the Mauldons name and launching the beer in bottle.

Black Adder

- **ABV 5.3%** ▪ **BOTTLE SIZE 500 ml** ▪ **SERVE cool**
- **INGREDIENTS Maris Otter and Pearl pale malt/crystal malt/black malt/Fuggle hops**

First brewed in 1988, when the Rowan Atkinson *Blackadder*

TV series was in its prime, this beer takes its name also from its dark appearance and its bite, according to Steve Sims. It makes an ideal partner for a ploughman's lunch, he adds. The beer is brewed at Mauldons but bottled, straight from the cask, by Iceni Brewery.

Tasting Notes

Near-black, with ruby tints, Black Adder has banana notes alongside coffeeish dark malt in the nose and follows this with a complex taste of mellow dark malt, hints of banana and a pleasant bitterness that increases in the nutty, roasted malt aftertaste. Easy to drink for its strength.

Major stockist Local Waitrose

MEADS OF MERCIA

Meads of Mercia, c/o Orchard, Hive & Vine,
4 High Street, Leominster HR6 8LZ.
Tel. (01568) 611232 Fax (01568) 620224
E-mail: enquiries@ohv.wyenet.co.uk
Website: www.orchard-hive-and-vine.co.uk

Meads of Mercia is not a brewery, but, as its name suggests, a mead- and other honey products-making venture. The honey beer below is contract brewed, the most recent batch at Teme Valley Brewery, with Wessex Craft Brewers (now Integrated Bottling Solutions) handling the bottling.

The Bees Knees

- **ABV 6.2%** ▪ **BOTTLE SIZE 500 ml** ▪ **SERVE cool**
- **INGREDIENTS Pale malt/chocolate malt/black malt/ wheat malt/Fuggle hops/honey**

The Bees Knees is an accidental beer. Meads of Mercia proprietor Geoff Morris misunderstood a request from a customer who wanted a 'mead ale' to serve at a historical re-enactment. A mead ale is apparently a half-strength mead (around 7%), produced using beer yeast rather than wine yeast, but Geoff instead commissioned this ale brewed with Warwickshire honey. Pasteurised honey is added – at a ratio of about 7 kg per brewers' barrel – during the last 15 minutes of the copper boil and becomes the first element to be fermented, leaving honey flavour but not too much sweetness. As the beer migrates from brewery to brewery, the recipe tends to be tweaked.

Tasting Notes

A red beer with a complex aroma, featuring butterscotch, chocolate, honey and a hint of perfume. The initial sweet promise fades as dryness emerges to balance the malt, alcohol, perfume, chocolate and a suggestion of fruit, all wrapped up in a honey softness. Nutty, honeyed finish.

MEANTIME

Meantime Brewing, 2 Penhall Road, London SE7 8RX.
Tel. (020) 8293 1111 Fax (020) 8293 4004
E-mail: alastair@meantimebrewing.co.uk
Website: www.meantimebrewing.co.uk

Meantime Brewing was set up by continental beer specialist Alastair Hook, who re-creates classic European beer styles (Belgian ales, kölsch, Viennese lagers, wheat beers, etc.) at his Greenwich base. Courtesy of Sainsbury's supermarkets, several of his bottled beers now grace the national stage, and three are bottle conditioned.

Strawberry

- **ABV 4%** ▪ **BOTTLE SIZE 330 ml** ▪ **SERVE cold**
- **INGREDIENTS Pale malt/wheat malt/strawberries/hops may vary**

A new beer, launched in Sainsbury's in summer 2004 and supplied in an elegant vase-like bottle. The recipe contains 20% wheat malt as well as strawberries, which are added to the conditioning tank to provoke a secondary fermentation (25% of the alcohol comes from this stage of the process).

Tasting Notes

A golden beer with a blush of red. Gentle strawberry dominates the aroma and the crisp, nicely acidic taste, before a dry, bitter strawberry finish. Quaffable and not over-fruity.

Major stockist (all beers) Sainsbury

Raspberry Wheat Beer

- **ABV 5%** ▪ **BOTTLE SIZE 330 ml** ▪ **SERVE cold**
- **INGREDIENTS Pale malt/wheat malt/raspberry fruit extract/hops may vary**

Part of Sainsbury's *Taste the Difference* collection, Meantime's Raspberry Wheat Beer was launched in 2003, following the success of the brewery's other beers for the supermarket chain (most of these are filtered, but not pasteurised). The malt grist is split 50/50 between low-colour malt and wheat malt, and raspberry fruit extract is used for flavouring and to help the bottle fermentation. A treat with a bar of chocolate, claims Alastair.

Tasting Notes
A hazy red beer with raspberries and a hint of banana in the nose. A raspberry sharpness in the mouth is tempered by just enough sweetness to make this a tart, but quenching, drink, with a little banana lingering in the background. Dry, increasingly bitter, raspberry finish.

Bavarian Style Wheat Beer

■ ABV 5% ■ BOTTLE SIZE 330/660 ml ■ SERVE cold
■ INGREDIENTS Pale malt/wheat malt/hops may vary
Taste the Difference Wheat Beer – which includes a hefty 65% wheat malt in its grist – is traditionally decoction mashed (the wort is pumped between vessels and subjected to varying temperatures to extract the best brewing sugars), fermented with a German wheat beer yeast and kräusened with active wort before bottling. The hop content having little impact on the flavour, apart from adding balancing bitterness, Alastair may vary the strains used in all these three bottled beers. Choose from a small bottle or one to share.
Tasting Notes
A cloudy yellow beer with banana, hints of pineapple, bubblegum and spice in the nose. Citrous notes, banana and gentle spice fill the bittersweet taste before a dry, bitter orange finish.

MOOR

Moor Beer Company, Whitley Farm, Ashcott, Somerset TA7 9QW. Tel./Fax (01458) 210050
E-mail: arthur@moorbeer.co.uk
Website: www.moorbeer.co.uk
Mail order service
Moor Beer Company was founded on a dairy farm (now a pig farm) by Arthur Frampton in 1996. Arthur's daughter, Holly, is now the brewer. Some 40 pubs currently take the cask beers locally. The three beers listed here are bottled by Leek Brewery, with best before dates set at six months.

Merlins Magic

■ ABV 4.3% ■ BOTTLE SIZE 500 ml ■ SERVE cool
■ INGREDIENTS Maris Otter pale malt/crystal malt/amber malt/Fuggle and Liberty hops
Conjuring up dreamy images of the myths and legends of the South West, Merlins Magic, already an established cask ale,

was first bottle conditioned back in spring 1999.

Tasting Notes

An orange-gold beer with a toffeeish, fruity hop aroma. Dry, fruity and malty to taste, it also has a lime-citrous hoppiness and light toffee notes. Dry, bitter finish.

Peat Porter

- **ABV 4.5% ▪ BOTTLE SIZE 500 ml ▪ SERVE cool**
- **INGREDIENTS Maris Otter pale malt/crystal malt/amber malt/chocolate malt/Bramling Cross and Fuggle hops**

First brewed in 1997, but only recently bottled, this beer remembers the 'peat porters', the workers who carried peat from the local moorland in years gone by and stacked it ready for use. Despite the name, there is no peated malt in the recipe, so don't expect any smoky, whisky-like flavours.

Tasting Notes

A ruby beer with an aroma that combines fruitiness with dark malt. The interesting taste has sweet, hoppy fruitiness to the fore with plenty of dark malt flavours behind and an increasing bitterness. Dry, bitter, roasted malt and hop finish.

Old Freddy Walker

- **ABV 7.3% ▪ BOTTLE SIZE 500 ml ▪ SERVE cool**
- **INGREDIENTS Maris Otter pale malt/crystal malt/black malt/Nugget and Liberty hops**

Old Freddy Walker, Moor's first bottled beer, appeared in 1998 and is named after an old seaman living in the brewery's village. It is also available in cask form and is one of the more unusual and novel beers in this book, being brewed with Nugget hops, which are known for their high alpha acid content. Alpha acids are responsible for bitterness, so, generally speaking, you don't need so many of them to make an impact. Blended with Liberty hops into a mash produced from a complex dark malt grist, they produce a dangerously drinkable, deceptively strong brew with a full fruitiness. These attributes helped Old Freddy collect the silver medal at the *Tucker's Maltings Bottled Beer Competition* (for beers brewed in the South West) in 1999. The cask version was voted CAMRA's *Champion Winter Beer of Britain* in 2004.

Tasting Notes

A very dark brown ale with a coffee-coloured head. The vinous, malty aroma is followed by a full, complex taste in which sweet dark malt flavours are topped with vinous, fruity, citrous notes. The aftertaste is bittersweet, roasted and fruity.

MOULIN

Moulin Hotel & Brewery, Kirkmichael Road, Moulin, by Pitlochry, Perthshire & Kinross PH16 5EH.
Tel. (01796) 472196 Fax (01796) 474098
E-mail: enquiries@moulinhotel.co.uk
Website: www.moulinhotel.co.uk
Mail order service

Moulin Brewery was opened in 1995 at the Moulin Hotel in Pitlochry, during celebrations for the hotel's 300th anniversary (the hotel housed a brewery when it opened in 1695, so it was deemed fitting to recommence brewing on the site). Brewing has been relocated since to the Old Coach House opposite the main building.

Ale of Atholl

- **ABV 4.5%** ■ **BOTTLE SIZE 500 ml** ■ **SERVE cool**
- **INGREDIENTS Maris Otter pale malt/crystal malt/chocolate malt/Fuggle hops**

Ale of Atholl (taking its name from the brewery's location in the Vale of Atholl, an area in which it is more common to find whisky distilleries than breweries) was first bottle conditioned in late 1996. The beer is allowed to settle in tank and then bottled, with a little sugar added, in glassware neatly overprinted with the history of Moulin village. Brewer Chris Tomlinson suggests you try a glass with venison (Scottish, of course).

Tasting Notes

A ruby-coloured beer with a fruity, malty, lightly chocolatey nose with hop resin notes. Fruity, citrous hops and dark malt are well balanced in the dry taste. Dark malt and hops emerge again in the dry, gently bitter aftertaste.

Where to Buy Real Ale in a Bottle

Beers in this book are generally sold locally, through farmers' markets, small grocers, craft shops, delicatessens and some restaurants. Some breweries also sell direct to the public, but this may be by the case only, and some offer a mail order service, which is mentioned in each entry, if relevant. Otherwise beers can be obtained through specialist off-licences or mail order companies, many of which are listed in the Beer Shops section at the back of the book. If a beer has a listing with a major supermarket or off-licence chain, this is indicated at the end of the entry.

NETHERGATE

Nethergate Brewery Co. Ltd., 11–13 High Street, Clare, Suffolk CO10 8NY.
Tel. (01787) 277244 Fax (01787) 277123
Mail order service

Established in 1986, Nethergate has produced some award-winning ales and has never been afraid to experiment. The coriander-flavoured beer mentioned below is normally only on sale in the USA, but bottles can be obtained from the brewery. Filtered and re-seeded with fresh yeast prior to filling, it is bottled under contract by Hepworth & Co. in Horsham.

Augustinian

- **ABV 5.2%** ▪ **BOTTLE SIZE 500 ml** ▪ **SERVE cool**
- **INGREDIENTS Maris Otter pale malt/crystal malt/Fuggle hops/coriander seeds**

This Augustinian bears no similarity to Nethergate's cask beer of the same name, which weighs in at 4.5% and does not include coriander spicing. This bottled beer is actually a bespoke beer for the American market, brewed to order for importers who liked the name but wanted a different sort of brew.

Tasting Notes

An amber-coloured ale with a piney, spicy, coriander aroma. The same piney spiciness continues through into the taste and the aftertaste, overlaid at all times by perfumed orange notes.

NORTH YORKSHIRE

North Yorkshire Brewing Company Ltd., Pinchinthorpe Hall, Guisborough, North Yorkshire TS14 8HG. Tel./Fax (01287) 630200
E-mail: nyb@pinchinthorpe.freeserve.co.uk
Website: www.pinchinthorpehall.co.uk
Mail order service

North Yorkshire was founded in Middlesbrough in 1989 and moved in 1998 to Pinchinthorpe Hall, a moated, listed house that was home to the noble Lee family and their descendants for centuries until 1957. The house now also includes a hotel and restaurant, and its own spring water is used for brewing. All the beers are now registered as organic.

Best Bitter

■ ABV 3.6% ■ BOTTLE SIZE 500 ml ■ SERVE cool
■ INGREDIENTS Pale malt/crystal malt/Hallertau hops

A pale bitter showcasing organic Hallertau hops from New Zealand. Like the other beers, it is bottled on site.

Tasting Notes

A golden beer with a lightly hoppy, bubblegum aroma. In the mouth it is clean, bittersweet and fruity, with a crisp, but light, hop edge. Hops and bitterness grow, but fruit lingers, in the drying finish.

Prior's Ale

■ ABV 3.6% ■ BOTTLE SIZE 500 ml ■ SERVE cool
■ INGREDIENTS Pale malt/Hallertau and First Gold hops

A beer commemorating the fact that one of the Lee family was once a prior of Guisborough, where the hall stands.

Tasting Notes

Light malt and hop compete with bubblegum in the nose of this golden session ale. The taste balances malt and tangy hop, giving a hint of tart fruit. Tangy hop lingers in the finish.

Archbishop Lee's Ruby Ale

■ ABV 4% ■ BOTTLE SIZE 500 ml ■ SERVE cool
■ INGREDIENTS Pale malt/crystal malt/chocolate malt/ Hallertau and First Gold hops

There was not only a prior in the family, but an Archbishop of York, too. The beer is described on the label as 'northern, rounded and full bodied'.

Tasting Notes

An amber ale with a spicy malt nose. Malt also leads in the bittersweet taste, supported by citrous hop, before a dry, bittersweet, hoppy finish.

Boro Best

■ ABV 4% ■ BOTTLE SIZE 500 ml ■ SERVE cool
■ INGREDIENTS Pale malt/crystal malt/Hallertau and First Gold hops

The label calls it a 'traditional, dark Northern bitter'; the name refers back to the brewery's first home over on Teesside.

Tasting Notes

Amber in colour, this best bitter has a malt and bubblegum nose and a sweetish, gentle taste of malt and hops. More hop adds some bitterness to the aftertaste.

Fools Gold

■ ABV 4.6% ■ BOTTLE SIZE 500 ml ■ SERVE cool
■ INGREDIENTS Pale malt/First Gold hops

The name of this premium ale combines the historic setting of the brewery and the use of rare, organic First Gold hops. A cross-eyed, medieval jester ('a fool') features on the label.

Tasting Notes

Suggestions of bubblegum are once again found in the aroma of this golden beer, which also has a light, hoppy, melon-fruity fragrance. The taste is notably hoppy and fruity, but well balanced. Hops dominate the aftertaste.

Golden Ale

■ ABV 4.6% ■ BOTTLE SIZE 500 ml ■ SERVE cool
■ INGREDIENTS Pale malt/crystal malt/Hallertau and First Gold hops

As for all the other beers, this strong pale ale carries a certification stamp from the Organic Food Federation.

Tasting Notes

Light tart fruit features in the nose, while sweetish malt is countered by fruity hop in the taste but retains the upper hand. Bittersweet, fruity finish, with increasing hop.

Flying Herbert

■ ABV 4.7% ■ BOTTLE SIZE 500 ml ■ SERVE cool
■ INGREDIENTS Pale malt/crystal malt/chocolate malt/ Hallertau and First Gold hops

One of North Yorkshire's earliest brews, with a daft name plucked out of the air by brewer George Tinsley's sister. The airborn hero in the name is depicted on the label.

Tasting Notes

Another amber beer with malt and hop in the aroma. There's a good hop counterbalance to sweet malt in the taste, and a hoppy, drying finish.

Lord Lee's

■ ABV 4.7% ■ BOTTLE SIZE 500 ml ■ SERVE cool
■ INGREDIENTS Pale malt/crystal malt/chocolate malt/ Hallertau and First Gold hops

Joint strongest of the bottled beers, named after Roger Lee, a family member who became Lord Mayor of London.

Tasting Notes

Amber, with a dense, creamy head, Lord Lee's is spicy and

malty to the nose, with a fine balance of malt and hops in the mouth. Bitterness grows in the malty finish.

O'HANLON'S

O'Hanlon's Brewing Company Ltd., Great Barton Farm, Whimple, Devon EX5 2NY.
Tel. (01404) 822412 Fax (01404) 823700
Website: www.ohanlons.co.uk

O'Hanlon's was set up in 1996 to serve John O'Hanlon's pub in Clerkenwell, London, but quickly expanded to supply other outlets. In 2000, he sold the pub and moved the brewery to Devon. The bottling operation has expanded considerably and the brewery has now secured the contract to brew and market the revered Thomas Hardy's Ale, as well as its old stablemate, Royal Oak. Beers are imported into the US by Phoenix Imports.

Double Champion Wheat Beer

- **ABV 4%** ▪ **BOTTLE SIZE 500 ml** ▪ **SERVE cool**
- **INGREDIENTS Optic pale malt/wheat malt/caramalt/ Challenger, First Gold and Cascade hops/coriander seeds**

A wheat beer in the Belgian style, low on bitterness but laced with aromatic hops (First Gold and Cascade are the late hops) and spiced with coriander seeds. Prior to bottling, the beer is filtered and re-seeded with dried bottling yeast. Winner of SIBA's *Wheat Beer Challenge* 1999 and 2002, hence the addition of 'Double Champion' to the beer's name. Drink with oriental foods or even good old fish and chips, suggest the brewers.

Tasting Notes
A golden beer with a lightly spiced, lemon-orange peel aroma. The taste is orange peel bitter, lightly perfumed and dry, and the finish is dry, bitter and slightly bready, with lingering orange and perfume notes.
Major stockist Safeway

Organic Rye Beer

- **ABV 4.5%** ▪ **BOTTLE SIZE 500 ml** ▪ **SERVE cool**
- **INGREDIENTS Pale malt/crystal malt/rye flakes/ Hallertau hops**

Despite being wholly organic, this beer is sold under the name of Original Rye in the US, because of difficulties in getting the Soil Association accreditation recognised in the States. Try with pizza or pasta.

Tasting Notes

A copper ale with a nutty, malty, 'crispbread' nose that gives way to light fruit. The taste is also nutty, but with some citrus fruit in the hop balance. Nutty, bitter finish.

Major stockists Local Sainsbury and Waitrose

Yellowhammer

- **ABV 4.5%** ▪ **BOTTLE SIZE 500 ml** ▪ **SERVE cool**
- **INGREDIENTS Optic pale malt/caramalt/First Gold and Cascade hops**

A golden beer with a complex hopping regime: First Gold hops are used for bitterness, Cascades are the late hop and then the beer is dry-hopped with more First Gold. Runner-up at the *Tucker's Maltings Bottled Beer Competition* in 2003.

Tasting Notes

A soft, malty beer with a light 'sherbet lemons' fruitiness. Well-balanced and clean.

Major stockist Safeway

Original Port Stout

- **ABV 4.8%** ▪ **BOTTLE SIZE 500 ml** ▪ **SERVE cool**
- **INGREDIENTS Optic pale malt/crystal malt/caramalt/ roasted barley/flaked barley/Phoenix and Styrian Golding hops/port**

A 'corpse reviver', in the Irish tradition of hang-over cures, this dry stout is enhanced by the addition of Ferreira port prior to bottling, at a ratio of two bottles per brewer's barrel (36 gallons), which raises the strength from 4.6 to 4.8%. The cask version was one of O'Hanlon's early beers – the port was added to mark out the cask beer from a popular keg stout John's pub also sold – and this bottled equivalent was introduced in 2000. In 2001, it claimed the gold medal at *Tucker's Maltings Bottled Beer Competition*. The draught version then took the top stout prize in CAMRA's *Champion Winter Beer of Britain* awards for 2002, while this bottled version was CAMRA's *Champion Bottled Beer* in 2003. Phoenix is the main bittering hop, with Styrian Goldings added late for aroma. The beer is lightly fined prior to bottling.

Tasting Notes

A near-black beer with a biscuity, roasted barley nose. This is a classic, dry, bitter stout in the mouth, with a trace of winey fruit. The dry, roasty, bitter finish has the same hint of fruit.

Major stockists Booths, Morrisons, Safeway

Royal Oak

■ ABV 5% ■ BOTTLE SIZE 500 ml ■ SERVE cool
■ INGREDIENTS Optic pale malt/crystal malt/torrefied wheat/Challenger, Northdown and Golding hops

Like the celebrated Hardy's Ale featured below, Royal Oak – first brewed in 1896 – was another great beer that Eldridge Pope threw away when it left brewing. O'Hanlon's has revived the brew and made it bottle conditioned for the first time. The label recommends it with grilled meats or a cheeseboard.

Tasting Notes
An amber beer with pleasant sweet esters at first on the nose, followed by malt and apricots. The taste is robust, hoppy and malty, with apricot notes, although perhaps not quite as sweet and fruity as the Royal Oak of old. Big, hoppy finish.

Major stockists Booths, local Sainsbury

Thomas Hardy's Ale

■ ABV 11.7% ■ BOTTLE SIZE 330 ml ■ SERVE cool
■ INGREDIENTS Low-colour pale malt/crystal malt/ Northdown, Challenger, Styrian Golding and Golding hops

A bottled classic, Hardy's Ale was created by Dorchester brewer Eldridge Pope in 1968 to commemorate the 40th anniversary of the death of Wessex writer Thomas Hardy. Its inspiration was a passage in Hardy's novel *The Trumpet-Major*, which described Dorchester's strong beer thus:

'It was of the most beautiful colour that the eye of an artist in beer could desire; full in body, yet brisk as a volcano; piquant, yet without a twang; luminous as an autumn sunset; free from streakiness of taste but, finally, rather heady.'

This famous quote was recalled on the label of each individually numbered bottle of Hardy's Ale. The beer seemed lost forever when Eldridge Pope (now no longer in brewing) lost interest in the beer after the 1999 vintage. However, following an absence of four years, Hardy's has now been brought back to life by O'Hanlon's, in conjunction with Phoenix Imports, which bought the brand and sees a great future for it in the US. UK supplies have been limited in the short term (available largely direct from Tucker's Maltings beer shop in Devon), but it is hoped that the second O'Hanlon's vintage will be more easily sourced. The beer enjoys two-and-a-half weeks of primary fermentation, three months of secondary fermentation, and a month of cold conditioning and dry hopping, before being fined and bottled. O'Hanlon's recommends ageing the beer for at least nine months before sampling.

Tasting Notes

From the red hue of its 'autumn sunset luminosity' to its sweet, fruity finish and lingering hop tang, this re-creation is as complex and absorbing as the original Hardy. The big taste has pronounced melon flavours and loads of warm, malty sweetness, and hints of cherry poke through the estery fruit that emerges. Probably needs more time in the bottle and should mature nicely.

OAKLEAF

Oakleaf Brewing Company Ltd., 7 Clarence Wharf Industrial Estate, Mumby Road, Gosport, Hampshire PO12 1AJ. Tel. (023) 9251 3222 Fax (023) 9251 0148
E-mail: info@oakleafbrewing.co.uk
Website: www.oakleafbrewing.co.uk

Ed Anderson, a former Firkin brew pub brewer, set up Oakleaf with his father-in-law, Dave Pickersgill. Their industrial unit home stands on the side of Gosport harbour, but they hope to relocate to former munitions buildings around the bay in the near future. They brew the following bottled beer themselves, but it is packaged at Hop Back, where it is filtered, re-seeded with fresh yeast and given a best before date 12 months after bottling.

Hole Hearted

- **ABV 4.7%** ■ **BOTTLE SIZE 500 ml** ■ **SERVE cool**
- **INGREDIENTS Optic pale malt/caramalt/torrefied wheat/Cascade hops**

This golden ale (good with spicy foods, white meats and fish, it is claimed) takes its name from the fact that it was originally brewed for sale at the Hole in the Wall pub in Southsea. The cask version was CAMRA's *Champion Beer of Hampshire* in 2002 and 2003, while this bottled companion was a SIBA regional champion in 2003. Vegan friendly.

Tasting Notes

An explosion of grapefruit notes awaits you in the aroma and taste of this premium ale, with a light malty sweetness in the background. The bitter, tangy Cascade hops linger on in the finish.

Major stockist Local Waitrose

OLD BEAR

Old Bear Brewery, Unit 4B, Atlas Works, Pitt Street, Keighley, West Yorkshire BD21 4YL.
Tel./Fax (01535) 637451
E-mail: sales@oldbearbrewery.com
Website: www.oldbearbrewery.com
Brewery founded in 1993 as Old White Bear Brewery, and since undergoing a change of ownership as well as name. A move to the new premises listed above was scheduled for summer 2004. The beer below is actually bottled and marketed by Clarke's Organic (see separate entry).

Hibernator

- **ABV 5%** ▪ **BOTTLE SIZE 500 ml** ▪ **SERVE cool**
- **INGREDIENTS Maris Otter pale malt/crystal malt/black malt/torrefied wheat/flaked barley/Pioneer hops**

An obvious name for a winter beer from a bear brewery: brewed since October 2002 and a beer festival award-winner.

Tasting Notes

A big, tasty, ruby beer with a malty, roasted aroma. Roasted malt lies over a bed of sweeter malt in the mouth, followed by a dry, roasted, bittersweet finish.

OLD CHIMNEYS

Office: Old Chimneys Brewery, The Street, Market Weston, Diss, Norfolk IP22 2NZ. Tel. (01359) 221411
Brewery: Hopton End Farm, Church Road, Market Weston, Diss, Norfolk IP22 2NX. Tel. (01359) 221013
Suffolk brewery, despite the postal address, founded by former Greene King and Broughton brewer Alan Thomson in 1995. His first bottles came out in autumn 2000, majoring on strong beers for sipping, but more quaffable brews have found their way into bottle in recent years. All the beers are matured in cask and sometimes kräusened or primed prior to bottling. Bottles are then given three weeks' secondary fermentation at the brewery before they go on sale. All beers are declared suitable for vegetarians, but Black Rat, with its milk-derived lactose, does not conform to vegan standards. Best before dates are generally 12 months after bottling (18 months for Good King Henry). The beers are now also sold direct from the brewery shop, which is open Friday, 2–7pm, and Saturday, 10am–1pm. Old Chimneys no longer provides a regular range of railway-inspired beers for the Mid-Suffolk

Light Railway, but does produce occasional commemorative beers for the cause.

Meadow Brown Ale

- **ABV 3.4%** ■ **BOTTLE SIZE 500 ml** ■ **SERVE cool**
- **INGREDIENTS Pale malt/crystal malt/roasted barley/ Fuggle and Challenger hops**

Replacing Victorian Brown Ale, part of the railway selection, Meadow Brown Ale takes its name from a rare type of butterfly but is in fact a bottled version of Old Chimneys' cask Military Mild. The beer is parti-gyled (brewed as part of the same batch) with Black Rat Stout.

Tasting Notes

A thinnish, but clean beer, with various shades of maltiness, from sweetness to hints of chocolate. Malty, chocolatey aroma; malty, bittersweet finish with light roasted notes.

Black Rat Stout

- **ABV 4.5%** ■ **BOTTLE SIZE 500 ml** ■ **SERVE cool**
- **INGREDIENTS Pale malt/crystal malt/roasted barley/ lactose/Fuggle and Challenger hops**

Black Rat takes over from Leading Porter in the Old Chimneys range. Although it is brewed alongside Meadow Brown Ale, it differs considerably in strength and also in the inclusion of lactose. Lactose is not fermentable by standard brewers' yeast and so the sugars remain in the brew adding body and sweetness (the best known beer to include lactose is Mackeson, the classic milk stout).

Tasting Notes

A deep ruby stout with a coffeeish, malty aroma, a malty, bittersweet taste, with coffee undertones, and a coffeeish, malty, lightly bitter finish.

Great Raft Bitter

- **ABV 4.1%** ■ **BOTTLE SIZE 500 ml** ■ **SERVE cool**
- **INGREDIENTS Pearl pale malt/crystal malt/caramalt/ Fuggle, Challenger and Target hops**

One of the brewery's three original draught beers, Great Raft has been available in bottle-conditioned form only since 2002. The beer takes its name from Britain's rarest and largest spider, which inhabits a local fen. The strength has been lowered from 4.3% in the past year.

Tasting Notes

A copper ale with a toffeeish malt aroma. Malt and toffee

lead again in the taste, but well balanced by clean bitterness and light fruitiness. Bitter, malty finish with spicy hops.

Golden Pheasant

- **ABV 4.7%** ■ **BOTTLE SIZE 500 ml** ■ **SERVE cool**
- **INGREDIENTS Pearl pale malt/caramalt/Challenger and Target hops**

Named after the oriental bird which lives in a nearby forest, Golden Pheasant is also sold in cask form but has been bottled since 2002. Like other Old Chimneys beers, this is now a touch weaker than before.

Tasting Notes

A dark golden ale that pours with a white collar of foam. Malt, fruit and a little spice feature in the nose, while the taste offers malt, hops, fruit, nuts and estery traces of almond. A complex, flavour-packed beer with a nutty, bitter and dry finish.

Natterjack

- **ABV 5.2%** ■ **BOTTLE SIZE 500 ml** ■ **SERVE cool**
- **INGREDIENTS Pearl pale malt/crystal malt/caramalt/ Fuggle hops**

Inspired by the heathland toad, Natterjack – a single-varietal hop beer, based on the classic English bittering hop, Fuggle – is another of Old Chimneys' original cask brews. Bottling started in 2002, but the ABV is now down from the original 5.4%.

Tasting Notes

Red-brown in colour, Natterjack has a nose of chocolate, malt and a touch of spice. Fairly sweet, nutty malt and spicy bitterness lead in the taste, with some estery notes. Toasted malt, hops and bitterness combine in the aftertaste.

India Pale Ale

- **ABV 5.6%** ■ **BOTTLE SIZE 500 ml** ■ **SERVE cool**
- **INGREDIENTS Pale malt/amber malt/caramalt/Target and Challenger hops**

Originally known as Lord Kitchener's India Pale Ale, when it was brewed for railway sales (Lord Kitchener opened the old railway line and was Commander-in-Chief in India, 1902–9). This authentic IPA is strong and well hopped, as beers intended for the long sea journey to India needed to be in the 19th century. Only Target hops are boiled in the copper, but Alan allows Challenger hops to sit in the hop back as the wort is run off, infusing their own character into the brew and enhancing the aroma. Kitchener still appears on the label, in familiar 'Your country needs you' pose.

Tasting Notes

A dark golden beer that is everything an authentic IPA should be, having plenty of body and filled with tangy, fruity hops. Rich, fruity aroma; hoppy, tangy, bitter finish with lingering malt in support.

Brimstone

- **ABV 6.5%** ■ **BOTTLE SIZE 275 ml** ■ **SERVE cold**
- **INGREDIENTS Lager malt/sugar/Hallertau and Northern Brewer hops**

This strong lager is named after a yellow butterfly and was first brewed in 2000.

Tasting Notes

A golden lager with a big fruity nose. The full-bodied taste has a piney hoppiness over smooth malt and a little fruit. Hoppy, bitter finish.

Greenshank

- **ABV 7%** ■ **BOTTLE SIZE 275 ml** ■ **SERVE cool**
- **INGREDIENTS Pale malt/caramalt/unrefined sugar/ Hallertau hops**

A strong, pale bitter brewed with organic ingredients. It was first produced in 2001 and is named after a bird.

Tasting Notes

A crisp but potent beer with a dark golden hue. Orange hop notes lead in the aroma, with a hint of tropical fruit, and the same orangey hops balance out the sweetness of the abundant malt in the taste. Bittersweet, fruity finish.

Redshank

- **ABV 8.7%** ■ **BOTTLE SIZE 275 ml** ■ **SERVE cool**
- **INGREDIENTS Pale malt/crystal malt/Fuggle and Challenger hops**

Redshank is another strong ale to treat with respect. Like Greenshank, it shares its name with a wading bird.

Tasting Notes

A red beer with an estery aroma. Estery fruit flavours are tempered by hop, roasted bitterness and alcohol in the taste. The finish is hoppy, with lingering malt and winey fruit, but on the bitter side of bittersweet.

Good King Henry

- **ABV 9.6%** ▪ **BOTTLE SIZE 275 ml** ▪ **SERVE cool**
- **INGREDIENTS Pale malt/crystal malt/roasted barley/ Fuggle and Challenger hops**

Although this is an imperial Russian stout, with all its court connections, apparently this beer takes its name not from a ruler but from an unusual, rarely-grown vegetable. The re-creation of the style is very welcome and the beer should develop interestingly in the bottle. Watch out, too, for Good King Henry Special Reserve. This 11% version, aged for six months on oak and for two years in the bottle, is due to be released for the brewery's tenth anniversary. Only 1,000 bottles will be available.

Tasting Notes

A very dark ruby beer with a dark beige head. The aroma features a little estery fruit and some roasted malt, while the taste is clean and well balanced, with sweetness, alcohol, dark malt, estery fruit and almonds. Sweet, roasted barley and hop finish.

OLD LUXTERS

Old Luxters Vineyard, Winery & Brewery, Hambleden, Henley-on-Thames, Oxfordshire RG9 6JW.
Tel. (01491) 638330 Fax (01491) 638645
E-mail: enquiries@chilternvalley.co.uk
Website: www.chilternvalley.co.uk
Mail order service

Old Luxters was set up in 1990 in a 17th-century barn by David Ealand, owner of Chiltern Valley Wines. A new bottling line was installed in spring 1998 and the brewery has since expanded its contract brewing and bottling services for other producers. In total, conditioning and maturation for bottled beers at the brewery take five weeks, with beers filtered and re-seeded with primary fermentation yeast. Best before dates are generally set one-year from bottling.

Fortnum & Mason Summer Ale

- **ABV 4.5%** ▪ **BOTTLE SIZE 330 ml** ▪ **SERVE cool**
- **INGREDIENTS Maris Otter pale malt/crystal malt/ chocolate malt/Fuggle and Golding hops/elderflowers**

In 1999 Old Luxters began bottling beer for exclusive London store Fortnum & Mason (see Fortnum's Ale overleaf). In 2002 this seasonal brew was added, given a summery fragrance with elderflowers. A good accompaniment for fish or poultry, thinks brewery founder David Ealand.

Tasting Notes

A golden beer with a strong, herbal aroma (slightly earthy and perfumed). The taste matches the aroma, although with sweet elderflower flavour emerging, while the finish is drying, with a touch more bitterness.

Major stockist Fortnum & Mason, London

Old Windsor Gold Ale

- **ABV 4.5%** ▪ **BOTTLE SIZE 500 ml** ▪ **SERVE cool**
- **INGREDIENTS Maris Otter pale malt/crystal malt/Fuggle and Golding hops**

Added to the range in 2001, this is one of two beers prepared for Royal Farms, for sale at Windsor Farm Shop.

Tasting Notes

A smooth, copper-gold beer with a creamy, nutty aroma. Creamy malt, a little nut and a light, citrous hoppiness follow in the mouth, finished by a creamy, bitter, malty aftertaste.

Dark Roast

- **ABV 5%** ▪ **BOTTLE SIZE 500 ml** ▪ **SERVE cool**
- **INGREDIENTS Maris Otter pale malt/crystal malt/chocolate malt/Fuggle and Golding hops**

This cask and bottled brew arrived in 1997.

Tasting Notes

A dark chestnut beer with a malty aroma tinged with cocoa and citrous hops. Crisp, malty and gently roasty in the mouth, it is well balanced and has orangey citrous notes. Dry, bittersweet, mellow roast finish. Not as strong in roast flavour as its name implies.

Fortnum's Ale

- **ABV 5%** ▪ **BOTTLE SIZE 330 ml** ▪ **SERVE cool**
- **INGREDIENTS Maris Otter pale malt/crystal malt/chocolate malt/Fuggle and Golding hops**

Another beer exclusively for Fortnum & Mason. The royal grocers approached Old Luxters for this special brew, having already sold Chiltern Valley's wines.

Tasting Notes

A copper beer with orange and malt in the aroma. Silky, nutty malt and fruity hops combine in the clean, bittersweet taste, while the aftertaste is hoppy, toasty, nutty and gently bitter.

Major stockist Fortnum & Mason, London

Luxters Gold

■ ABV 5% ■ BOTTLE SIZE 330 ml ■ SERVE cool
■ INGREDIENTS Maris Otter pale malt/Fuggle and Golding hops

In 1997, Old Luxters secured a contract with the Gilbey's wine importer/restaurateur company, to produce Gilbey's Gold (ABV 5%), a 'farmhouse ale' in dark green 330 ml bottles. The beer proved so successful that it was added to the permanent range, with the name changed accordingly. A good accompaniment for spicy foods, claims David Ealand.

Tasting Notes
A golden beer with spicy hops edging out malt in the aroma. The taste nicely balances malt and spicy hops, and there is a hint of grapefruit, too. Hoppy, dry finish.

Old Windsor Dark Ale

■ ABV 5% ■ BOTTLE SIZE 500 ml ■ SERVE cool
■ INGREDIENTS Maris Otter pale malt/crystal malt/ chocolate malt/Fuggle and Golding hops

The second Royal Farms beer, as its name implies, darker and stronger.

Barn Ale

■ ABV 5.4% ■ BOTTLE SIZE 500 ml ■ SERVE cool
■ INGREDIENTS Maris Otter pale malt/crystal malt/ chocolate malt/Fuggle and Golding hops

Taking its name from the brewery's rustic location, Barn Ale, first brewed in 1993, is considerably stronger than the cask Barn Ale Special (4.5%) on which it is based. The brewery reckons it's a good match for strong-flavoured foods, such as a robust cheese or even a curry.

Tasting Notes
A dark copper beer, combining fruit, silky, chocolatey malt and hops in a good body. Malty, chocolatey, orange fruit nose; dry, fruity, bittersweet finish.

Major stockist Local Waitrose

Winter Warmer

■ ABV 6% ■ BOTTLE SIZE 500 ml ■ SERVE cool
■ INGREDIENTS Maris Otter pale malt/crystal malt/ chocolate malt/Fuggle and Golding hops/spices

A beer first bottled in 2001, Winter Warmer is sold in frosted glass bottles and features cinnamon among its mysterious spices. One batch is produced each winter, with best before dates set at two years.

Tasting Notes

A rich amber ale with a perfumed aroma of oranges and spice. The perfumed, floral, bitter orange taste also has malt for balancing sweetness. Bitter, hoppy, scented finish.

Damson Ale

■ ABV 7% ■ BOTTLE SIZE 500 ml ■ SERVE cool
■ INGREDIENTS Maris Otter pale malt/crystal malt/ chocolate malt/damson juice/Fuggle and Golding hops

Old Luxters used to bottle Damson Beer for Strawberry Bank Brewery (now closed) in Cumbria. Its successor lives on in this brew, in which Cumbrian damson juice is added to the beer 24 hours after primary fermentation has begun. Savour with fine cheeses or robust sausages and mash, says David Ealand.

Tasting Notes

A red-amber brew reminiscent of Belgian fruit beers. Damsons feature strongly in the otherwise musty, spicy aroma, and dominate in the same way in the warming, bittersweet taste. Drying, bittersweet, damson finish.

ORGANIC

The Organic Brewhouse, Unit 1, Higher Bochym Workshops, Cury Cross Lanes, Mullion, Helston, Cornwall TR12 7AZ. Tel. (01326) 241555
E-mail: a.hamer@btclick.com

This entirely organic brewery was set up by Andy Hamer in 2000 in a former slaughterhouse in the shadow of Goonhilly Downs radio station in Cornwall. It is the southernmost brewery in mainland Britain. The first bottle-conditioned beer was brewed in 2001 and three more have been added since. The beers are filled from a cask or conditioning tank on site and may be kräusened if necessary. They carry a ten-month best before date (a year for Wolf Rock) and are all acceptable for vegans.

Lizard Point

■ ABV 4% ■ BOTTLE SIZE 500 ml ■ SERVE cool
■ INGREDIENTS Pale malt/crystal malt/Hallertau hops

Named after the most southerly point on the British mainland (close to the brewery), Lizard Point was one of Andy's first cask brews. Good with fish, he says.

Serpentine

- **ABV 4.5%** ▪ **BOTTLE SIZE 500 ml** ▪ **SERVE cool**
- **INGREDIENTS Pale malt/crystal malt/chocolate malt/wheat malt/Hallertau hops**

Taking its name from the local bedrock, which is often shaped into decorative tourist souvenirs, Organic's first bottled beer.

Tasting Notes

A tawny ale with a malty, chocolate-biscuit nose and a malty, sweet taste countered by a little roast grain and chocolate. Bitter, roasted, malty finish.

Black Rock Stout

- **ABV 4.7%** ▪ **BOTTLE SIZE 500 ml** ▪ **SERVE cool**
- **INGREDIENTS Pale malt/crystal malt/chocolate malt/wheat malt/Hallertau hops**

A stout introduced in December 2001 and named after an island at the entrance to Falmouth harbour. The hops used, as in the other beers, are imported from New Zealand.

Wolf Rock

- **ABV 5%** ▪ **BOTTLE SIZE 500 ml** ▪ **SERVE cool**
- **INGREDIENTS Pale malt/crystal malt/wheat malt/Hallertau hops**

Another beer from late 2001, named after the famous Wolf Rock lighthouse that can be seen from the brewery.

Tasting Notes

A copper beer with a soft fruity aroma (sweet apple and strawberry). Although the taste is fruity and sweetish, there are enough hop resins and bitterness for balance, and a little warmth to expose the strength. Bitter, hoppy, fruity finish.

OULTON

Oulton Ales Ltd., Lake Lothing Brewery, Oulton Broad, Suffolk NR32 3LZ. Tel. (01502) 587905
E-mail: wayne@oultonales.co.uk
Website: www.oultonales.co.uk
Mail order service

Oulton Ales brews on the site formerly used by Green Jack Brewery (former partner Tim Dunford left in 2002 and now owns the Green Jack name). All the beers are presented in swing-topped bottles, although different glassware may be employed in future.

Sunrise

■ ABV 4% ■ BOTTLE SIZE 500 ml ■ SERVE cool
■ INGREDIENTS Pearl pale malt/crystal malt/caramalt/ maize/Challenger and Styrian Golding hops

A summer cask beer, first put into bottle in 2003. Like the other beers, this is hand-filled on site, after kräusening.

Nautilus

■ ABV 4.2% ■ BOTTLE SIZE 500 ml ■ SERVE cool
■ INGREDIENTS Pearl pale malt/crystal malt/chocolate malt/caramalt/Challenger and Styrian Golding hops

Formerly Green Jack's Grasshopper, introduced in 1997.

Tasting Notes

An amber-red beer with a hoppy nose, a fresh, hoppy taste, well balanced with malt, and a dry, hoppy, moreish finish.

Gone Fishing

■ ABV 5% ■ BOTTLE SIZE 500 ml ■ SERVE cool
■ INGREDIENTS Pearl pale malt/crystal malt/chocolate malt/caramalt/Fuggle hops

A strong, single-varietal hop bitter, in bottle since 2002.

Roaring Boy

■ ABV 8.5% ■ BOTTLE SIZE 500 ml ■ SERVE cool
■ INGREDIENTS Pearl pale malt/caramalt/maize/candy sugar/Challenger and Styrian Golding hops

This the beer Green Jack used to call Ripper, which was first produced in 1995. Prior to bottling, it is matured for at least ten months.

Tasting Notes

An amber beer with a hoppy nose with hints of bitter orange. The robust flavour is sweetish, malty and full of tangy, fruity hops. Hoppy, tangy, warming finish with a little nut.

PARADISE

Paradise Brewery, The Old Creamery, Wrenbury, Nantwich, Cheshire CW5 8EX. Tel./Fax (01270) 780916
E-mail: john@gillmorgan.go-plus.net

Beers bottled under the name of The Old Creamery Bottling Company originate from Paradise Brewery, a business set up by John Wood in 2000 and operating from just such premises.

The first regular bottles rolled out in 2004 and tend to be sold at farmers' markets in the North-West.

Mild

■ **ABV 3.6%** ■ **BOTTLE SIZE 500 ml** ■ **SERVE cool**
■ **INGREDIENTS Maris Otter pale malt/crystal malt/chocolate malt/First Gold and Golding hops**

A beer first brewed in cask form in 2000 to mark CAMRA's annual May Mild Month. Like the other bottled beers, Mild is filtered and kräusened prior to filling.

Dabbers

■ **ABV 5%** ■ **BOTTLE SIZE 500 ml** ■ **SERVE cool**
■ **INGREDIENTS Maris Otter pale malt/wheat malt/Styrian Golding hops**

A Dabber, in local terms, is a person who originates in Nantwich, the nearest major town to the brewery. Another of the earliest brews, this strong bitter was first on sale as a cask beer in 2000.

Nantwich Ale

■ **ABV 5.6%** ■ **BOTTLE SIZE 500 ml** ■ **SERVE cool**
■ **INGREDIENTS Maris Otter pale malt/crystal malt/First Gold and Fuggle hops**

A new beer, introduced on draught for a Christmas beer festival in 2003 and first bottled in March 2004.

PARISH

Parish Brewery, 6 Main Street, Burrough-on-the-Hill, Leicestershire LE14 2JQ. Tel. (01664) 454801

Parish Brewery is one of Britain's great survivors among microbreweries. Founded in 1983 in Burrough-on-the-Hill, it later moved to Somerby in the same county of Leicestershire, but now has returned home. Owner Barrie Parish has dabbled in bottled beers, but only recently produced a regular range.

PSB (Parish Special Bitter)

■ **ABV 4.3%** ■ **BOTTLE SIZE 500 ml** ■ **SERVE cool**
■ **INGREDIENTS Maris Otter pale malt/crystal malt/wheat malt/Golding and Fuggle hops**

Barrie's first ever brew and still going strong. Like the other bottled beers, PSB is kräusened in cask and then filled using a three-head bottling machine. Labels are applied by hand.

Tasting Notes

A light amber beer with a hoppy, malty aroma. The taste features nutty malt and citrous hops, before a dry, nutty, citrous aftertaste.

Burrough Bitter

■ ABV 4.8% ■ BOTTLE SIZE 500 ml ■ SERVE cool
■ INGREDIENTS Maris Otter pale malt/crystal malt/wheat malt/Golding and Fuggle hops

Brewed to celebrate the return of Parish Brewery to its home town, this beer was new in both cask and bottle in 2003. It follows basically the same recipe as PSB, apart from the greater strength and the extra half-hour boil it enjoys in the copper, for more robust flavours.

Tasting Notes

An orange-gold beer with a fruity, malty nose. Malt and sharp hops feature in the taste, before a dry, bitter, hop and malt finish.

Baz's Bonce Blower

■ ABV 11.5% ■ BOTTLE SIZE 500 ml ■ SERVE cool
■ INGREDIENTS Maris Otter pale malt/crystal malt/black malt/Golding, Fuggle and Willamette hops

The beer that made Barrie Parish famous. When the brewery was established at The Stag & Hounds pub (making it the first brew pub of the modern era in Leicestershire), Barrie needed something a little out of the ordinary to draw the punters out to the country. He found it in this notorious beer, which requires a double fermentation to achieve its giddy, 11.5% strength (sometimes even a touch stronger). After Parish's yeast has given up the ghost during the first fermentation, fresh yeast is pitched and kept alive by the addition of a secret 'yeast food' to enable it to venture into territory where beer yeasts normally fear to tread. A good mix of hops provides a counterbalance to all the alcohol. But if you think this is a strong beer, you should have tried Baz's Super Brew. In 1995 it featured in the *Guinness Book of Records* as the strongest beer in the world (23%). The famous Bonce Blower doesn't do badly for publicity either and has other strings to its bow. Specialist sausage and pork pie makers Dickinson & Morris of Melton Mowbray employ it in their Parish Sausages, and Barrie extols its virtues as a fine accompaniment to some of the excellent local Stiltons.

Tasting Notes
A ruby beer with a malty, alcoholic aroma with a whiff of almonds. The taste is sweetish, almondy, malty and alcoholic, with a sherry-like fruitiness. Warm, sweetish, malty and fruity aftertaste.

PITFIELD

Pitfield Brewery, The London Beer Company Ltd.,
14 Pitfield Street, Hoxton, London N1 6EY.
Tel. (020) 7739 3701
Website: www.pitfieldbeershop.co.uk
Mail order service
Pitfield was founded way back in 1981 and, after several years out of production, was revived in 1996, next to Hoxton's well-known Beer Shop. In 2000 the brewery was certified to be an organic producer, but a new range of historic re-creation beers are not organic (authentic ingredients not being available in organic form). These historic beers are listed separately at the end of the Pitfield entry. Through such initiatives, the bottled beer range keeps on growing, but, as Pitfield has a specialist off-licence attached, it has the distinct advantage of being able to bottle beers to demand (around 70 bottles at a time). The beers are matured in cask for two–three weeks before being racked mostly bright. New yeast is added as required, with maltose syrup primings used to encourage good secondary fermentation. The bottles are then kept at the brewery for at least two weeks before release. Six months are specified as a best before date. Because finings (which are usually made from fish swim bladders and are used to help clear beer of yeast) have been omitted, the beers hold no fears for vegetarians or vegans, but they may be a little hazy as a result. Special one-off brews are occasionally produced, such as Pumpkin Porter (5%) for Hallowe'en, Valentine Ale (5%) in February and beers for major football tournaments.

Pitfield Original Bitter

- **ABV 3.7%** ▪ **BOTTLE SIZE 500/750 ml** ▪ **SERVE cool**
- **INGREDIENTS Maris Otter pale malt/crystal malt/wheat malt/Fuggle, Challenger and East Kent Golding hops**

Pitfield's standard session bitter was one of its first ever brews. It was renamed 'Pitfield Original' in 1999.
Tasting Notes
An orange/gold-coloured beer with a hoppy nose. The taste is

dry and hoppy with gentle malt behind. Very dry, hoppy finish.

Shoreditch Stout

- **ABV 4%** ▪ **BOTTLE SIZE 500/750 ml** ▪ **SERVE cool**
- **INGREDIENTS Maris Otter pale malt/roasted barley/flaked barley/Fuggle, Challenger and Target hops**

Not as 'stout' as some, this brew was added in 1997.

Tasting Notes

A very dark brown beer with a smoky aroma. It is a little sour in the mouth but also fruity and malty. Gently roasty, bitter malt finish.

East Kent Goldings

- **ABV 4.2%** ▪ **BOTTLE SIZE 500/750 ml** ▪ **SERVE cool**
- **INGREDIENTS Maris Otter pale malt/crystal malt/wheat malt/flaked maize/East Kent Golding hops**

This single-varietal hop beer, using the UK brewers' favourite aroma hop, was first produced in 1999 and is now a permanent part of the range.

Tasting Notes

An orange-gold ale with a fruity, peppery hop nose. Fruity hop is well balanced by smooth malt in the taste, which is not too bitter. Dry, gently bitter finish.

Eco Warrior

- **ABV 4.5%** ▪ **BOTTLE SIZE 500/750 ml** ▪ **SERVE cool**
- **INGREDIENTS Chariot pale malt/sugar/Hallertau hops**

This beer, launched in 1998, set the Pitfield organic ball rolling. It quickly found itself a niche and has been stocked by several health food shops.

Tasting Notes

A hazy golden beer with a fruity hop bouquet (hints of tinned peaches). In the mouth, the initially sweetish taste is balanced by delicate, soft, orangey-peachy hops which provide slowly increasing bitterness. Dry, fruity hop finish.

Hoxton Best Bitter

- **ABV 4.8%** ▪ **BOTTLE SIZE 500/750 ml** ▪ **SERVE cool**
- **INGREDIENTS Maris Otter pale malt/crystal malt/dried pale malt/roasted barley/Northdown, Challenger and East Kent Golding hops**

Designed as a pseudo-Scottish brew, with typically strong

malty characteristics, this beer was formerly known as Hoxton Heavy. The use of a little dried malt adds a touch of sweetness and balances out the roasted barley flavours.

Tasting Notes

A dark copper beer with a malty, chocolatey nose, a malty but citrous taste, with balancing bitterness, and a bitter malt finish.

Black Eagle

- **ABV 5% ■ BOTTLE SIZE 500/750 ml ■ SERVE cool**
- **INGREDIENTS Maris Otter pale malt/crystal malt/black malt/wheat malt/Fuggle, Challenger and Styrian Golding hops**

Black Eagle may ring a few bells with drinkers acquainted with Pitfield beers of old. It is reminiscent of the brewery's famous Dark Star, *Champion Beer of Britain* in 1987, which is now produced by the Dark Star brewery (see separate entry).

Tasting Notes

A dark ruby beer, with an aroma of ripe red berry fruits. The taste is smooth and fruity but with some dark malt flavour and good hop balance. Quite dry, it doesn't drink its strength. Dry, mostly bitter, lingering finish.

N1

- **ABV 5% ■ BOTTLE SIZE 500 ml ■ SERVE cool**
- **INGREDIENTS Pale malt/wheat malt/Hallertau hops/ coriander**

Brewed with a genuine wheat beer yeast, this new addition to the organic range is Pitfield's version of a Belgian wit bier, complete with coriander spicing.

Tasting Notes

A hazy yellow beer with a bready, lemon juice aroma. Lemon tartness, sweetness, spice and a touch of warmth combine in the mouth, before a drying, lemony, slightly chewy finish.

1850 London Porter

- **ABV 5% ■ BOTTLE SIZE 500 ml ■ SERVE cool**
- **INGREDIENTS Maris Otter pale malt/brown malt/ roasted barley/Golding hops**

Pitfield had been producing this porter off and on for a few years before it decided to include it in the new range of beers based on historic beer styles. The recipes for these brews have been inspired by the work of the Durden Park Beer Circle, a dedicated and enthusiastic group of private brewers (one reluctantly uses the titles 'amateur' or 'home brewers', such is their proficiency and attention to detail). The Circle goes to extreme lengths to re-create beers that have long ceased to be part of the portfolio of brewers today, unearthing the truth about how beers used to taste.

Tasting Notes

A deep ruby beer with a coffeeish aroma. The taste is nutty and bittersweet with light roasted notes amidst the malt. Dry, nutty, coffeeish, gently bitter finish.

1830 Amber Ale

- **ABV 6% ▪ BOTTLE SIZE 500 ml ▪ SERVE cool**
- **INGREDIENTS Maris Otter pale malt/amber malt/ chocolate malt/Fuggle, Golding and Styrian Golding hops**

In Victorian times, amber malt was widely used in brewing but it died out in the 20th century. It is now proving popular among brewers keen to resurrect old-fashioned beers.

Tasting Notes

Actually ruby in colour, with soft, juicy pineapple and malt in the nose. Pineapple again features in the taste, overlaying plenty of malt, with nutty, toasted notes emerging on the swallow. Dry, roasted malt aftertaste.

1824 Mild Ale

- **ABV 6.5% ▪ BOTTLE SIZE 500 ml ▪ SERVE cool**
- **INGREDIENTS Maris Otter pale malt/black malt/wheat malt/Golding hops**

Mild – an endangered species among beer styles – is most commonly found as a weak beer, around 3–3.5% alcohol, these days. There are some stronger milds around, as this book illustrates, and this particular beer serves as a reminder that, in days gone by, mild was not only Britain's most popular brew but a rather potent drink, too.

Tasting Notes

Another ruby beer with some light fruit in the creamy, malty nose. Smooth malt leads in the mouth, with hints of darker malt and some fruit. Dry, bitter, roasted malt finish.

1837 India Pale Ale

- **ABV 7% ▪ BOTTLE SIZE 500 ml ▪ SERVE cool**
- **INGREDIENTS Maris Otter pale malt/roasted barley/ Northdown and Golding hops**

A powerful IPA in the traditional style, emulating the sort of beer that was strong and hoppy enough to withstand the rough sea crossing to India in the 19th century.

Tasting Notes

An amber ale with a big, hoppy and fruity aroma, with malt in support. The taste is full and sweetish, with lots of hops and fruit (including tropical). Drying, bittersweet, hoppy, warming finish, with lingering tropical fruit.

1792 Imperial Stout

- **ABV 9.3%** ▪ **BOTTLE SIZE 500 ml** ▪ **SERVE cool**
- **INGREDIENTS Maris Otter pale malt/roasted barley/ wheat malt/Northdown hops**

Helping to fill a gap vacated by Courage's renowned Imperial Russian Stout, this strong, complex brew is typical of the beers that crossed the Baltic to warm the hearts of the imperial Russian court at the turn of the 19th century.

Tasting Notes

As black as night, this potent brew has a clean, slightly savoury aroma, with a hint of liquorice in its roasted notes and a light whiff of fruit. Smooth, oily malt leads in the taste, which is sweetish with a tinge of raisin and coffee notes. Easy to drink for its strength. Mellow, sweetish, dark malt finish.

1896 XXXX Stock Ale

- **ABV 10%** ▪ **BOTTLE SIZE 500 ml** ▪ **SERVE cool**
- **INGREDIENTS Maris Otter pale malt/crystal malt/ Northdown hops**

A beer to lay down and enjoy in a couple of years' time. Stock ales were designed for such keeping, having the alcohol and body to mature long after brewing.

Tasting Notes

A dark golden beer with a rich, vinously fruity, malty nose. The big, warming taste is sweet and fruity, yet complex and spicy. Long, bittersweet, fruity finish. Dangerously drinkable.

PLASSEY

Plassey Brewery, Eyton, Wrexham LL13 0SP.
Tel. (01978) 781111 Fax (01978) 781279
E-mail: plasseybrewery@globalnet.co.uk
Website: web-nexus.com/plassey
Mail order service

Plassey Brewery was established in 1985 on the 250-acre Plassey estate, which also includes a caravan park, a golf course, craft shops and licensed premises. A new brewery was completed in 1996 and includes a shop.

Fusilier

■ ABV 4.5% ■ BOTTLE SIZE 500 ml ■ SERVE cool
■ INGREDIENTS Maris Otter pale malt/crystal malt/ chocolate malt/carapils malt/Cascade, Styrian Golding, Saaz and Pacific Gem hops

Fusilier is the regimental ale of the Royal Welch Fusiliers, the oldest infantry regiment in Wales (raised in 1689). The bottle depicts Billy, the regimental goat mascot, and provides a little of his history. 'Serve with pride', instructs the label. Although brewed by Plassey, the beer is bottled by Hanby Ales.

Tasting Notes

A dark amber beer with a malty, fruity nose. The taste is sweetish and malty with a gentle hop seasoning. Bittersweet, malty, hoppy finish.

POACHERS

Poachers Brewery, Unit 4, Camp Road, Swinderby, Lincolnshire LN6 9TW. Tel. (01522) 868889
Website: www.poachersbeer.co.uk

Poachers was opened in May 2001 by former home brewer Ian Baker and ex-RAF man George Batterbee, which ties in nicely as their home is a unit on a former RAF base. The lads publicised their business by opening a real ale off-licence in Lincoln (see Beer Shops) but, as the brewery workload increased in summer 2003, this was sold. The range of bottled beers are all matured in cask before being racked bright and kräusened for bottling.

Trembling Rabbit Mild

■ ABV 3.4% ■ BOTTLE SIZE 500 ml ■ SERVE cool
■ INGREDIENTS Maris Otter pale malt/crystal malt/ chocolate malt/Cascade and Mount Hood hops

Stuck for a name for their new mild, Ian and George threw it open to regulars at The Eight Jolly Brewers pub in Gainsborough, who took part in a competition to devise a suitable title.

Tasting Notes

A red beer with a malty, sharply fruity nose, a malty taste, with roasted grain on the swallow, and a bitter, roasted malt aftertaste.

Shy Talk Bitter

▪ ABV 3.7% ▪ BOTTLE SIZE 500 ml ▪ SERVE cool
▪ INGREDIENTS Maris Otter pale malt/crystal malt/ Challenger, Cascade and Mount Hood hops
A new, pale golden session beer, named after a boat spotted in Whitby harbour.

Poachers Pride

▪ ABV 4% ▪ BOTTLE SIZE 500 ml ▪ SERVE cool
▪ INGREDIENTS Maris Otter pale malt/crystal malt/ Cascade and Mount Hood hops
An amber beer, apparently inspired by the Chris Rea song 'Too Much Pride'.

Poachers Den

▪ ABV 4.2% ▪ BOTTLE SIZE 500 ml ▪ SERVE cool
▪ INGREDIENTS Maris Otter pale malt/roasted barley/ Challenger, Cascade and Mount Hood hops
A best bitter named after Ian's father, Dennis Baker, who introduced the grateful Ian to cask ale. His cartoon features on the bottle.

Tasting Notes
A golden ale with a spicy hop-fruit aroma. The taste is also hoppy, spicy and fruity, but dry. Dry, hoppy, fruity finish.

Poachers Trail

▪ ABV 4.2% ▪ BOTTLE SIZE 500 ml ▪ SERVE cool
▪ INGREDIENTS Maris Otter pale malt/roasted barley/ Golding and Styrian Golding hops
This was the brewery's first commercial brew. At the time it didn't have a name and was just listed as 'Trial', which later evolved into Trail.

Tasting Notes
A copper beer with an orangey, malty aroma. The taste is full of juicy fruit (slightly tart lemon), with good malt balance and a touch of roast. Dry, roasted, pleasantly bitter aftertaste.

Black Crow Stout

▪ ABV 4.5% ▪ BOTTLE SIZE 500 ml ▪ SERVE cool
▪ INGREDIENTS Maris Otter pale malt/roasted barley/ Challenger, Chinook and Styrian Golding hops
The first beer Ian ever brewed was a stout (he was, at the

time, a Guinness drinker). This one was named after the birds in the small wood behind the brewery, although it has been revealed since that they are actually rooks.

Tasting Notes

Ruby, with a mellow, biscuity, dark malt nose, a soft, almost burnt, grainy, bitter flavour and a bitter, roasted grain finish.

Poachers Dick

- **ABV 4.5% ▪ BOTTLE SIZE 500 ml ▪ SERVE cool**
- **INGREDIENTS Maris Otter pale malt/crystal malt/ Golding, Cascade, Mount Hood, Challenger and Styrian Golding hops**

This brew is named, in turn, after George's dad, Richard Batterbee, who is caricatured on the label.

Tasting Notes

A tawny/amber ale with a fruit aroma (rhubarb and gooseberries) and a bittersweet, fruity taste. Dry, hoppy, increasingly bitter finish.

Jock's Trap

- **ABV 5% ▪ BOTTLE SIZE 500 ml ▪ SERVE cool**
- **INGREDIENTS Maris Otter pale malt/roasted barley/ Cascade and Mount Hood hops**

A Scottish pun for a beer featuring American hops.

Tasting Notes

An orange-golden beer with an aroma of toffee-malt and fruity hops. The same hoppy flavours continue in the sweetish, fruity taste, while the finish is dry, bitter and hoppy with lingering fruit and toffee.

Trout Tickler

- **ABV 5.5% ▪ BOTTLE SIZE 500 ml ▪ SERVE cool**
- **INGREDIENTS Maris Otter pale malt/crystal malt/ chocolate malt/Mount Hood and Cascade hops**

A dark, malty ale said to have liquorice undertones.

POINTS WEST

Points West Brewery, Plymouth College of Further Education, Kings Road, Devonport, Plymouth, Devon PL1 5QG. Tel. (01752) 305700 Fax (01752) 305888
E-mail: jfitzge@pcfe.ac.uk
Website: www.pcfe.ac.uk

There's no substitute for hands-on experience when brewing and that's what the students at Plymouth College of Further Education appreciate. Their little (five-barrel) Points West Brewery gives them a weekly understanding of the skills of brewing, as they brew beers to set recipes and occasionally conjure up their own special beers. The two bottled beers mentioned below are produced under supervision and sold in the college restaurant as well as in The National Trust's Buckland Abbey shop. Bottles are filled directly from a cask that has been primed to guarantee a good secondary fermentation.

Medieval Porter/Kitchen Porter

- **ABV 4.4%** ▪ **BOTTLE SIZE 275 ml** ▪ **SERVE cool**
- **INGREDIENTS Lager malt/black malt/roasted barley/ Golding hops**

Now here's a novelty. I'm sure Ralph Harwood, the 18th-century London brewer who is said to have created the beer we now know as porter, would have been impressed to know that it existed way back in the Middle Ages, and that it was produced with lager malt. College brewing chief Roger Pengelly is the first to acknowledge such anachronisms but merely responded to the National Trust's request for a beer of this name. At the college itself, the beer is known more fittingly as Kitchen Porter.

Tasting Notes

A ruby beer with dark malt dominant throughout, from the aroma, through the reasonably thin, drying, slightly salty taste to the modest, dry finish.

Drake's Drum

- **ABV 4.8%** ▪ **BOTTLE SIZE 275 ml** ▪ **SERVE cold**
- **INGREDIENTS Lager malt/Saaz and Tettnanger hops**

Roger says that this beer is brewed as an IPA, but the ingredients reveal how it is marketed to the mostly lager-drinking college students. Its name is derived from the drum attributed to the naval hero Drake, which is housed at 13th-century Buckland Abbey and is said to sound whenever England is in danger of invasion. Too late, Sir Francis: lager's already taken over by the looks of it.

Tasting Notes

A pale golden beer with spicy hops and malt in the nose, and a bittersweet malt and hop taste. Light, gently hoppy aftertaste.

POTTON

The Potton Brewery Co., 10 Shannon Place, Potton, Bedfordshire SG19 2PZ. Tel. (01767) 261042
E-mail: info@potton-brewery.co.uk
Website: www.potton-brewery.co.uk

Reviving the Potton Brewery Co. name after it disappeared following a take-over in 1922, this brewery was set up in 1999, by two former Greene King employees. The beers are conditioned in casks, decanted bright, kräusened and then bottled. One-off, 'own label' beers are also produced.

Butlers' Ale

- **ABV 4.3%** ▪ **BOTTLE SIZE 330 ml** ▪ **SERVE cool**
- **INGREDIENTS Pearl pale malt/crystal malt/Target and First Gold hops**

Brewed for Wimpole Hall, a National Trust property in Cambridgeshire, this beer is dedicated to the loyal butler, who traditionally savoured a glass of home brew downstairs after a hard day's service upstairs.

Tasting Notes

An amber ale with malt and fruit in the nose, a pleasant, mostly bitter and nutty taste, and a dry, bitter aftertaste.

Shambles Bitter

- **ABV 4.3%** ▪ **BOTTLE SIZE 500 ml** ▪ **SERVE cool**
- **INGREDIENTS Pearl pale malt/crystal malt/Target and Styrian Golding hops**

The Shambles – a series of trading stalls – in Potton's market place were reconstructed in the late 18th century by the Lord of the Manor, one Samuel Whitbread. As the label of this beer reports, the stalls were used by farmers and other merchants until the end of the 19th century and were eventually demolished in 1954.

Tasting Notes

An amber bitter with a fruit cocktail aroma. There's a hint of pear drop in the taste, countered by crisp bitterness and malt sweetness. Dry, bitter finish with some lingering fruit.

No-ale Spiced

- **ABV 4.8%** ▪ **BOTTLE SIZE 500 ml** ▪ **SERVE cool**
- **INGREDIENTS Pearl pale malt/crystal malt/carapils malt/roasted barley/Target and First Gold hops/seasonal spices**

The festive bottle, this beer is based on the brewery's Christmas cask ale, but with added seasonal spices (including ginger, cinnamon, mace and cloves).

PRINCETOWN

Princetown Breweries Ltd., The Brewery, Tavistock Road, Princetown, Devon PL20 6QF. Tel. (01822) 890789 Fax (01822) 890719

Princetown Brewery was established in 1994 by former Gibbs Mew and Hop Back brewer Simon Loveless. The brewery was scheduled to move to a greenfield site, 300 yards from its original base, in autumn 2004.

Jail Ale

- **ABV 4.8%** ▪ **BOTTLE SIZE 500 ml** ▪ **SERVE cool**
- **INGREDIENTS Pipkin pale malt/crystal malt/wheat malt/Challenger and Progress hops**

Based, as it is, just a short tunnelling distance from the famous prison, what else could the brewery call its premium beer? This bottled version of an award-winning cask ale is racked bright and re-seeded with yeast and fresh wort before bottling. Winner of the *Tucker's Maltings Bottled Beer Competition* in 1999.

Tasting Notes

An amber beer with a floral, fruity aroma with light pear drops. The taste is malty, sweetish, fruity and flower-scented but has good hop balance. Bittersweet, malty finish.

RCH

RCH Brewery, West Hewish, Weston-super-Mare, Somerset BS24 6RR. Tel. (01934) 834447 Fax (01934) 834167
E-mail: rchbrew@aol.com
Website: www.rchbrewery.com

This brewery was originally installed behind the Royal Clarence Hotel at Burnham-on-Sea in the early 1980s, but since 1993 brewing has taken place on a commercial basis on this rural site, a couple of fields away from the rumble of the M5 motorway. The beers are shipped in conditioning tanks to Integrated Bottling Solutions in Gloucestershire (formerly Wessex Craft Brewers) for bottling, with the best before date for all brews set at six months. Pitchfork and Old Slug Porter are distributed in the USA by B United.

On the Tiles

■ ABV 3.9% ■ BOTTLE SIZE 500 ml ■ SERVE cool
■ INGREDIENTS Pale malt/crystal malt/Fuggle and Progress hops

On the Tiles is a bottled version of RCH's draught bitter, PG Steam, and was launched initially as part of a pack for sale in British Home Stores in 1998.

Tasting Notes

A pale brown beer with a fine hoppy nose, backed with fruit and a little toffee. The taste is hoppy, with plenty of fruit. Hoppy, bitter finish.

Pitchfork

■ ABV 4.3% ■ BOTTLE SIZE 500 ml ■ SERVE cool
■ INGREDIENTS Pale malt/Fuggle and Golding hops

First produced in 1993, this beer's name was derived from the unsuccessful Pitchfork Rebellion against King James II by the followers of the Duke of Monmouth. They challenged the King's forces at nearby Sedgemoor in July 1685. The single malt beer is also available in cask (*Champion Best Bitter* at CAMRA's *Champion Beer of Britain* awards in 1998).

Tasting Notes

A golden beer with a mouth-wateringly fruity nose. Initially soft and fruity to taste, it soon gains a solid, slightly perfumed, orangey hop edge. Hoppy, bitter and dry finish.

Major stockists Safeway, Sainsbury

Old Slug Porter

■ ABV 4.5% ■ BOTTLE SIZE 500 ml ■ SERVE cool
■ INGREDIENTS Pale malt/crystal malt/black malt/Fuggle and Golding hops

It took a brave brewery to name a beer this, but it doesn't seem to have deterred drinkers. Old Slug was named after the pesky little creatures that enjoyed the sandy soil around RCH's old brewery. The slugs are now a thing of the past, but the beer still has a dedicated following in both cask and bottle. Gold medalist in the *Tucker's Maltings Bottled Beer Competition* in 1998.

Tasting Notes

A ruby porter with a mellow coffee nose. Not too full-bodied, it nonetheless has bags of taste – good, bitter coffee with some sweetness, nuttiness and hops behind. Big, dry finish of bitter coffee.

Major stockists Unwins

Double Header

■ ABV 5.3% ■ BOTTLE SIZE 500 ml ■ SERVE cool
■ INGREDIENTS Pale malt/Golding hops

The winner of Asda's first bottled beer competition, Double Header is named after a train pulled by two engines (as illustrated on the label, which also declares the beer to be 'ideal with roast meats, casseroles or cheese').

Tasting Notes

A strong, golden ale with a complex fruity nose (orange, melon, pear and grapefruit all seem to come through). The taste is immediately citrus-fruity but then a big kick of hops arrives to add tangy, bitter notes. Dry, lipsmackingly tangy, hop finish. A hop feast.

Major stockist Asda

Ale Mary

■ ABV 6% ■ BOTTLE SIZE 500 ml ■ SERVE cool
■ INGREDIENTS Pale malt/chocolate malt/Progress and Target hops/ginger/cloves/cinnamon/coriander/ nutmeg/pimento

Ale Mary is RCH's Firebox (see below), but with spice oils and essences added prior to bottling. It was first 'created' for Christmas 1998 and has remained a festive favourite. Voted CAMRA's *Champion Bottle-conditioned Beer* in 2001.

Tasting Notes

Orange fruit overlaid with exotic, peppery spice dominates the perfumed nose of this strong amber beer. The spices impart an unusual taste, with the citrous qualities of Firebox exaggerated by the coriander in particular, and the other flavourings providing a peppery, gingery warmth. Dry, scented, bitter orange finish with a light ginger burn.

Major stockist Safeway

Firebox

■ ABV 6% ■ BOTTLE SIZE 500 ml ■ SERVE cool
■ INGREDIENTS Pale malt/chocolate malt/Progress and Target hops

RCH's premium strength cask- and bottle-conditioned beer. Its name reflects the steam-powered nature of the brewery, plus the fascination with the golden age of railways shared by director Paul Davey and brewer Graham Dunbavan.

Tasting Notes

A flavoursome, red-amber, strong bitter with a fruity, malty nose. The taste is sweet and fruity, backed with hop

bitterness and some dark malt. Dry, tangy, bitter fruit finish, with a hint of dark malt.
Major stockist Waitrose

REBELLION

Rebellion Beer Company, Bencombe Farm, Marlow Bottom, Buckinghamshire SL7 3LT. Tel. (01628) 476594 Fax (01628) 476617 E-mail: tim@rebellionbeer.co.uk Website: www.rebellionbeer.co.uk
Mail order service
Rebellion was the company that brought brewing back to Marlow, following the closure of Wethereds by Whitbread. Opened in 1993, the brewery has since moved locally and expanded, serving a sizeable pub trade. Although the beer featured below is brewed in Marlow, bottling takes place off-site, at Hepworth & Co. in Horsham.

White

- **ABV 4.5%** ▪ **BOTTLE SIZE 500 ml** ▪ **SERVE cold**
- **INGREDIENTS Pale malt/wheat malt/First Gold and Cascade hops/coriander/orange peel/lemon peel**

This spiced wheat beer was first brewed in 2001 and claimed that year's SIBA (Society of Independent Brewers) *Wheat Beer Challenge* award for Belgian-style wheats, followed up by a category gold medal in the *International Beer Competition* in 2002. In 2003 and 2004, it was voted overall champion in the *Wheat Beer Challenge*. It's not available on draught and, for bottling, the beer is filtered and re-seeded with fresh yeast. The best before date is fixed at 12 months.
Tasting Notes
A hazy gold beer with a gingery spiciness to the nose, along with a hint of perfumed, bitter orange and clove. Crisp and easy-drinking, it tastes bittersweet with cloves dominating and a backdrop of tart lemon. Scented finish of bitter oranges.
Major stockists Safeway, Waitrose, local Unwins

REEPHAM

Reepham Brewery, Unit 1, Collers Way, Reepham, Norfolk NR10 4SW. Tel. (01603) 871091
Reepham is one of the longest established breweries in Norfolk, founded in 1983. Its contribution to the bottle-

conditioned beer scene is not entirely conventional, as the beer mentioned is packaged only in 2-litre PET bottles for sale in local off-licences, with a best before date set at just six weeks after filling.

Rapier Pale Ale

- **ABV 4.2%** ■ **BOTTLE SIZE 2 litres** ■ **SERVE cool**
- **INGREDIENTS Maris Otter pale malt/crystal malt/ Whitbread Golding Variety, Fuggle and Bramling Cross hops**

Effectively fresh beer for quick consumption. Rapier, in its cask form, is a former award-winner at the Norwich Beer Festival. This bottled version is aged in cask for a couple of weeks prior to packaging.

REFRESH UK

Refresh UK PLC, Wychwood Brewery, Eagle Maltings, The Crofts, Witney, Oxfordshire OX28 4DP.
Tel. (01993) 890800 Fax (01993) 772553
E-mail: info@refreshuk.com
Website: www.refreshuk.com

Refresh UK was founded by former Bass and Morland sales executive Rupert Thompson as a marketing company for the products of various breweries, primarily the Ushers brands, following the closure of the Trowbridge brewery in 2000. Refresh has since purchased Wychwood's brewery and also the Brakspear beer brands, which were initially brewed at Burtonwood under contract after the Brakspear board decided to close the historic brewery to cash in on the value of the central site in Henley-on-Thames. Now Refresh has built a new brewhouse at Wychwood (incorporating former Brakspear brewing kit) to produce the Brakspear's beers, although the company's sole bottle-conditioned beer is still outsourced.

Brakspear Organic Beer

- **ABV 4.6%** ■ **BOTTLE SIZE 500 ml** ■ **SERVE cool**
- **INGREDIENTS Optic pale malt/crystal malt/Hallertau, Golding and Target hops**

Winner of the first ever *Organic Beer Challenge*, in 2000, Live Organic (as the beer was then known) has survived the depressing closure of Brakspear and is now produced under contract for Refresh UK by Brakspear's former head brewer,

Peter Scholey. He brews the beer personally at Hepworth & Co. in Horsham, using the old Henley yeast and filtering the beer prior to re-seeding with fresh yeast of the same strain. The beer is bottled at 4.3% alcohol, but ferments in the bottle over three months up to its declared 4.6%. The best before date is set at a year, after which, being organic, says Peter, it may become hazy. He also recommends it with spicy foods. The world's first organic Golding hops were specially grown for Brakspear in Belgium to produce this brew. Also featured are organic German Hallertau and organic Target hops, the latter used for dry hopping. A beer that is acceptable to vegans.

Tasting Notes
A copper ale with a rich, orange and apricot aroma. The taste is fairly bitter and crisp with lots of fruity, tangy hops and a spicy overlay, but always a sweet malt balance. Dry, bitter, hoppy finish.

Major stockists Asda, Booths, Morrisons, Safeway, Unwins

RIDGEWAY

Ridgeway Brewing, South Stoke, Oxfordshire RG8 0JW.
Tel./Fax (01491) 873474
E-mail: info@ridgewaybrewery.co.uk

Ridgeway Brewing is run by Peter Scholey, former head brewer at Brakspear, who, in addition to brewing the Coniston and Refresh UK bottle-conditioned beers mentioned elsewhere in this book, also brews for his own business, using equipment at Hepworth & Co. in Horsham. The Ridgeway long-distance footpath passes just a few hundred yards from Peter's front door in South Oxfordshire – hence the brewery name.

Ridgeway Bitter

- **ABV 4%** ■ **BOTTLE SIZE 500 ml** ■ **SERVE cool**
- **INGREDIENTS Maris Otter pale malt/crystal malt/ Challenger and Boadicea hops**

This bitter features the new Boadicea strain of aphid-resistant hops. Like all Peter's bottle-conditioned beers, the beer is sterile filtered before being re-seeded with fresh yeast for bottling. It is also sold in cask form locally.

Tasting Notes
A golden-amber beer with a fruity, floral hop aroma. The taste is also floral, clean and well-balanced, leading on to a drying, floral, bitter finish.

RINGWOOD

Ringwood Brewery Ltd., 138 Christchurch Road, Ringwood, Hampshire BH24 3AP.
Tel. (01425) 471177 Fax (01425) 480273
E-mail: info@ringwoodbrewery.co.uk
Website: www.ringwoodbrewery.co.uk
Mail order service

Ringwood was set up in 1978 and moved in 1986 to attractive 18th-century buildings, formerly part of the old Tunks brewery. It has since become one of the stalwarts of the UK brewing scene, overtaking in size many established regional brewers. The bottled beers are brewed in the same way as the cask versions, except that a week's cold-conditioning (3°C) is employed to bring down the yeast count prior to bottling (which is carried out under contract at Hop Back Brewery). The beer is then kräusened. Twelve months' shelf life is indicated on the labels. In addition to the beers listed below, other Ringwood beers may be available soon in bottle-conditioned form.

Bold Forester

- **ABV 4.2%** ▪ **BOTTLE SIZE 500 ml** ▪ **SERVE cool**
- **INGREDIENTS Maris Otter pale malt/crystal malt/amber malt/Challenger and Progress hops**

Bold Forester was launched as a seasonal cask beer for spring 2003, but was also bottled as a way of commemorating the brewery's 25th birthday. It will now continue as an annual bottled offering produced in springtime. The Maris Otter malt included is grown exclusively in Hampshire by farmers directly contracted by the brewery. Amber malt helps add dryness to the brew while late and dry hopping (in the conditioning tank) with Challenger hops adds to the spicy fruit character.

Tasting Notes

An amber beer with chocolate notes in its malty nose. The taste balances chocolate, malt, fruit and hops. Dry, bitter finish with lingering chocolate.

XXXX Porter

- **ABV 4.7%** ▪ **BOTTLE SIZE 500 ml** ▪ **SERVE cool**
- **INGREDIENTS Maris Otter pale malt/crystal malt/chocolate malt/roasted barley extract/Challenger, Progress and Golding hops**

Cask XXXX Porter has been a favourite among local drinkers since 1981 but the brewery has only ever brewed it in the winter months. However, following its introduction in bottled form in November 2000, fans can now enjoy this dark brew at any time, as stocks bottled while the cask beer is in production should last through to the next winter run (November to February).

Tasting Notes

A near-black, dark ruby beer with an aroma of lightly roasted malt. Clean and tasty, it is easy to drink, with hints of orange and pleasantly bitter roasted notes, plus some sweetness throughout. Roasted malt and fruit feature in the dry, bittersweet aftertaste.

Major stockists Local Co-op

Fortyniner

- **ABV 4.9%** ▪ **BOTTLE SIZE 500 ml** ▪ **SERVE cool**
- **INGREDIENTS Maris Otter pale malt/crystal malt/ chocolate malt/Challenger, Progress and Golding hops**

Fortyniner first appeared in cask form in 1978, taking its name from its 1049 original gravity. This bottled version only made its debut in 1996 and was increased in strength from 4.8 to 4.9% in 1998.

Tasting Notes

Orange gold in colour, this beer has a lovely, zesty aroma of oranges and hops. Malty orange fruit is prominent in the mouth, with some sweetness, although bitterness increases as the hops kick in. The body is good and solid, but this is an easy drinking and deceptively strong ale. Dry, bitter orange peel finish.

Major stockists Safeway, Sainsbury, Tesco, local Co-op

ST AUSTELL

St Austell Brewery Company Ltd., 63 Trevarthian Road, St Austell, Cornwall PL25 4BY.
Tel. (01726) 74444 Fax (01726) 68965
E-mail: info@staustellbrewery.co.uk
Website: www.staustellbrewery.co.uk
Mail order service

St Austell joined the band of bottle-conditioned beer brewers in spring 2000, when it won the *Tesco Beer Challenge* with Clouded Yellow. The beer is brewed at St Austell but bottled by Hepworth & Co. in Horsham, where it is sterile filtered and re-seeded with its original yeast strain. The best before date is set at 12 months.

Clouded Yellow

■ ABV 4.8% ■ BOTTLE SIZE 500 ml ■ SERVE cold
■ INGREDIENTS Maris Otter pale malt/wheat malt/ Willamette hops/vanilla pods/cloves/coriander/ maple syrup

St Austell stages an annual Celtic Beer Festival, for which it prepared two novel brews in 1999. This beer, known as Hagar the Horrible at the time, was one. Brewer Roger Ryman popped down to his local supermarket to pick up the ingredients to make his vision of a German-style wheat beer become reality. He didn't want foreign yeast strains in his brewhouse, where there might be a chance of St Austell's own prized yeast becoming contaminated, and so set about recreating weissbier flavours artificially, by adding various spices to the beer after the boil, as it strained through the hops in the hop back. Vanilla pods, whole cloves and coriander seeds are the key flavourings, as well as maple syrup which is mixed with sugar for priming, and they blended together so well that Roger decided to submit the beer for the Tesco contest. Rave reviews followed. In June 2003, the beer was re-formulated. The alcohol was dropped to 4.8% from 5%, the clove content was reduced and a touch more vanilla (four pods per barrel) completed the revamp. For a while, this new format beer – re-packaged in a slender green bottle – was exclusive once again to Tesco. The name is shared with a rare butterfly, which, just like German wheat beers, is a popular continental visitor to Britain in summer. Drink with fragrant, lightly spiced foods such as a Thai curry, or a dessert like crème brûlée, Roger suggests. Acceptable to vegetarians.

Tasting Notes
A golden beer with rich banana and vanilla in the nose. Crisper and thinner than before, this new version still has plenty of banana and vanilla flavour, but noticeably less clove. Dry finish, with light banana and vanilla.

Major stockists Asda, Safeway, Tesco

SALOPIAN

The Salopian Brewing Company Ltd., The Brewery, 67 Mytton Oak Road, Shrewsbury, Shropshire SY3 8UQ. Tel. (01743) 248414 Fax (01743) 358866

Salopian began production in 1995. After closing briefly in 1997, it re-opened in new hands, retaining its inspiration, brewer Martin Barry. Bottle-conditioned beers were introduced in 1996 and were initially brewed on site. These were later brewed by Martin using the equipment at Hepworth & Co. and bottled there under contract, allowing the Shrewsbury brewery to focus on cask products. However, changes introduced in recent years in the way that beer duty is levied mean that tax concessions are no longer available on beer brewed under contract, and therefore large-scale bottling has been suspended temporarily. Plans are in place to resume bottling the following beers in small runs at Shrewsbury.

Proud Salopian

▪ABV 4.5% ▪BOTTLE SIZE 500 ml ▪SERVE cool
▪INGREDIENTS Maris Otter pale malt/crystal malt/ Fuggle, Golding and Styrian Golding hops

This ale was one of Salopian's first cask beers and has been sold in bottled form since 1996 (albeit initially under the name of Minsterley Ale). The current title is a reference to legendary Shropshire brewer Thomas Southam, who was known as the 'Proud Salopian'.

Tasting Notes

A dark copper-coloured ale with a big, fruity, slightly peppery aroma. The malty, fruity taste is reasonably sweet, but also features hoppy bitterness. A dry, hoppy, bitter fruit finish rounds off.

Gingersnap

▪ABV 4.7% ▪BOTTLE SIZE 500 ml ▪SERVE cool
▪INGREDIENTS Pale malt/crystal malt/pale chocolate malt/wheat malt/root ginger/East Kent Golding, Hersbrucker, Saaz and Styrian Golding hops

There's no mistaking the key ingredient of this brew. The ginger snaps out at you in the aroma and the initial taste but the acclaim the beer has received indicates that this is a better-balanced drink than most ginger-flavoured beers. It's actually a dark wheat beer (the mash is 40% wheat) with fresh root ginger added to the copper. Drink it cloudy and try it with chocolate or a dessert.

Tasting Notes

A bronze-coloured beer with a powerful ginger nose with some lemon in the background. The taste is surprisingly hoppy, a little citrous and ginger warm, with sound malt but little sweetness. Ginger warmth and bitterness fill the very dry finish.

Entire Butt

■ABV 4.8% ■BOTTLE SIZE 500 ml ■SERVE cool
■INGREDIENTS Maris Otter pale malt/crystal malt/dark crystal malt/amber malt/pale chocolate malt/dark chocolate malt/brown malt/black malt/lager malt/carapils malt/wheat malt/malted oats/roasted barley/torrefied wheat/Fuggle, Styrian Golding and Golding hops

Count the malts! This mammoth beer is a tribute to a beer style which originated nearly 300 years ago. In the early 1700s, drinkers favoured a blend of three beers – pale ale, brown ale and stock ale – laboriously drawn from three separate casks (or butts). A London brewer, Ralph Harwood, hit upon the idea of combining the three brews in one cask and gave it the name Entire Butt (the brew being entirely in one butt, so to speak). Its popularity with local street porters allegedly saw the new brew re-christened 'porter'.

Tasting Notes
Dark ruby with a mellow, lightly citrous, coffee/chocolate aroma. The full and smooth taste is deeply malty and fairly sweet, with citrous hop notes. Dry, bittersweet, malty finish.

Puzzle

■ABV 4.8% ■BOTTLE SIZE 500 ml ■SERVE cool
■INGREDIENTS Lager malt/wheat malt/ginger/coriander/orange peel/Saaz and Hersbrucker hops

According to brewer Martin Barry, Puzzle is the negative version of Jigsaw, a black wheat beer that Salopian produced for a few years, but which is no longer available. No finings are used in this intriguing brew, which is lagered for two weeks before bottling. Sixty per cent of the grist is wheat.

Tasting Notes
Hazy yellow, with a ginger, lemon and bitter orange nose. The taste has teasing citrous sharpness, peppery spiciness, orange peel bitterness and underlying ginger warmth. Dry, lemony, scented hop aftertaste, with a little burn from the ginger.

Firefly

■ABV 5% ■BOTTLE SIZE 500 ml ■SERVE cool
■INGREDIENTS Maris Otter pale malt/dark crystal malt/peated malt/Golding and Styrian Golding hops

Peated malt, which gives this beer an unusual smoky taste, is not liked by many brewers because, if used to excess, it can give the beer an antiseptic, 'TCP' edge. Martin seems to have hit the right balance in creating an ale that has more than a hint of Scotch whisky. The beer is usually bottle conditioned but it has been seen on sale in filtered form, too.

Tasting Notes

A bronze beer with a peaty, smoky nose. The same attributes come through in the taste, which also has full malt, citrous sharpness and fruity hop bitterness. Tangy, smoky, dry finish.

SCARECROW

Scarecrow Brewery Ltd., c/o Dairyman's Daughter, Arreton Barn, Newport Road, Arreton, Isle of Wight PO30 3AA. Tel. (01983) 856161

Scarecrow Brewery – set up by the lads at Ventnor Brewery – is located at Arreton Craft Village, a tourist magnet alongside the Dairyman's Daughter Inn, in the middle of the Isle of Wight. The 3.5-barrel brewery can be seen from the adjacent shop, which stocks beers from all the island's breweries.

Best

- **ABV 4.2%** ▪ **BOTTLE SIZE 500 ml** ▪ **SERVE cool**
- **INGREDIENTS Pale malt/crystal malt/wheat malt/ Bramling Cross hops**

The only beer to date from the brewery that uses the punning slogan 'Outstanding in our field' to advertise its presence. Apparently, this beer 'pulls the birds'.

Tasting Notes

A golden ale tasting bittersweet, malty and nutty, but with a spritzy hop kick. Dry, roasted nut, bitter finish.

SHARDLOW

Shardlow Brewing Co. Ltd., Old Brewery Stables, British Waterways Yard, Cavendish Bridge, Leicestershire DE72 2HL. Tel./Fax (01332) 799188

Shardlow Brewing was set up in 1993 and was taken over by its present ownership in 1996.

Best Bitter

- **ABV 3.9%** ▪ **BOTTLE SIZE 500 ml** ▪ **SERVE cool**
- **INGREDIENTS Maris Otter pale malt/crystal malt/ Phoenix and Golding hops**

Bottling of Shardlow's Best Bitter, like the others listed here, started at the end of 2003 (under contract at Leek Brewery), with bottles sold in the brewery's two pubs, local shops and at Chatsworth House.

Cavendish Gold

■ ABV 4.5% ■ BOTTLE SIZE 500 ml ■ SERVE cool
■ INGREDIENTS Maris Otter pale malt/Golding and Phoenix hops
A single malt brew, resulting in a premium pale bitter.

Narrowboat

■ ABV 4.5% ■ BOTTLE SIZE 500 ml ■ SERVE cool
■ INGREDIENTS Maris Otter pale malt/crystal malt/ Phoenix hops
A beer recalling Shardlow's history as the one-time busiest inland port in England (on the Trent and Mersey Canal).

Reverend Eaton's

■ ABV 4.5% ■ BOTTLE SIZE 500 ml ■ SERVE cool
■ INGREDIENTS Maris Otter pale malt/Golding and Phoenix hops
In the early 19th century, the site of the brewery once belonged to the Eaton family, one of whom was also the local vicar. He now gives his name to this dark golden ale which has been issued by Leek Brewery as part of its 'guest bottled ales' series.

Whistlestop

■ ABV 5% ■ BOTTLE SIZE 500 ml ■ SERVE cool
■ INGREDIENTS Maris Otter pale malt/Phoenix hops
A pale bitter reflecting Shardlow's proximity to the railway city of Derby.
Tasting Notes
A golden beer with fruit in the nose and taste, back by a soft malty sweetness. Dry, bittersweet, fruity-hop aftertaste.

Stedman Tipple

■ ABV 5.1% ■ BOTTLE SIZE 500 ml ■ SERVE cool
■ INGREDIENTS Maris Otter pale malt/crystal malt/dark crystal malt/Cascade hops
An occasional bottling of a beer that derives its name from Fabian Stedman, the 17th-century father of bellringing. One

of Shardlow's pubs, The Blue Bell at Melbourne, stands by a church that once hosted a round of a national campanology competition.

Tasting Notes

A light amber ale with malt and fruit in the aroma and taste, and a dry, bitter finish.

SHOES

Shoes Brewery, The Three Horse Shoes Inn, Norton Cannon, Hereford HR4 7BH.
Tel./Fax (01544) 318375

Three Horse Shoes landlord Frank Goodwin had been a home brewer long before deciding to brew for his own pub. His sole bottle-conditioned ale is sold in tiny numbers (no wholesaler calls, please!), and has smashed its way to the top of the list of the strongest beers featured in this book.

Farrier's Beer

- **ABV 15.2%** ▪ **BOTTLE SIZE 330 ml**
- **SERVE at room temperature**
- **INGREDIENTS Malt extract/sugar/Fuggle hops**

Farriers is bottled and labelled by Frank himself in very small quantities. He has now managed to raise the strength to a mighty 15.2%, up from the modest 13.4% dealt out by the beer when it was first brewed in 2000. Beware, therefore: this is not a beer for the faint-hearted. Even the brewery's yeast surrenders in the face of so much alcohol, which means Frank needs to finish off the fermentation with a wine yeast.

Tasting Notes

Amber, with an alcoholic nose. The taste is sweet and fiercely alcoholic, with estery almond notes and a persistent warmth. Warm, sweet, alcoholic finish with a sherry-like dryness.

SPRINGHEAD

Springhead Brewery, Old Great North Road, Sutton on Trent, Newark, Nottinghamshire NG23 6QS.
Tel. (01636) 821000 Fax (01636) 821150
E-mail: info@springhead.co.uk
Website: www.springhead.co.uk

Springhead – taking its name from a tidal bend in the River Trent – was founded in 1991 as the smallest brewery in Britain but has changed hands and moved premises since. It introduced bottle-conditioned beers in 1998, but, thanks to demand for cask beers, more or less stopped bottling in 2003. With new capacity added at the brewery, bottling is back on the agenda, with beers filled under contract by Leek Brewery.

Roundheads' Gold

■ ABV 4.4% ■ BOTTLE SIZE 500 ml ■ SERVE cool
■ INGREDIENTS Pale malt/Northdown and Saaz hops/wild honey

Most of Springhead's beer names have connections with the English Civil War, a legacy of brewery founder Alan Gill, who is a Civil War enthusiast (he now runs Broadstone Brewery). The Roundheads – members of Fairfax's New Model Army – fought on the Parliamentarian side and reputedly used their helmets as drinking vessels.

Tasting Notes
A golden beer with a spicy hop and honey nose. The taste is sweetish and malty with spicy hop and tart lemon overtones. Bitterness grows as hops develop in the finish, along with a honey softness and lemon.

The Leveller

■ ABV 5% ■ BOTTLE SIZE 500 ml ■ SERVE cool
■ INGREDIENTS Pale malt/amber malt/roasted malt/ Northdown hops

The Levellers were an extreme group of London-based Parliamentarians who advocated major constitutional changes, including the separation of the Church and State. The beer itself is in the style of a Belgian dubbel Trappist beer.

Tasting Notes
A beer the colour of burnished copper, with a malty, chocolatey, nutty and lightly smoky aroma. Although the taste is rich, malty and nutty, there is also a surprisingly tangy hop edge. The finish is dry, malty, nutty and notably hoppy.
Major stockist Local Waitrose

Roaring Meg

■ ABV 5.7% ■ BOTTLE SIZE 500 ml ■ SERVE cool
■ INGREDIENTS Pale malt/Northdown hops

This Belgian-influenced blonde ale is named after a huge cannon used by the Roundheads to destroy and capture Goodrich Castle, near Monmouth, in 1646.

Tasting Notes
A golden ale with a bready, perfumed aroma. The taste is

also bready, bitter and drying, with a light, malty sweetness and a touch of perfume and lemon from the hops. Dry, bitter, slightly chewy finish.
Major stockist Local Waitrose

Cromwell's Hat

- **ABV 6.2%** ▪ **BOTTLE SIZE 500 ml** ▪ **SERVE cool**
- **INGREDIENTS Pale malt/crystal malt/Northdown hops/ cinnamon/juniper**

Oliver Cromwell was finally offered the Crown 'to curtail his powers', but rejected it, preferring to keep his hat on his head instead – hence the name of this strong, spiced ale.

STORM

Storm Brewing Co., 2 Waterside, Macclesfield, Cheshire SK11 7HJ. Tel./Fax (01625) 431234
Storm Brewing was set up in 1998, with a little help from Brian Rides of Wickwar Brewery. It now supplies around 60 pubs in the Manchester/Cheshire/Peak District area with cask beer and has started sending beer to Leek Brewery for bottling within the last year.

Bosley Cloud

- **ABV 4.1%** ▪ **BOTTLE SIZE 500 ml** ▪ **SERVE cool**
- **INGREDIENTS Pale malt/lager malt/wheat malt/Cluster and Fuggle hops**

It fits in with Storm's weather theme, but Bosley Cloud is actually named after a rocky outcrop near the brewery's home in Macclesfield.

Tasting Notes
A golden ale with a modest malt aroma but plenty of taste. Sweetish orange fruit and a little counter-bitterness from hops ensure a crisp, light drink, with a drying, increasingly bitter and hoppy finish.

Ale Force

- **ABV 4.2%** ▪ **BOTTLE SIZE 500 ml** ▪ **SERVE cool**
- **INGREDIENTS Pale malt/crystal malt/chocolate malt/ Fuggle hops**

Storm's first ever brew, Ale Force made its debut in cask form in 1998. As for the other Storm entries, bottles are simply filled from the cask, maintaining the same yeast used in primary fermentation, with best before dates set at nine months.

Tasting Notes

A copper ale with an aroma of malt, oranges and a pinch of chocolate. The taste is full of earthy hops but quite sweet and fruity behind, while the hoppy, drying, bitter finish has hints of dark malt.

Silk of Amnesia

- **ABV 4.7%** ▪ **BOTTLE SIZE 500 ml** ▪ **SERVE cool**
- **INGREDIENTS Pale malt/crystal malt/chocolate malt/ Cluster and Fuggle hops**

Like Bosley Cloud, this brew incorporates American Cluster hops. Its name, an obvious play on words with a well-known dyspepsia remedy, also reflects Macclesfield's former importance as a major silk industry centre.

Tasting Notes

A deep amber beer, toffee-flavoured from nose to finish, yet not sweet, with a sharp, balancing bitterness in the taste and a dry, bitter finish.

STRANGFORD LOUGH

Strangford Lough Brewing Company Ltd., Braidleigh Lodge, 22 Shore Road, Killyleagh, Co. Down BT30 9UE.
Tel. (02844) 821461 Fax (02844) 821273
E-mail: office@slbc.ie
Website: www.slbc.ie

A new enterprise founded by two management consultants who have started to build brands without running to the cost of setting up a brewery. The beers listed (introduced in May 2004) are contract brewed and are themed around the area of Northern Ireland's Strangford Lough, burial place of Magnus, King of Norway from 1093, one of the area's early invaders. Also buried close by is St Patrick, and a series of beers related to his story is scheduled. Plans are also in hand to have Strangford beers contract brewed in the USA, too.

Barelegs Brew

- **ABV 4.5%** ▪ **BOTTLE SIZE 500 ml** ▪ **SERVE cool**
- **INGREDIENTS Pale malt/lager malt/caramalt/flaked maize/Northern Brewer, First Gold and Perle hops**

Barelegs was the nickname of Magnus, who was killed in battle near the lough and buried on Downpatrick Marshes in

1103. His Viking ship is seen approaching on the label.

Tasting Notes

A pale golden ale with a big lemon-lime aroma. The crisp, bittersweet taste is lightly warming, a tangy mix of hop fruit and malt. Dry, gently bitter, hoppy aftertaste.

Legbiter

■ ABV 4.8% ■ BOTTLE SIZE 500 ml ■ SERVE cool
■ INGREDIENTS Lager malt/caramalt/flaked maize/ Northern Brewer, First Gold, Golding and Styrian Golding hops

Legbiter was the name of Magnus's trusty sword, said to have been adorned with ivory and gold-thread.

Tasting Notes

This pale golden premium ale has a clean aroma of succulent fruit. Tangy hops lead in the mouth, but sweet malt is in support, along with fruit. Hoppy, tangy, bitter, drying finish.

SUTHWYK

Suthwyk Ales, Offwell Farm, Southwick, Fareham, Hampshire PO17 6DX. Tel./Fax (023) 9232 5252
E-mail: mjbazeley@suthwykales.com
Website: www.suthwykales.com
Mail order service

Suthwyk Ales does not brew itself. It is run by barley farmer Martin Bazeley, who decided to go the whole hog and complete the 'field to table' cycle by commissioning a beer brewed from malt kilned by Warminster Maltings from his own Optic barley. Produced by Hop Back Brewery, Skew Sunshine Ale proved to be a hit and was followed up by a second offering, Bloomfields, and then a third, Liberation. The beers – with best before dates set at 12 months – are still bottled by Hop Back but are brewed now by Oakleaf Brewing, in Gosport. All are also available in cask form.

Bloomfields

■ ABV 3.8% ■ BOTTLE SIZE 500 ml ■ SERVE cool
■ INGREDIENTS Optic pale malt/crystal malt/Challenger, Fuggle and Golding hops

Sidney Bloomfield was the man who tended Martin's land back in the 1920s, dying at the tender age of 40 in 1926 – a sad consequence perhaps of the fact that the 700 acres in his care were farmed only with horsepower. One field on the estate still bears his name and it is here that the barley that is turned into crystal malt for this session ale is grown (and, according to the label, blessed with evening sunshine and chalky soil).

Tasting Notes

A golden ale with spicy hop and malt leading in the aroma, but melon and citrous fruitiness emerging later. Spicy and very drinkable, it tastes crisp and clean, with good backing malt sweetness and a light melon and peach fruitiness. The dry, bitter and fruity finish turns hoppy.

Liberation

■ ABV 4.2% ■ BOTTLE SIZE 500 ml ■ SERVE cool
■ INGREDIENTS Optic pale malt/crystal malt/Liberty hops

Launched to commemorate the 60th anniversary of D-Day, on 6 June 2004. Montgomery and Eisenhower planned Operation Overlord (the D-Day offensive) in nearby Southwick House and enjoyed a pint or two from the local Hunt's brewery, which closed in 1957, after their talks. The label shows the military masterminds examining a bottle of Liberation.

Tasting Notes

A pale golden beer with a fresh, citrussy, hoppy nose, becoming a touch biscuity. The light, bittersweet, slightly perfumed taste makes it very quaffable. Hoppy, drying finish.

Skew Sunshine Ale

■ ABV 4.6% ■ BOTTLE SIZE 500 ml ■ SERVE cool
■ INGREDIENTS Optic pale malt/Challenger hops

The barley malted for this premium ale is grown in what is known as Skew Field, on Portsdown Hill. The field faces south and catches the sun – hence the beer's name.

Tasting Notes

A pale golden ale with a creamy, malty, lightly fruity nose with a hint of sulphur. Light-bodied and fairly spritzy, it tastes citrus-fruity with lightly scented hops crisping up smooth malt. Bitter, fruity, hoppy finish.

SUTTON

Sutton Brewing Company, Stokeley Barton Farm, Stokenham, Kingsbridge, Devon TQ7 2SE.
Tel./Fax (01548) 581151

Sutton Brewery was built alongside Plymouth's Thistle Park Tavern in 1993 and began production the following year. The first bottle-conditioned beer appeared in spring 2001 and is bottled for Sutton by Keltek Brewery. In 2004 the brewery moved to Stokenham and bottling was suspended for a while, with plans to resume in the winter.

Madiba Stout

- **ABV 5%** ▪ **BOTTLE SIZE 500 ml** ▪ **SERVE cool**
- **INGREDIENTS Maris Otter pale malt/crystal malt/ chocolate malt/black malt/roasted malt/wheat malt/ Bramling Cross hops**

Nelson Mandela features on the label of this stout, the name 'Madiba' being an African word meaning 'old father who is respected and wise'. The South African connection is via the brewery's owner, Quintin Style, who hails from the country.

Tasting Notes

This dark ruby stout has a roasted, fruity-hoppy aroma, followed by a nicely rounded, bittersweet, fruity taste, with plenty of dark grain flavour, and then a bittersweet, fruity, roasted finish.

TEIGNWORTHY

Teignworthy Brewery, The Maltings, Teign Road, Newton Abbot, Devon TQ12 4AA.
Tel./Fax (01626) 332066
Mail order service (via Tucker's Maltings)

Teignworthy Brewery was founded in 1994 with a 15-barrel plant by former Oakhill and Ringwood brewer John Lawton, using part of the historic Victorian malthouse of Edward Tucker & Sons. (Tucker's Maltings is now a fascinating tourist attraction, enjoyed by thousands of holidaymakers each year.) The bottled beers are the same as John's cask beers, except that usually they are filtered and re-pitched with new yeast. A 12-month best before date is marked on each bottle.

Reel Ale/Edwin Tucker's Devonshire Prize Ale

- **ABV 4%** ▪ **BOTTLE SIZE 500 ml** ▪ **SERVE cool**
- **INGREDIENTS Maris Otter pale malt/crystal malt/ Willamette, Golding, Bramling Cross and Challenger hops**

Reel Ale is Teignworthy's standard cask bitter. When bottle conditioned, it is sold under the same name and also as Edwin Tucker's Devonshire Prize Ale in the Tucker's Maltings bottled beer shop, largely as an attempt to catch the eye of the many holidaymakers the Maltings attracts.

Tasting Notes

An orange/gold-coloured beer with a dry flavour of orange fruit, malt and hops, preceded by a gentle aroma of fruit, malt and orangey hops. Moderately dry, bitter orange finish.

Spring Tide

- **ABV 4.3%** ▪ **BOTTLE SIZE 500 ml** ▪ **SERVE cool**
- **INGREDIENTS Maris Otter pale malt/crystal malt/ Willamette, Golding, Bramling Cross and Challenger hops**

Named after the high tides that wash up the Teign estuary close to the brewery, this best bitter is brewed every four months or so.

Tasting Notes

A crisp, refreshing and enjoyable, copper beer with a zesty orange nose. Fruit and malt continue into the taste, which has a light, citrous hop balance and grassy, herbal notes. Dry, bitter orange finish.

Major stockist Local Tesco

Old Moggie

- **ABV 4.4%** ▪ **BOTTLE SIZE 500 ml** ▪ **SERVE cool**
- **INGREDIENTS Maris Otter pale malt/crystal malt/wheat malt/torrefied wheat/Golding, Bramling Cross and Fuggle hops**

Forget brewery cats: this beer, first brewed in January 2000, is named after the Morris Minor motor car owned by former underbrewer Mark Bayley and is a tribute to the heyday of the British motor trade. The beer may appear hazy in the glass, as it is not fined (and therefore acceptable to vegans).

Tasting Notes

An amber ale with a fruity, malty aroma. In the mouth it is toffeeish and malty-sweet with a fruity hop balance. The finish is also sweet and malty, with light hop-fruit.

Beachcomber

- **ABV 4.5%** ▪ **BOTTLE SIZE 500 ml** ▪ **SERVE cool**
- **INGREDIENTS Maris Otter pale malt/Willamette, Golding, Bramling Cross and Challenger hops**

Described as a lager on the label, Beachcomber was devised as a pale beer for swigging at barbecues on warm summer evenings. A bottom-fermenting yeast is used and bottles are now prepared approximately every four months.

Tasting Notes

A golden beer with a rich, citrous hop nose with sweet malt behind. The full taste combines light malt and excellent hoppiness with hints of blackcurrant. Bittersweet, hoppy, slightly tart finish.

Major stockist Local Tesco

Harvey's Special Brew

- **ABV 4.6%** - **BOTTLE SIZE 500 ml** - **SERVE cool**
- **INGREDIENTS Pale malt/crystal malt/wheat malt/ Golding and Fuggle hops**

First brewed to celebrate the birth of John and Rachel Lawton's son, Harvey, on 8 April 2000 – hence the Baby Crockett lookalike character on the blue label.

Tasting Notes

An orange-gold beer with an aroma of bitter orange peel. The taste is fruity with silky malt and bitter orange peel notes throughout. Dry, bitter fruit finish.

Amy's Ale

- **ABV 4.8%** - **BOTTLE SIZE 500 ml** - **SERVE cool**
- **INGREDIENTS Pale malt/crystal malt/wheat malt/ Bramling Cross and Golding hops**

A beer named after the Lawtons' first child (who drew the label, by the look of it), brewed first in March 2003.

Tasting Notes

A light amber beer with a floral, honeyed aroma backed with soft malt. The taste is equally flowery, with hints of sweet tropical and citrus fruits. Pleasantly bitter, gently fruity finish.

Maltster's Ale

- **ABV 5%** - **BOTTLE SIZE 500 ml** - **SERVE cool**
- **INGREDIENTS Maris Otter pale malt/crystal malt/ Willamette, Golding, Bramling Cross and Challenger hops**

This was a innovative brew when first prepared in 1996, as it used the new barley strain Regina, but John has now switched to Maris Otter. The beer is sold on draught in winter and is bottled twice a year.

Tasting Notes

A mellow, bronze beer that lives up to its name with a malty nose that features traces of treacle and citrus. Richly malty in the mouth, it is finely balanced by lemony hops and pear drop flavour. The pleasant aftertaste is gentle, dry and bittersweet.

Martha's Mild

- **ABV 5.3%** - **BOTTLE SIZE 500 ml** - **SERVE cool**
- **INGREDIENTS Pale malt/crystal malt/amber malt/chocolate malt/wheat malt/Fuggle and Golding hops**

Another baby celebration, this time for Martha, born on 27 March 2002. On the label, John declares that he brewed it as a tonic for Rachel when she was feeding the baby. The beer is now inked in as a regular brew for May.

Tasting Notes

A deep ruby, strong mild with an aroma of coffeeish, biscuity malt. The taste is smooth and quite sweet, with oily roasted malt notes and a hint of hop fruit. Bitterness increases and roasted flavour persists in the aftertaste.

Edwin Tucker's Maris Otter

- **ABV 5.5%** - **BOTTLE SIZE 500 ml** - **SERVE cool**
- **INGREDIENTS Maris Otter pale malt/crystal malt/wheat malt/Willamette, Golding, Bramling Cross and Challenger hops**

First produced in 1998, as a tribute to the most highly regarded strain of malting barley ('the master brewer's choice around the world'), Maris Otter is part of Edwin Tucker's 'Premium Malt Selection' series, although no other such beers have yet arrived.

Tasting Notes

A dark copper beer with an estery (bananas and pear drops), malty nose. Rich and malty in the mouth, with estery fruit and a hint of lemon, it is smooth and clean tasting. Bitter hops come through to provide a pleasant, bittersweet finish with a hint of liquorice.

Christmas Cracker

- **ABV 6%** - **BOTTLE SIZE 500 ml** - **SERVE cool**
- **INGREDIENTS Maris Otter pale malt/crystal malt/Willamette, Golding, Bramling Cross and Challenger hops**

This strong seasonal brew is also sold in cask form.

Tasting Notes

A malty nose preludes a malty, fruity beer with balancing bitterness. Malty, bitter finish. Red-brown in colour.

Edwin Tucker's East India Pale Ale

- **ABV 6.5%** ▪ **BOTTLE SIZE 500 ml** ▪ **SERVE cool**
- **INGREDIENTS East India malt/wheat malt/Bramling Cross and Golding hops**

This well-researched replica of a true India pale ale – bursting with hops and packing the alcoholic punch such beers needed in order to cope with the long sea journey to India – includes malt specially kilned to match the colour of malt used in the Empire days (close to the colour of lager malt).

Tasting Notes

A copper ale with a relatively modest, orangey aroma, but a crisp, zingy, orange-hoppy taste, well balanced with a little sweetness. The same orangey hops add bitterness in the lingering, dry, lipsmacking finish.

Edwin Tucker's Celebrated Arctic Ale

- **ABV 9%** ▪ **BOTTLE SIZE 275 ml** ▪ **SERVE cool**
- **INGREDIENTS Maris Otter pale malt/crystal malt/ Bramling Cross, Golding and Challenger hops**

Like the other Edwin Tucker ales, this beer's label is enhanced by a faded old photograph of the man himself. This beer is a throwback to Edwin Tucker's times, inspired by the creation of the first ever arctic ale in 1852. Brian Gates, who runs Tucker's excellent bottled beer shop, discovered the beer in the records of 19th-century brewing historian Alfred Barnard, who recalled how Allsopp's in Burton had produced a special brew for the voyage of *HMS Assistance* to the frozen North. On the journey, despite freezing at one point, the beer proved to be a 'great blessing' to the crew, according to ship's captain Sir Edward Belcher. Brian and John Lawton together came up with this recipe (which involves a six-and-a-quarter-hour copper boil and generous quantities of crystal malt and hops) to give an indication of how the arctic ale might have tasted.

Tasting Notes

A cherry-coloured ale with hops giving a peppery fruitiness to the malty aroma. Not as full bodied as expected, but with a good smack of peppery, fruity bitterness throughout.

Edwin Tucker's Empress Russian Porter

- **ABV 10.5%** ▪ **BOTTLE SIZE 275 ml** ▪ **SERVE cool**
- **INGREDIENTS Maris Otter pale malt/chocolate malt/oat malt/roasted barley/Willamette, Golding, Bramling Cross and Challenger hops**

This re-creation of the Baltic porter style was necessitated in part by the demise of the classic Courage Imperial Russian Stout, once sold in the Tucker's beer shop. It's the sort of strong, warming brew that was shipped to Russia during the 18th and 19th centuries and became known for its medicinal qualities. The beer is not produced every year, but has come out in 1998, 2000, 2001 and 2003.

Tasting Notes

(1998 vintage, tasted after one year) A mellow, very dark brown beer with caramel and fruit in the nose. Thick, smooth and sweetish on the palate, it has a creamy rum-and-raisin toffee taste with orange-citrus flavours and gentle roasted, bitter notes. Dry, lingering, deep and warming finish, with caramel, toffee and fruit balancing a gentle bitterness.
(2000 vintage, tasted after six months) Near-black, with malt, polished leather and coffee in the nose. The taste is sweetish and deep: strong hops for bitterness, coffee and a little fruit, with persistent malt. Sweetish, roasted, hoppy finish.

TEME VALLEY

Teme Valley Brewery, The Talbot, Knightwick, Worcestershire WR6 5PH.
Tel. (01886) 821235 Fax (01886) 821060
E-mail: temevalley@aol.com
Website: www.the-talbot.co.uk
Mail order service

The Talbot Inn at Knightwick is owned by the Clift family, who farmed hops locally from the 19th century to the year 2000. The hops they cultivated are still used in the pub's brewery, which was set up in 1997. Brewer Chris Gooch produces a range of cask and bottled beers to the same recipes, but beer for bottling is fermented with a dried, bottom-fermenting yeast which remains in the beer when it is bottled straight from cask by Integrated Bottling Solutions. New labels have been introduced in the past year.

This

- **ABV 3.7%** ▪ **BOTTLE SIZE 500 ml** ▪ **SERVE cool**
- **INGREDIENTS Pale malt/chocolate malt/wheat malt/ Challenger, Fuggle and Golding hops**

The Talbot Inn's own wine list has included, since spring 2003, a 'Beer and Food' page, suggesting ideal matches for Teme Valley beers. Here, This is recommended as the ideal accompaniment for sandwiches or a ploughman's lunch.

Tasting Notes
A golden beer with malt and hop-fruit in the nose. The taste balances silky malt, fruit and crisp, but only moderately bitter, hops before a dry, bitter, hoppy finish with a hint of roast.

The Hop Nouvelle

- **ABV 4.1%** ▪ **BOTTLE SIZE 500 ml** ▪ **SERVE cool**
- **INGREDIENTS Pale malt/wheat malt/Golding and First Gold hops**

Brewed once a year, time permitting, during the hop harvest, this is an ale equivalent to wine's Beaujolais Nouveau. The hops are plucked from bines less than half a mile from the brewery and, within the hour, without kilning, are cast green into the copper, delivering a sappier, more resin-like flavour to the beer than standard dried hops. Chris has now expanded the idea to include two further green-hop beers (see below). They are all showcased (alongside cask beers) at The Talbot's green-hop beer festival each October.

Tasting Notes
(*2003 version*) A pale golden beer with a sappy, sweet-lemon aroma. Delicate malt leads in the mouth, overlaid with a sappy, pea-pod hop dominance which has lemon undertones. There's a little burnt flavour in the finish, but bitterness and sappy, green-hop flavours dominate.

Lulsley Court

- **ABV 4.1%** ▪ **BOTTLE SIZE 500 ml** ▪ **SERVE cool**
- **INGREDIENTS Pale malt/chocolate malt/wheat malt/ Pilgrim and Golding hops**

At Lusley Court (formerly the Clift family's hop garden), they had never grown Pilgrim hops before. Brewer Chris Gooch had never brewed with Pilgrim before, either, so this beer was a voyage of adventure, especially as all the hops were green.

Tasting Notes
(*2003 version*) A bitter beer with lots of hop tang and a bite of burnt flavour on the swallow. There's a hint of bubblegum alongside the spicy hop in the aroma, and the finish is dry, bitter and hoppy.

Northdown Nouvelle

- **ABV 4.1%** ▪ **BOTTLE SIZE 500 ml** ▪ **SERVE cool**
- **INGREDIENTS Pale malt/crystal malt/wheat malt/ Northdown hops**

A further green hop beer, showcasing the Worcestershire

Northdown hop, which is becoming harder to source (this batch, as it happens, was grown only 500 yards from the brewery).

Tasting Notes

(*2003 version*) A pale golden beer with lemon-citrus hop notes and light, biscuity malt in the aroma. Robust, tangy, sappy, hop character overlays a light malt base in the mouth, becoming dry, bitter and hoppy in the finish.

That

■ABV 4.1% ■BOTTLE SIZE 500 ml ■SERVE cool
■INGREDIENTS Pale malt/crystal malt/wheat malt/ roasted barley/Challenger and Fuggle hops

A perfect match for stews or game dishes, according to The Talbot's beer menu, the hop bitterness lightening rich sauces and gravies.

Tasting Notes

A malty, lemony aroma paves the way for this amber ale. Hops lie over a clean, nutty, malty base in the taste, with lemon notes emerging. Dry, hoppy, bitter finish with again a trace of lemon.

Wotever Next?

■ABV 5% ■BOTTLE SIZE 500 ml ■SERVE cool
■INGREDIENTS Pale malt/crystal malt/chocolate malt/ wheat malt/Northdown and Fuggle hops

The complex fruit and roasted malt flavours of Wotever Next? are suggested as the ideal partners for a dessert like a rich chocolate pudding or gateau. Although produced once (in 1999) in cask, it is now only sold in bottled form.

Tasting Notes

A tawny ale with fruit in the nose (lemon and blackcurrant). Hop fruit dominates the taste and runs into the drying, bitter finish where roasted malt lingers.

Hearth Warmer

■ABV 6% ■BOTTLE SIZE 500 ml ■SERVE cool
■INGREDIENTS Pale malt/crystal malt/chocolate malt/ wheat malt/roasted barley/Northdown and Fuggle hops

For Christmas 2002 Teme Valley's Christmas beer, Wass Ale, was made available in bottle, but now this has been renamed Hearth Warmer and is being sold at other times of the year. Since its debut on draught in 1997, the beer has been aged in casks every year for eight or nine months. Sip a glass instead of a port, suggests brewer Chris Gooch.

Tasting Notes

A red beer with almonds at first in the aroma then fruit and malt. Sweetish and reasonably fruity, it has a smooth malt base and a bittersweet, malty, fruity finish with roasted grain.

TINDALL

Tindall Ales, Toad Lane, Seething, Norfolk NR35 2EQ.
Tel. (01508) 483844
E-mail: greenangela5@aol.com

Tindall Ales is a family-run business founded in 1998 close to historic Tindall Wood (hence its name). In 2002, Tindall moved to new premises in a former stable block, just outside the village of Seething. Bottling began in 1999 and all the beers are kräusened before filling. Best before dates are set at four months later.

Summer Loving

- **ABV 3.6%** ■ **BOTTLE SIZE 500 ml** ■ **SERVE cool**
- **INGREDIENTS Maris Otter and Fanfare pale malt/Mount Hood hops**

Only brewed June–September, Summer Loving is designed as a refreshing summer beer, and is seasoned with American hops. The brewers suggest it's the sort of beer to drink with Mediterranean food.

Tasting Notes

A clean and quaffable, golden beer with a fresh, hoppy aroma and plenty of taste for its strength, balancing fruity hop (light bitter orange) and malt sweetness. Gentle, hoppy, dry aftertaste.

Best Bitter

- **ABV 3.7%** ■ **BOTTLE SIZE 500 ml** ■ **SERVE cool**
- **INGREDIENTS Maris Otter and Halcyon pale malt/Golding hops**

Like the other bottled beers, Best Bitter – Tindall's first ever beer – is also available in cask form.

Tasting Notes

A very drinkable, copper ale with a hoppy, lightly perfumed nose and plenty of tangy hops and light orange-fruit in the taste. Dry, hoppy finish. Lots of flavour for its strength.

Mild

■ **ABV 3.7%** ■ **BOTTLE SIZE 500 ml** ■ **SERVE cool**
■ **INGREDIENTS Halcyon and Maris Otter pale malt/crystal malt/chocolate malt/Golding and Fuggle hops**

The bottled version of a popular cask dark mild.

Tasting Notes

Attractively ruby in the glass, Tindall's Mild has an aroma of soft, dark malts. The smooth malt and gentle fruit continue in the bittersweet taste, with more fruit arriving on the swallow. Dry, bittersweet finish, with hops emerging.

Liberator

■ **ABV 3.8%** ■ **BOTTLE SIZE 500 ml** ■ **SERVE cool**
■ **INGREDIENTS Maris Otter and Pearl pale malt/Cascade hops**

Tindall's new brewery stands opposite Seething USAAF air base, home to the 448 Bombardment (H) Group and their Liberator aircraft from 1943 to 1948 – hence the name of this American-hopped bitter, which the brewer thinks goes well with a curry.

Tasting Notes

A golden ale with an aroma of hops and juicy fruit. The crisp taste is hoppy, tangily fruity and bittersweet, although bitterness gradually takes over, leading to a dry, bitter finish.

Resurrection

■ **ABV 3.8%** ■ **BOTTLE SIZE 500 ml** ■ **SERVE cool**
■ **INGREDIENTS Halcyon pale malt/Cascade hops**

A session beer infused with American hops, launched at Easter 1999, as implied by its name.

Alltime

■ **ABV 4%** ■ **BOTTLE SIZE 500 ml** ■ **SERVE cool**
■ **INGREDIENTS Maris Otter and Halcyon pale malt/Golding hops**

An unusually-named beer, with a clock-face label. This was a seasonal cask beer brought back permanently because of demand, and hence now available 'alltime'.

Tasting Notes

A chestnut-coloured beer with a lightly toffeeish, malty aroma. The same malt and toffee feature in the taste, with a gentle fruitiness behind, before a moderate, malty and increasingly hoppy finish.

Christmas Cheers

■ **ABV 4%** ■ **BOTTLE SIZE 500 ml** ■ **SERVE cool**
■ **INGREDIENTS Maris Otter and Halcyon pale malt/crystal malt/Golding hops**

Available in December, Christmas Cheers is one of the more quaffable festive beers, at a modest 4%.

Ditchingham Dam

■ **ABV 4.2%** ■ **BOTTLE SIZE 500 ml** ■ **SERVE cool**
■ **INGREDIENTS Maris Otter pale malt/roasted malt/ chocolate malt/Golding and Mount Hood hops/ liquorice/ginger**

A spiced premium ale, taking its name from an area near the brewery. Ditchingham Dam was a scene of some controversy in 2000 when the local authority proposed to cull the wild chickens that roamed the area, considering them to be a danger to road users. (The chickens had lost their earlier home near Simpson's Maltings when it burned down.) The brewery stepped in and offered to give £5 for every firkin sold of this beer to provide signs to warn motorists of the hazard, and the chickens were saved. Note the picture of a rooster on the label.

Tasting Notes
A red beer with a fruity, herbal aroma. The taste is fruity, herbal and finely balances bitterness and sweetness, with traces of lemon-ginger throughout. Dry, bitter, herbal finish.

Extra

■ **ABV 4.5%** ■ **BOTTLE SIZE 500 ml** ■ **SERVE cool**
■ **INGREDIENTS Maris Otter and Halcyon pale malt/ Golding hops**

The brewery's second ever beer, with extra colour, extra flavour and extra strength. It bears much the same label as Best Bitter, featuring a bird on a twig, except the border around the picture is red instead of green.

Norfolk 'n' Good

■ **ABV 4.6%** ■ **BOTTLE SIZE 500 ml** ■ **SERVE cool**
■ **INGREDIENTS Halcyon pale malt/Cascade hops**

Be careful how you ask for this stronger version of the 3.8% Resurrection! The risqué name is derived from a song popular with a local folk band, who have now written a new last verse specifically about the beer.

Tasting Notes
Dark golden with a floral, peppery hop aroma. Floral hops and soft malt combine in the mouth for a good bittersweet balance. Hops eventually take over and lead in the dry finish.

Norwich Dragon

- **ABV 4.6%** ■ **BOTTLE SIZE 500 ml** ■ **SERVE cool**
- **INGREDIENTS Halcyon pale malt/Cascade and Golding hops**

A new premium ale named after Norwich's Dragon Hall, a 13th-century merchant's hall that was rediscovered in the 1970s and is said to be the only building of its type still surviving in western Europe.

Honey Do

- **ABV 5%** ■ **BOTTLE SIZE 330 ml** ■ **SERVE cool**
- **INGREDIENTS Halcyon pale malt/Cascade hops/honey**

A Norwich Beer Festival award-winner, laced with clear honey.

Tasting Notes
A dark golden beer with honey leading over malt in the aroma. The taste is bittersweet, with a honeyed softness, but with enough hop character to prevent it from cloying. Slightly warming, bittersweet finish with the mellowness of honey.

TITANIC

The Titanic Brewery, Unit 5, Callender Place, Lingard Street, Burslem, Stoke-on-Trent, Staffordshire ST6 1JL.
Tel. (01782) 823447 Fax (01782) 812349
E-mail: titanic@titanicbrewery.co.uk
Website: www.titanicbrewery.co.uk

This brewery, named in honour of the *Titanic*'s Captain Smith, who hailed from Stoke, was founded in 1985 but fell into difficulties until rescued by the present owners. A move to larger premises took place in 1992 and new brewing plant was installed in 1995. The brewery moved yet again in 2002.

Stout

- **ABV 4.5%** ■ **BOTTLE SIZE 500 ml** ■ **SERVE cool**
- **INGREDIENTS Maris Otter pale malt/wheat malt/ roasted barley/Northdown, Willamette and Golding hops**

Titanic Stout (also a cask beer) was the winner of *The Guardian's Best Bottle-Conditioned Beer* in 1994, although the recipe has been tweaked a little since, removing crystal malt and replacing it with a greater quantity of roasted barley. Stylish new labels arrived in 2003. The beer is now brewed at Titanic but bottled by Hepworth & Co. in Horsham and carries a best before date of 16 months. A West Midlands CAMRA gold award-winner in 2003.

Tasting Notes

A deep ruby beer with coffee and a whiff of liquorice in the biscuity nose. Bitter roasted grain leads in the mouth, but there is a slightly fruity, malty sweetness, too. Smoky coffee, nut and smooth roasted bitterness feature in the finish.

Major stockist Local Sainsbury

Christmas Ale

- **ABV 7.2%** ■ **BOTTLE SIZE 330 ml** ■ **SERVE cool**
- **INGREDIENTS Maris Otter pale malt/crystal malt/wheat malt/invert sugar/Galena and Golding hops**

Christmas Ale is a bottled version of Titanic's strong ale, Wreckage (7.2%). Only small runs are produced each year, with the bottle size likely to vary. The most recent batch was bottled at Hobsons Brewery.

Tasting Notes

A red beer with a deeply fruity, alcoholic nose. Slightly tart in the mouth, it is fruity, malty and fairly sweet, with a warming, sweetish, malt and fruit finish.

UNCLE STUART'S

Uncle Stuart's Brewery, Antoma, Pack Lane, Lingwood, Norwich, Norfolk NR13 4PD. Tel. (01603) 716998
E-mail: stuartsbrewery@aol.com
Mail order service

Stuart Evans has been brewing bottled beers in very small quantities at his home in beautiful rural Norfolk since spring 2002. His brewplant is only capable of turning out 100 litres at a time.

Pack Lane

- **ABV 4%** ■ **BOTTLE SIZE 500 ml** ■ **SERVE cool**
- **INGREDIENTS Pale malt/crystal malt/black malt/chocolate malt/Golding and Progress hops**

A mild, brewed weekly, like the other beers, and named after the lane that is home to the brewery. Best before dates for this and the other beers are set at one year.

Tasting Notes

A light-drinking, red-brown ale with a malty, herbal, lightly fruity aroma. The taste and the aftertaste are both sweet and malty.

Excelsior

- **ABV 4.5%** ▪ **BOTTLE SIZE 500 ml** ▪ **SERVE cool**
- **INGREDIENTS Pale malt/crystal malt/Golding and Progress hops**

A beer that recalls in its name a fishing smack on which Stuart's grandfather worked and which is still used today by a charity trust.

Tasting Notes

A dark golden beer with piney hops in the nose and taste, which is light-bodied and backed with a gentle sweetness. Piney, bittersweet finish.

Church View

- **ABV 4.7%** ▪ **BOTTLE SIZE 500 ml** ▪ **SERVE cool**
- **INGREDIENTS Pale malt/crystal malt/Progress and Golding hops**

Each of Stuart's bottled beers is first matured in, and then filled from, a cask, with the addition of priming sugars to ensure good carbonation. A percentage of the proceeds from this brew is donated to a fund for the extension of the local church.

Tasting Notes

A red beer with a herbal (minty), malty character, right from the aroma, through the bittersweet taste to the finish.

Buckenham Woods

- **ABV 5.6%** ▪ **BOTTLE SIZE 500 ml** ▪ **SERVE cool**
- **INGREDIENTS Pale malt/crystal malt/flaked maize/ Golding and Progress hops**

A dark, strong bitter, with a name derived from a local beauty spot.

Tasting Notes

A deep ruby-coloured beer with a malty, biscuity, herbal aroma. The taste is also malty and herbal, with a touch of coffee, the same flavours carrying through into the bittersweet aftertaste.

Strumpshaw Fen

- **ABV 5.7%** ■ **BOTTLE SIZE 500 ml** ■ **SERVE cool**
- **INGREDIENTS Pale malt/crystal malt/Progress and Golding hops**

A beer named after a local RSPB nature reserve.

Tasting Notes

Dark golden, this is another beer with a herbal aroma, mixed with malt and fruit. The sweet, fruity taste is followed by a sweet, malty finish. Modest body for its strength.

Christmas Ale

- **ABV 7%** ■ **BOTTLE SIZE 500 ml** ■ **SERVE cool**
- **INGREDIENTS Pale malt/crystal malt/black malt/ Progress and Golding hops**

A strong old ale, sold only between October and January.

VALE

Vale Brewery Company, Thame Road,
Haddenham, Buckinghamshire HP17 8BY.
Tel. (01844) 290008 Fax (01844) 292505
E-mail: valebrewery@yahoo.co.uk
Website: www.valebrewery.co.uk
Mail order service

Vale Brewery was opened in 1995 by brothers Mark and Phil Stevens, both of whom had previously worked for other breweries and related industries. Their brewery is housed in an industrial unit on the fringe of one of the most attractive villages in Buckinghamshire. The brewplant was expanded in 1996 and bottling began a year later. All the beers are matured in casks, filtered, primed with sweet wort and re-seeded with fresh yeast. Best before dates are set at six months. 'Own label' bottles are also supplied for individual customers. All beers are vegan friendly.

Black Swan Dark Mild

- **ABV 3.3%** ■ **BOTTLE SIZE 500 ml** ■ **SERVE cool**
- **INGREDIENTS Maris Otter pale malt/crystal malt/ roasted barley/Golding and Fuggle hops**

Bottle-conditioned milds are extremely rare, as conventional wisdom has it that more alcohol is needed for the beer to mature and survive in the bottle. However, the Stevens brothers have taken the plunge with this version of an award-winning cask brew. The name and the label play on the brewery logo (actually based on the Buckinghamshire county emblem) of a swan, but making it black to match the beer.

Tasting Notes

Pouring ruby, with a white foam collar, Black Swan has a light, chocolatey malt nose and a gentle fruitiness in the taste, balanced by soft, sweetish malt and bitterness from both hops and roasted barley. Dry, bitter aftertaste.

Wychert Ale

- **ABV 3.9%** ▪ **BOTTLE SIZE 500 ml** ▪ **SERVE cool**
- **INGREDIENTS Maris Otter pale malt/crystal malt/Fuggle and Challenger hops**

'Wychert', meaning 'white earth', is the substance from which many of the oldest buildings in the lovely village of Haddenham (the brewery's home) were constructed. You see them all around the sprawling village green.

Tasting Notes

An amber ale with orange fruit and a little toasted malt in the aroma. The taste is nutty and lightly fruity, with a good, hoppy, bitter balance. Dry, bitter, hoppy finish.

Black Beauty Porter

- **ABV 4.3%** ▪ **BOTTLE SIZE 500 ml** ▪ **SERVE cool**
- **INGREDIENTS Maris Otter pale malt/roasted barley/ Fuggle and Golding hops**

A dark horse. Unlike the other beers, there are no Saxon or local connections: the name just describes the beer inside.

Tasting Notes

Another ruby-coloured beer, this time with subtle dark malt and juicy fruit leading in the nose. The lightish body supports a slightly tropical fruitiness from the hops, roasted barley and gentle bitterness. Dry, bitter, roasted finish.

Edgar's Golden Ale

- **ABV 4.3%** ▪ **BOTTLE SIZE 500 ml** ▪ **SERVE cool**
- **INGREDIENTS Maris Otter pale malt/Fuggle and Golding hops**

Edgar is a Stevens family name, traditionally passed down to the first son of the first son over the generations. The beer was formerly sold also as Halcyon Daze.

Tasting Notes

A clean and tasty, golden beer with a hoppy aroma of fruit cocktail. The same juicy fruit cocktail flavours continue in the mouth, tempered by a crisp, spicy hop bitterness. Fruity, bitter, hoppy finish.

Grumpling Premium

- **ABV 4.6%** ▪ **BOTTLE SIZE 500 ml** ▪ **SERVE cool**
- **INGREDIENTS Maris Otter pale malt/crystal malt/ roasted malt/Challenger and Golding hops**

Grumpling stones are the large, foundation stones upon which wychert houses are constructed (see Wychert Ale).

Tasting Notes

Amber in colour, Grumpling Premium is a bitter but fruity beer with excellent malty body and a bitter, hoppy finish. The aroma offers both soft, juicy fruit and malt.

Hadda's Head Banger

- **ABV 5%** ▪ **BOTTLE SIZE 500 ml** ▪ **SERVE cool**
- **INGREDIENTS Maris Otter pale malt/crystal malt/ Challenger and Fuggle hops**

Hadda was the Saxon king who settled in (and gave his name to) the village of Haddenham and Hadda's Head Banger is just one of a range of seasonal cask beers Vale produces under his banner. This, however, is the only Hadda in bottle. The label shows a Saxon warrior, complete with axe.

Tasting Notes

Malt and a hint of fruit combine in the nose of this amber ale. There's a slightly salty note behind the hops, fruit, malt and lightly roasted bitterness, making it rather moreish. The same savoury note lingers with fruit in the dry, bitter finish.

Good King Senseless

- **ABV 5.2%** ▪ **BOTTLE SIZE 500 ml** ▪ **SERVE cool**
- **INGREDIENTS Maris Otter pale malt/crystal malt/ chocolate malt/Fuggle and Golding hops**

This Christmas warmer is bottled each November.

VENTNOR

Ventnor Brewery, 119 High Street, Ventnor, Isle of Wight PO38 1LY. Tel. (01983) 856161 Fax (01983) 856404
Website: www.ventnorbrewery.co.uk
Mail order service

The former Burts Brewery was put back into production by new ownership in 1996 and now supplies up to 100 pubs on the Isle of Wight with cask beers. The first bottle-conditioned beer was St Boniface Golden Spring Ale (ABV 6%), which was produced in 1997 as a limited edition in antique quart bottles discovered on the site. However, apart from Old Ruby, featured below, the brewery's wide-ranging bottled output is no longer naturally conditioned. See also Scarecrow Brewery.

Old Ruby Bitter

- **ABV 4.7%** ▪ **BOTTLE SIZE 500 ml** ▪ **SERVE cool**
- **INGREDIENTS Pale malt/crystal malt/wheat malt/ Golding and Challenger hops**

Designed as an old-style beer, Old Ruby is bottled for Ventnor by Integrated Bottling Systems in Gloucestershire (formerly Wessex Craft Brewers).

Tasting Notes
Not really ruby in colour, more a light red/brown, this premium ale opens with a malty, fruity aroma (hint of blackcurrant). The palate has lots of clean, nutty malt but is not particularly sweet, and a light fruitiness persists. Toasted malt provides bitterness in the finish.

WARCOP

Warcop Brewery, 9 Nellive Park, St Brides Wentlooge, Gwent NP10 8SE. Tel./Fax (01633) 680058
Brewery established in September 1998 by chemist and experienced home brewer Bill Picton, who renovated a former milking parlour just outside Newport for the purpose. The six-barrel plant came from the Ross Brewery brew pub in the town and the name of the brewery is derived from Bill's family's initials. The quoted address is the home/office; the brewery is a few miles away. The bottled beers are produced whenever Bill is running short of stock and may include any of his extensive draught range. What follows is a listing of the bottled beers the *Guide* has been able to track down. Each is bottled straight from the cask after two months' maturation and primed with sugar. Bottled beers are also brewed to order for private celebrations and other events.

Drillers

- **ABV 4%** ▪ **BOTTLE SIZE 500 ml** ▪ **SERVE cool**
- **INGREDIENTS Maris Otter and Halcyon pale malt/crystal malt/Golding hops**

Local industry features strongly in the names of most of

Warcop's cask and bottled beers, hence the title of this orange-golden ale.

Steelers

■ ABV 4.2% ■ BOTTLE SIZE 500 ml ■ SERVE cool
■ INGREDIENTS Maris Otter and Halcyon pale malt/crystal malt/chocolate malt/Golding hops
A amber-coloured tribute to the steel workers of Llanwern, on the eastern side of Newport.

YA No.3

■ ABV 4.3% ■ BOTTLE SIZE 500 ml ■ SERVE cool
■ INGREDIENTS Maris Otter pale malt/Fuggle hops
'YA' stands for Yellow Ale – to avoid confusion with Bill's other beer, 'YB' ('Yellow Bitter')! It's called No.3 because it weighs in at 4.3% ABV.

Zen

■ ABV 4.4% ■ BOTTLE SIZE 500 ml ■ SERVE cool
■ INGREDIENTS Maris Otter and Halcyon pale malt/crystal malt/Golding hops
One more golden brew, its name derived from the contemplation given by Bill Picton over what to call the beer.

Riggers

■ ABV 4.5% ■ BOTTLE SIZE 500 ml ■ SERVE cool
■ INGREDIENTS Maris Otter and Halcyon pale malt/crystal malt/Golding hops
Riggers is a less potent version of the 5% Dockers (see opposite).

Rockers

■ ABV 4.8% ■ BOTTLE SIZE 500 ml ■ SERVE cool
■ INGREDIENTS Maris Otter and Halcyon pale malt/lager malt/Fuggle hops
The flippant counterpart to Rollers (another beer that Bill produces with name origins in the steel industry).

Tasting Notes
A golden beer with a malt and hop nose. Sweet, honeyish malt and crisp, dry hop bitterness feature in the mouth, before a dry, gently hoppy, honeyed finish.

Deep Pit

- **ABV 5%** ■ **BOTTLE SIZE 500 ml** ■ **SERVE cool**
- **INGREDIENTS Maris Otter and Halcyon pale malt/ crystal malt/chocolate malt/Golding hops**

Deep Pit clearly reflects the mining heritage of South Wales.

Tasting Notes

A red-brown ale with a malty, roasty, hoppy aroma. Malt, roast malt and citrous hops feature in the taste, too, before a dry, roasty, bitter finish.

Dockers

- **ABV 5%** ■ **BOTTLE SIZE 500 ml** ■ **SERVE cool**
- **INGREDIENTS Maris Otter and Halcyon pale malt/crystal malt/Golding hops**

Newport has long been an important docks town.

Black and Amber Extra

- **ABV 6%** ■ **BOTTLE SIZE 500 ml** ■ **SERVE cool**
- **INGREDIENTS Halcyon pale malt/crystal malt/chocolate malt/Golding hops**

Locals will need no reminding that the Black and Ambers is the nickname of Newport Rugby Football Club. This 'Extra' is stronger than Warcop's 4% cask beer, Black and Amber.

Tasting Notes

A reddish brown ale with an alcoholic, malty, fruity aroma. The taste is malty, fruity and strong. Dry, bitter fruit and malt finish, with a hint of roast.

QE2

- **ABV 6%** ■ **BOTTLE SIZE 500 ml** ■ **SERVE cool**
- **INGREDIENTS Maris Otter and Halcyon pale malt/lager malt/Fuggle hops**

A beer initially brewed in 2002 for The Queen's Jubilee.

Tasting Notes

A golden beer with light spice and fruit in the nose. The taste is also lightly fruity and the finish is dry and hoppy.

Red Hot Furnace

- **ABV 9%** ■ **BOTTLE SIZE 330 ml** ■ **SERVE cool**
- **INGREDIENTS Maris Otter and Halcyon pale malt/crystal malt/chocolate malt/Golding hops**

Newport's steel connections (Llanwern again) once more

provide the inspiration for this powerful winter beer.

Tasting Notes

A ruby beer with a spicy, fruity, malty aroma. Although malty, sweet and fruity, it tastes nothing like its strength would suggest. Dry, bittersweet, fruit finish, with a hint of roast.

WARWICKSHIRE

Warwickshire Beer Co. Ltd., Queen Street, Cubbington, Leamington Spa, Warwickshire CV32 7NA.
Tel. (01926) 450747
E-mail: sales@warwickshirebeer.co.uk
Website: www.warwickshirebeer.co.uk
Mail order service

Warwickshire was set up in 1998 in a former village bakery (an earlier Warwickshire Brewery ran for a couple of years in the mid-1990s producing some beers of the same name). Its seven-barrel equipment turns out a wide range of cask beers, and some ales are also brewed under contract at Highgate Brewery. Four bottle-conditioned beers are now available, filled in-house from matured casks primed with sugar. One-year best before dates are set and the brewers indicate that all should be acceptable to vegetarians.

Best Bitter

■ ABV 3.9% ■ BOTTLE SIZE 500 ml ■ SERVE cool
■ INGREDIENTS Maris Otter pale malt/crystal malt/ torrefied wheat/First Gold and Golding hops

One of Warwickshire's first ever beers, depicting the bear and ragged staff emblem of the Earls of Warwick on its label.

Tasting Notes

An orange gold beer with modest malt and hops in the nose. Hops shade out malt in the taste, before a dry, hoppy, bitter finish, with a touch of roast grain.

Lady Godiva

■ ABV 4.2% ■ BOTTLE SIZE 500 ml ■ SERVE cool
■ INGREDIENTS Maris Otter pale malt/amber malt/ torrefied wheat/Cascade and Styrian Golding hops

A suitably blonde ale remembering the wife of Leofric, 11th-century Earl of Mercia, and the stand she made against his high-tax regime, riding naked through the streets of Coventry.

Tasting Notes

A hazy golden ale with a malty, resin-like aroma. Hop resins lead in the bitter taste, with a light malty sweetness for balance. Dry, hoppy, bitter aftertaste.

Churchyard Bob

- **ABV 4.9%** ■ **BOTTLE SIZE 500 ml** ■ **SERVE cool**
- **INGREDIENTS Maris Otter pale malt/amber malt/ chocolate malt/torrefied wheat/Fuggle hops**

Although the label of this porter portrays a rather ghoulish Magwitchian figure, its name actually refers to an old campanology term referring to a ringing call change (so the label also reveals). The beer is brewed to commemorate the centenary of the tower and bells at All Saints Church, Leamington Spa.

Tasting Notes

A ruby beer with a biscuity malt aroma. The taste is sweetish and malty, yet with a roasted grain bitterness beneath. Roasted, increasingly bitter, slightly liquorice-like finish.

Kingmaker

- **ABV 5.5%** ■ **BOTTLE SIZE 500 ml** ■ **SERVE cool**
- **INGREDIENTS Maris Otter pale malt/crystal malt/ torrefied wheat/Challenger and Golding hops**

A beer recalling Richard Neville (1428–71), Earl of Warwick, who earned the nickname of Kingmaker because of his influence during the Wars of the Roses (described by Shakespeare in *Henry VI, Part III* as 'Thou setter up and plucker down of Kings', as the purple label explains). A good match for strong cheeses and cold meats, reckon brewers Phil Page and Jerry Lewitt.

Tasting Notes

A dark amber brew with a malty, lightly fruity nose. The taste is full-bodied, malty-sweet and warming, with fruit and hops for balance. Hoppy, bitter, drying yet lingeringly malty finish.

WENTWORTH

**Wentworth Brewery Ltd., The Powerhouse,
The Gun Park, Wentworth, Rotherham,
South Yorkshire S62 7TF.
Tel. (01226) 747070 Fax (01226) 747050
E-mail: sales@wentworthbrewery.co.uk
Website: www.wentworthbrewery.co.uk**

Wentworth opened in 1999 on the site of the former anti-aircraft gun positions on the Wentworth Woodhouse estate.

WENTWORTH

The impressive, 18th-century facade of Wentworth Woodhouse (the longest in England) is depicted on the labels of all three bottled beers, which were introduced in November 2000 and are filled on site after kräusening. The brewery's Whistlejacket, at a powerful 8.4%, will be the next beer to find its way into the bottle.

Wentworth Pale Ale

■ABV 4% ■BOTTLE SIZE 500 ml ■SERVE cool
■INGREDIENTS Maris Otter pale malt/lager malt/wheat malt/Cascade and Fuggle hops

Light and refreshing, says the label, about Wentworth's standard bitter, commonly known as WPA or 'Woppa'.

Tasting Notes

A golden beer with an aroma of toffee-malt and hop fruit. The taste is crisp, bitter and aggressively hoppy, with fruit throughout. Bitter, hoppy finish.

Oatmeal Stout

■ABV 4.8% ■BOTTLE SIZE 500 ml ■SERVE cool
■INGREDIENTS Maris Otter pale malt/black malt/wheat malt/roasted barley/oatmeal malt/Golding hops

The cask equivalent of Oatmeal Stout was bronze medallist in CAMRA's 2003 *Champion Winter Beer of Britain* contest.

Tasting Notes

A near-black stout with a softly roasted, biscuity, slightly toffeeish aroma. The complex taste is crisp, dry, roasted and toasted, leathery, biscuity, creamy and bitter. Nicely bitter, long roasted grain finish.

Rampant Gryphon

■ABV 6.2% ■BOTTLE SIZE 500 ml ■SERVE cool
■INGREDIENTS Maris Otter pale malt/crystal malt/wheat malt/Challenger and Golding hops

A gryphon stands atop the coat of arms of the Wentworth estate and lends its name to two of the brewery's strong ales. Gryphon, at 5.1%, is not bottled, however, only this even more potent – hence 'rampant' – brew.

Tasting Notes

An orange-gold ale with a malty, orangey aroma. The taste is crisp and bitter but reveals the beer's strength, bursting with tangy, fruity hops, yet with lots of thick malt behind. The bitter, hoppy aftertaste has some lingering fruit.

WEST BERKSHIRE

The West Berkshire Brewery Company Ltd., The Old Bakery, Yattendon, Thatcham, Berkshire RG18 0UE. Tel./Fax (01635) 202968
E-mail: info@wbbrew.co.uk
Website: www.wbbrew.co.uk

Dave and Helen Maggs set up West Berkshire Brewery in a barn behind the idyllic Pot Kiln pub (a separate business), near Frilsham in Berkshire in 1995. They still brew there but have also opened a second, larger site in an old bakery in the estate village of Yattendon, a few miles away. They have produced occasional bottles of the popular cask ale Good Old Boy (4%) and the Christmas special, Spiced Porter (5%), but only Full Circle is a regular product.

Full Circle

- **ABV 4.5%** ▪ **BOTTLE SIZE 500 ml** ▪ **SERVE cool**
- **INGREDIENTS Maris Otter pale malt/crystal malt/wheat malt/hops not declared**

Brewed first as West Berkshire's 1,000th brew (and still also available as an award-winning cask ale), Full Circle incorporates locally-grown hops alongside local barley (with the spent grains going back to local farmers, the name Full Circle seemed appropriate). The strength of the brew has also been toyed with in the past year, briefly being raised to 5% before dropping back to 4.5. The beer is re-seeded with fresh yeast (the brewery's regular strain) prior to bottling. Bottles are kept for a month to condition before release and the best before date is set at nine months. Full Circle may also be found in carbonated form, so look out for the words 'bottle-conditioned' when you come across a bottle.

Tasting Notes

A copper ale with a strong hop nose. Fresh, fruity hops dominate gentle malt before a drying, hoppy finish.

WHEAL ALE

Wheal Ale Brewery, c/o The Bird in Hand, Trelissick Road, Hayle, Cornwall TR27 4HY.
Tel. (01736) 753974
E-mail: george@birdinhand-hayle.co.uk
Website: www.birdinhand-hayle.co.uk

The Bird in Hand is a large brew pub situated alongside the Paradise Park bird gardens in Hayle. This brewery is housed in outbuildings alongside the beer garden and produces a few cask beers, plus the bottle-conditioned beer below. This was introduced in summer 2001 and is bottled at Keltek Brewery.

Speckled Parrot

- **ABV 5.5%** ▪ **BOTTLE SIZE 500 ml** ▪ **SERVE cool**
- **INGREDIENTS Maris Otter pale malt/crystal malt/Fuggle and Golding hops**

There are no prizes for guessing the inspiration for the name of this strong ale, which ties in neatly with the bird park next door. It is also sold in cask form, but bottled in summer only. The yeast used is obtained from The Blue Anchor at Helston, and provides the same spicy notes as found in that brewery's Spingo beers.

Tasting Notes

A red-amber beer with an aroma of malt, plus a spicy yeast note. The soft, smooth body has loads of sweet malt, fruit and an earthy, spicy yeastiness, with bitterness in support. Toasted, malty, bittersweet finish.

WHITTINGTONS

Whittingtons Brewery, Three Choirs Vineyard, Newent, Gloucestershire GL18 1LS.
Tel. (01531) 890555 Fax (01531) 890877
E-mail: info@whittingtonsbrewery.co.uk
Website: www.whittingtonsbrewery.co.uk
Mail order service

Whittingtons Brewery was founded in spring 2003 on the Three Choirs Vineyard. It takes as its theme the character of Dick Whittington (and his cat), who was born in the area: hence the brewery's slogan, 'Purveyors of the purrfect pint'.

Cats Whiskers

- **ABV 4.2%** ▪ **BOTTLE SIZE 500 ml** ▪ **SERVE cool**
- **INGREDIENTS Maris Otter pale malt/crystal malt/chocolate malt/sugar/First Gold and Cascade hops**

Matured after fermentation, then filtered, primed with sugar and re-seeded with a fresh dose of the brewery's regular yeast, Cats Whiskers carries a nine-month best before date. The cask version was Gloucestershire CAMRA's *Beer of the Year* for 2004.

Tasting Notes

Amber-coloured, with an aroma of nutty, chocolatey malt until fruity/floral hops take over. Bittersweet and dry in the mouth, with a little lemon, nut and hop; very dry, bitter finish.

WICKED HATHERN

Wicked Hathern Brewery Ltd., 46 Derby Road, Hathern, Loughborough, Leicestershire LE12 5LD.
Tel. (01509) 842585 Fax (01509) 646393
E-mail: beer@hathern.com
Website: www.wicked-hathern.co.uk

It was the Reverend Edward Thomas March Phillips, apparently, who declared that the village of Hathern in Leicestershire was 'Wicked'. The 19th-century cleric despaired at the drunken brawls and the cockfighting that were common place in the town, not least between the gravestones of his churchyard, and after his condemnation of public standards the local nickname of Wicked Hathern stuck. This two-and-a-half-barrel brewery was opened early in 2000.

Doble's Dog

- **ABV 3.5%** ▪ **BOTTLE SIZE 500 ml** ▪ **SERVE cool**
- **INGREDIENTS Maris Otter pale malt/crystal malt/chocolate malt/wheat/Golding and Fuggle hops**

Inspired by the unfortunate tale of another of the village's vicars. The Reverend Doble, sadly, died, along with his wife, Violet, attempting to rescue their pet dog in rough seas off Hunstanton. The dog, however, survived. The story is recalled on a plaque in the village church. The late hopping on this beer is with Fuggles, Goldings being used early in the copper.

Tasting Notes

A ruby beer with a rich, malty aroma. There is light toffee in the sweetish, malty taste, with a touch of burnt grain. Gently bitter, malty finish with a lingering hint of roasted malt.

Hawthorn Gold

- **ABV 3.5%** ▪ **BOTTLE SIZE 500 ml** ▪ **SERVE cool**
- **INGREDIENTS Maris Otter pale malt/wheat/Fuggle and Golding hops**

The name Hathern is derived from the Saxon for hawthorn, the bushes that surrounded the village in pre-*Domesday Book* times – hence the title of this golden session bitter.

Tasting Notes

A pale golden ale with a hoppy nose, a dry, crisp taste of sweetness and lemony hop, and a dry, lemon-hoppy finish.

WHB (Wicked Hathern Bitter)

- **ABV 3.8%** ▪ **BOTTLE SIZE 500 ml** ▪ **SERVE cool**
- **INGREDIENTS Maris Otter pale malt/crystal malt/ chocolate malt/wheat malt/Fuggle and Golding hops**

WHB is the brewery's main cask bitter, brewed first in January 2000. Like all the bottled versions, this beer is filled in house, after being conditioned in casks and primed with sugar. Warm conditioning in bottle is then allowed for a week, followed by two further weeks at cellar temperature at the brewery, before the beers go on sale. Twelve months are stated in the best before dates.

Tasting Notes

Amber in colour, this bitter is robust for its strength. Light malt and fruity hops in the nose; plenty of bitterness in the taste, with malt behind. Bitter, drying aftertaste with roasted malt hints.

Cockfighter

- **ABV 4.2%** ▪ **BOTTLE SIZE 500 ml** ▪ **SERVE cool**
- **INGREDIENTS Maris Otter pale malt/crystal malt/ Golding hops**

So rife was the 'sport' of cockfighting in this area during the 19th century that an area on the outskirts of Hathern was the venue for countless challenge contests, apparently attracting among many visitors the famous Leicestershire outsize man, Daniel Lambert.

Tasting Notes

A golden beer with an aroma of fruit, creamy malt and hop resins. The taste is also malty and creamy, but well balanced by lightly fruity hops. Drying, hoppy finish with creamy malt lingering.

Albion Special

- **ABV 4.3%** ▪ **BOTTLE SIZE 500 ml** ▪ **SERVE cool**
- **INGREDIENTS Maris Otter pale malt/crystal malt/ wheat/Fuggle and Golding hops**

You can only try cask Albion Special if you visit The Albion Inn at Loughborough, or spot it at a beer festival. However, this bottled version is more widely available.

Tasting Notes

A copper ale with creamy malt in the nose and a sweetish taste of malt, light, grassy hops and some smoky/burnt grain. Dry, bittersweet finish.

Soar Head

- **ABV 4.8%** - **BOTTLE SIZE 500 ml** - **SERVE cool**
- **INGREDIENTS Maris Otter pale malt/crystal malt/ chocolate malt/wheat/Fuggle and Golding hops**

The River Soar flows through Hathern village.

Tasting Notes

An amber beer with a fruity, hoppy and malty aroma. The taste is a spritzy, malty, fruity mix, with a bit of everything from hops to roasted grain. Dry, bitter, lightly roasted finish.

Gladstone Tidings

- **ABV 5.3%** - **BOTTLE SIZE 500 ml** - **SERVE cool**
- **INGREDIENTS Maris Otter pale malt/crystal malt/ chocolate malt/Golding hops**

This is Wicked Hathern's Christmas ale, a dark bitter named after the village's Gladstone Street.

WICKWAR

The Wickwar Brewing Co., The Old Brewery, Station Road, Wickwar, Wotton-under-Edge, Gloucestershire GL12 8NB. Tel./Fax (01454) 294168
E-mail: bob@wickwarbrewing.co.uk
Website: www.wickwarbrewing.co.uk
Mail order service

Wickwar was launched in 1990 in the cooperage of the long-gone Arnold, Perrett & Co. Brewery. By summer 2004, however, the brewery had outgrown these limited premises and was about to move across the road into the main buildings. Although its bottled beers are brewed at Wickwar, bottling is carried out from casks by Integrated Bottling Solutions after the beer has been fined. Most bottles carry a 12-month best before date.

BOB (Brand Oak Bitter)/Dog's Hair

- **ABV 4%** - **BOTTLE SIZE 500 ml** - **SERVE cool**
- **INGREDIENTS Maris Otter pale malt/crystal malt/black malt/Fuggle and Challenger hops**

BOB, one of Wickwar's most popular beers, took its name from Brand Oak Cottage, where one of the founders was living at the time. This bottle-conditioned brew – which has also been packaged under the name of Dog's Hair – has been joined now by a filtered version called BOB Sparkling.

Tasting Notes
An amber ale with a fruity, malty nose. The taste is a dry, lightly apple-fruity mix of malt and hops, rounded off by a dry, bitter, malt and hops finish.

Cotswold Way

- **ABV 4.2%** ■ **BOTTLE SIZE 500 ml** ■ **SERVE cool**
- **INGREDIENTS Maris Otter pale malt/crystal malt/black malt/Fuggle hops**

A beer added to the bottled range at the end of 2002 to commemorate the Cotswold Way footpath.

Tasting Notes
Pear fruit and malt feature in the nose of this dark golden beer. Pear is well in evidence in the taste and finish, too, but so are malt and dry, soft bitterness.
Major stockist Local Tesco

Infernal Brew

- **ABV 4.8%** ■ **BOTTLE SIZE 500 ml** ■ **SERVE cool**
- **INGREDIENTS Maris Otter pale malt/crystal malt/chocolate malt/Fuggle and Challenger hops**

Another re-badge, Infernal Brew, for all its devilish packaging, is actually the brewery's Olde Merryford Ale in a bottle.

Tasting Notes
An amber ale with a hoppy aroma. The taste is also hoppy and fruity, but the malt renders it bittersweet rather than bitter, and it rounds off with a bittersweet, hoppy aftertaste.

Old Arnold

- **ABV 4.8%** ■ **BOTTLE SIZE 500 ml** ■ **SERVE cool**
- **INGREDIENTS Maris Otter pale malt/black malt/Fuggle and Challenger hops**

This premium ale was named after the Mr Arnold who founded the original brewery in Wickwar in 1800 and who merged his business with that of Mr Perrett, his near neighbour, in 1826. The stone tower brewhouse they constructed was employed for cider making from the 1920s and was eventually closed in 1969. The recipe for this brew is based on Mr Arnold's 'Strong Old Beer', which, so the label reveals, was sold for 12/- a firkin.

Tasting Notes
Dark golden with hops and light, chocolatey malt in the nose. Initially malty-sweet to taste, it becomes fruity and tangy as hops kick in. Bitter, hoppy finish with a hint of roasted malt.

Mr Perrett's

- **ABV 5.9%** ■ **BOTTLE SIZE 500 ml** ■ **SERVE cool**
- **INGREDIENTS Maris Otter pale malt/crystal malt/black malt/Fuggle hops**

A *Tesco Beer Challenge* winner in 2001, Mr Perrett's Traditional Stout, as it was then more fully known, was at first only available in cruelly small 330 ml bottles. Since the exclusive contract with Tesco ended, a standard half-litre bottle, with a two-year best before date, has been introduced. The beer has been twice voted *Champion Beer of Gloucestershire* in its cask form.

Tasting Notes

A very dark red/brown brew with coffee and tart dark fruits in the nose. The same flavours continue on the palate, but with a light liquorice bitterness poking through. Roasted malt leads in the dry finish. Gently smoky throughout.

Station Porter

- **ABV 6.1%** ■ **BOTTLE SIZE 500 ml** ■ **SERVE cool**
- **INGREDIENTS Maris Otter pale malt/crystal malt/black malt/Fuggle hops**

An award-winning cask beer (including two silver medals at CAMRA's Great Winter Beer Festival), named after Wickwar village's long-lost railway halt, Station Porter was first brewed in 1993 and first bottled in 1997. The original stencilled label design has now been superseded by something more serious and in keeping with the brewery's other labels.

Tasting Notes

Dark red with a fruity, chocolatey nose. The taste is smooth, sweet and fruity (hints of bitter orange), with nutty roast balance. Lightish body; roasted, bitter orange finish.

Where to Buy Real Ale in a Bottle

Beers in this book are generally sold locally, through farmers' markets, small grocers, craft shops, delicatessens and some restaurants. Some breweries also sell direct to the public, but this may be by the case only, and some offer a mail order service, which is mentioned in each entry, if relevant. Otherwise beers can be obtained through specialist off-licences or mail order companies, many of which are listed in the Beer Shops section at the back of the book. If a beer has a listing with a major supermarket or off-licence chain, this is indicated at the end of the entry.

WISSEY VALLEY

Wissey Valley Brewery, The Bluebell, Lynn Road, Stoke Ferry, King's Lynn, Norfolk PE33 9SW.
Tel. (01366) 500767
E-mail: info@wisseyvalleybrewery.co.uk
Website: www.wisseyvalleybrewery.co.uk

Formerly trading as Captain Grumpy's Beer Company, at The Ship pub at Brandon Creek, this enterprise moved to Stoke Ferry in 2003, changing its name to reflect its new geographical position. Now based behind The Bluebell pub, Tony Hook, the brewer, specialises in bottle-conditioned beers, producing a wide range of ales that he primarily sells at East Anglia's farmers' markets (yet more bottles may arrive on an occasional basis). The only cask-conditioned beers his four-barrel brewery turns out go to two regular pubs and beer festivals.

WVB (Wissey Valley Bitter)

- **ABV 3.6%** ■ **BOTTLE SIZE 500 ml** ■ **SERVE cool**
- **INGREDIENTS Pale malt/crystal malt/caramalt/Fuggle and Target hops**

A session bitter unusually adding Target hops late for aroma (this hop strain is most commonly employed for bitterness and used early).

Ratty Bob

- **ABV 3.7%** ■ **BOTTLE SIZE 500 ml** ■ **SERVE cool**
- **INGREDIENTS Pale malt/caramalt/Fuggle hops**

Ratty Bob was apparently a character who lived in Stoke Ferry in years gone by, as discovered by Tony in a local history book.

Captain Grumpy's Best Bitter

- **ABV 3.9%** ■ **BOTTLE SIZE 500 ml** ■ **SERVE cool**
- **INGREDIENTS Pale malt/crystal malt/caramalt/Target and Challenger hops**

A surviving bitter from the brewery's earlier incarnation at Brandon Creek. When Tony was based at The Ship pub, he was struck by the number of miserable people that were disembarking from boats on the rainy river, and decided that the name Captain Grumpy might help put a smile back on their faces and brighten up their day.

Bodger Brown

- **ABV 4%** ▪ **BOTTLE SIZE 500 ml** ▪ **SERVE cool**
- **INGREDIENTS Pale malt/crystal malt/caramalt/ Challenger and Target hops**

Late-hopped with Target, this is another beer inspired by a name found in the book chronicling the story of Stoke Ferry.

Old Wobbly

- **ABV 4.2%** ▪ **BOTTLE SIZE 500 ml** ▪ **SERVE cool**
- **INGREDIENTS Pale malt/crystal malt/caramalt/ chocolate malt/roasted barley/Target and Phoenix hops**

A dark amber ale, described by the brewer as 'smooth and hoppy'.

Wissey Dawn

- **ABV 4.3%** ▪ **BOTTLE SIZE 500 ml** ▪ **SERVE cool**
- **INGREDIENTS Pale malt/caramalt/Bramling Cross hops**

A malt-accented, pale-golden beer.

Busted Flush

- **ABV 4.4%** ▪ **BOTTLE SIZE 500 ml** ▪ **SERVE cool**
- **INGREDIENTS Pale malt/crystal malt/caramalt/Phoenix and Challenger hops**

An amber ale continued from the days of Captain Grumpy.

Stoked Up

- **ABV 4.4%** ▪ **BOTTLE SIZE 500 ml** ▪ **SERVE cool**
- **INGREDIENTS Pale malt/caramalt/Phoenix hops**

A pale ale named after the brewery's new village home.

Tasting Notes

A dark golden beer with a malty aroma, a malty, sweetish taste and a bittersweet, malty, drying aftertaste, with a hoppy edge.

Old Faithful

- **ABV 4.5%** ▪ **BOTTLE SIZE 500 ml** ▪ **SERVE cool**
- **INGREDIENTS Pale malt/crystal malt/caramalt/ Bramling Cross hops**

A premium bitter which, like all Wissey Valley's beers, is allowed to drop bright, transferred to a new cask, kräusened and then bottled on site, using a converted wine filler. Bottles are warm conditioned for at least a week before going on sale.

Old Grumpy

- **ABV 4.5%** ▪ **BOTTLE SIZE 500 ml** ▪ **SERVE cool**
- **INGREDIENTS Pale malt/crystal malt/caramalt/chocolate malt/roasted barley/Challenger and Target hops**

Old Grumpy is the brewery's porter.

Eel Catcher

- **ABV 4.8%** ▪ **BOTTLE SIZE 500 ml** ▪ **SERVE cool**
- **INGREDIENTS Pale malt/crystal malt/caramalt/chocolate malt/roasted barley/Fuggle, Target and Phoenix hops**

This dark bitter was a special brew for Ely Beer Festival and is now the latest addition to the regular range.

Wissey Sunset

- **ABV 5%** ▪ **BOTTLE SIZE 500 ml** ▪ **SERVE cool**
- **INGREDIENTS Pale malt/crystal malt/caramalt/Phoenix hops**

You get your money's worth of Phoenix with this brew, as the hop is added three times during the brewing process.

Golden Rivet

- **ABV 5.1%** ▪ **BOTTLE SIZE 500 ml** ▪ **SERVE cool**
- **INGREDIENTS Pale malt/crystal malt/caramalt/Challenger and Bramling Cross hops**

A golden ale; another relic from the Captain Grumpy days, late hopped with Bramling Cross.

Khaki Sergeant

- **ABV 6.7%** ▪ **BOTTLE SIZE 500 ml** ▪ **SERVE cool**
- **INGREDIENTS Pale malt/crystal malt/caramalt/chocolate malt/roasted barley/Target and Challenger hops**

This stout was inspired by a sepia picture of Tony's grandfather, an RSM in the Royal Artillery during World War I. The photograph now appears on the label.

WOLF

The Wolf Brewery Ltd., 10 Maurice Gaymer Road, Attleborough, Norfolk NR17 2QZ.
Tel. (01953) 457775 Fax (01953) 457776
E-mail: info@wolf-ales.co.uk
Website: www.wolf-brewery.ltd.uk
Mail order service

Brewery founded in 1996 by Wolfe Witham, former owner of Norfolk's Reindeer Brewery, and housed in an industrial unit on the former Gaymer's cider orchard. Beers are kräusened prior to bottling, bringing fresh Wolf yeast into each bottle.

Cavell Ale 9503

- **ABV 3.7%** ■ **BOTTLE SIZE 500 ml** ■ **SERVE cool**
- **INGREDIENTS Pearl pale malt/crystal malt/wheat malt/Fuggle and Challenger hops**

Brewed primarily for the Norwich lodge of The Buffaloes – number 9503, the Edith Cavell Lodge – this beer is largely sold at The Beehive, the lodge's meeting place in the city. The label includes a picture of the World War I nursing heroine, who was executed by the Germans.

Tasting Notes

Toasted malt and fruity hops dominate the aroma of this amber ale, which has a fruity, softly bitter taste, but also malt sweetness. The aftertaste is dry and bitter.

Festival Ale

- **ABV 3.7%** ■ **BOTTLE SIZE 500 ml** ■ **SERVE cool**
- **INGREDIENTS Pearl pale malt/crystal malt/wheat malt/Fuggle and Challenger hops**

Festival Ale is an annual brew for Norwich and Norfolk's Arts Festival, but with the recipe changed from year to year. Flavourings have included lavender honey and blackcurrants.

Norfolk Lavender

- **ABV 3.7%** ■ **BOTTLE SIZE 500 ml** ■ **SERVE cool**
- **INGREDIENTS Optic pale malt/crystal malt/wheat malt/Golding, Styrian Golding and Cascade hops/ lavender honey**

An unusual beer – brewed for Norfolk Lavender Ltd., Heacham – with the scented inclusion of local lavender honey.

Tasting Notes

A golden beer with a perfumed, honeyed aroma. In the

mouth, it is scented, citrous and bittersweet, with a light honey softness. A perfumed, bitter, hoppy finish rounds off.

Wolf in Sheep's Clothing

- **ABV 3.7%** ■ **BOTTLE SIZE 500 ml** ■ **SERVE cool**
- **INGREDIENTS Pearl pale malt/crystal malt/chocolate malt/wheat malt/Golding and Cascade hops**

From its name, you'd think that this beer had something to hide, but it's essentially just a fruity session ale.

Tasting Notes

Toffee notes to the malt and a raisin fruitiness feature in the aroma and taste of this ruby ale, which also has a moreishly dry, slight saltiness and finishes with bitter fruit and hops.

Wolf Ale

- **ABV 3.9%** ■ **BOTTLE SIZE 500 ml** ■ **SERVE cool**
- **INGREDIENTS Pearl pale malt/crystal malt/wheat malt/Golding, Challenger and Styrian Golding hops**

Formerly known simply as Best Bitter in cask and bottle.

Coyote Bitter

- **ABV 4.3%** ■ **BOTTLE SIZE 500 ml** ■ **SERVE cool**
- **INGREDIENTS Pearl pale malt/crystal malt/wheat malt/Golding, Styrian Golding and Cascade hops**

Cascade hops lend an American accent to this award-winning brew, which explains the presence of the Americanised wolf in the name. The coyote is featured howling at a desert moon on the colourful label.

Tasting Notes

Amber with a powerful fruity aroma, laced with hints of pears and juicy oranges. Big, peppery hops, more juicy fruit and a good malt base in the taste; dry, bitter, peppery-hop finish.

Lupine

- **ABV 4.5%** ■ **BOTTLE SIZE 500 ml** ■ **SERVE cool**
- **INGREDIENTS Pearl pale malt/crystal malt/amber malt/wheat malt/Styrian Golding and Golding hops**

A beer produced on draught and in bottle in October.

Tasting Notes

Orange fruit emerges in the aroma of this ruby beer, along with light, biscuity malt. Robust and full-bodied, its taste has bitterness to the fore, but also malt and a little fruit for balance. Long, bitter, hoppy finish.

Straw Dog

- **ABV 4.5%** - **BOTTLE SIZE 500 ml** - **SERVE cool**
- **INGREDIENTS Lager malt/wheat malt/Saaz and Hallertau hops**

A new beer containing 30% wheat, a SIBA *Wheat Beer Challenge* award-winner. It takes its name from the colour, the wolf association and from the fact that it was first brewed in the week that the film *Straw Dogs* was first shown on TV!

Granny Wouldn't Like It!!!

- **ABV 4.8%** - **BOTTLE SIZE 500 ml** - **SERVE cool**
- **INGREDIENTS Pearl pale malt/crystal malt/chocolate malt/wheat malt/Golding and Challenger hops**

Particularly popular at Christmas, as a novelty gift for granny, this is another acclaimed Wolf ale. Taking the fairy story as its inspiration, the label pictures Little Red Riding Hood and a menacing, red-eyed wolf.

Tasting Notes

A red-amber ale with a slightly piney, vinously fruity aroma. The taste is mostly bitter, but with plenty of malt, pepper, roasted malt and a little vinous fruit. Dry, roasted, bitter finish.

Woild Moild

- **ABV 4.8%** - **BOTTLE SIZE 500 ml** - **SERVE cool**
- **INGREDIENTS Pearl pale malt/crystal malt/chocolate malt/wheat malt/Fuggle, Golding and Challenger hops**

A strong mild, parti-gyled (brewed as part of the same batch) with Granny Wouldn't Like It!!!

Tasting Notes

A ruby ale with a fruity, coffeeish nose. Fruit and dark malts feature in the mouth, finishing smoky and bitter, with gentle roasted malt notes.

Timber Wolf

- **ABV 5.8%** - **BOTTLE SIZE 500 ml** - **SERVE cool**
- **INGREDIENTS Pearl pale malt/crystal malt/chocolate malt/wheat malt/Golding and Challenger hops**

A warming ale for the winter months.

Tasting Notes

A ruby beer with a fruity, vinous aroma. Light winey notes continue through this fruity, tangy drink to the finish, with dark malt lurking in the shadows.

Ported Timber Wolf

- **ABV 5.8%** ■ **BOTTLE SIZE 500 ml** ■ **SERVE cool**
- **INGREDIENTS Pearl pale malt/crystal malt/chocolate malt/wheat malt/Golding and Challenger hops/port**

Bearing the descriptive sub-title of 'Falling Down Water', this is a doctored version of Timber Wolf, in the style of an Irish stout-and-fortified-wine cocktail (a 'corpse reviver'). A whole bottle of port is added after fermentation to every firkin, and the beer is then left to age for at least nine months before it is bottled.

Tasting Notes
A ruby beer with an appetising, mellow fruit aroma. The taste is strong and bitter, but the fruitiness of the port shines through amid some roasted malt flavour. Very dry, bitter, roasted finish, with teasing hints of winey fruit.

WOODFORDE'S

Woodforde's Norfolk Ales (Woodforde's Ltd.), Broadland Brewery, Woodbastwick, Norwich, Norfolk NR13 6SW.
Tel. (01603) 720353 Fax (01603) 721806
E-mail: info@woodfordes.co.uk
Website: www.woodfordes.co.uk
Mail order service

Woodforde's was founded in 1981 in Drayton, near Norwich, and moved to a converted farm complex in the picturesque Broadland village of Woodbastwick in 1989. It brews a wide range of award-winning beers (including two former CAMRA *Champion Beers of Britain*), many of which are now also bottled (unfiltered and conditioned by the yeast remaining from primary fermentation). The best before dates are set at nine months after filling (except for Wherry and Headcracker – 12 months – and Norfolk Nip – two years).

Wherry

- **ABV 3.8%** ■ **BOTTLE SIZE 500 ml** ■ **SERVE cool**
- **INGREDIENTS Maris Otter pale malt/crystal malt/ Golding and Styrian Golding hops**

This is a bottled version of CAMRA's *Champion Beer of Britain* of 1996, and very well does it reflect the success of its cask-conditioned equivalent. A wherry – as depicted on the label – is a type of shallow-draught sailing boat once commonly seen crossing the Norfolk Broads.

Tasting Notes
A golden beer with a lusciously fruity, hoppy and slightly peppery nose. Bitter, zesty, hoppy orange fruit fills the mouth before a dry, bitter fruit finish.

Great Eastern

- **ABV 4.3%** ■ **BOTTLE SIZE 500 ml** ■ **SERVE cool**
- **INGREDIENTS Maris Otter pale malt/lager malt/ Progress hops**

A special brew to commemorate 150 years of the Great Eastern Railway in Norfolk, first brewed in 1994 in cask form as a souvenir for railway enthusiasts.

Tasting Notes
A light-bodied, pale golden beer with an appetising aroma of pear fruit. The taste is dry and pear-fruity with a little peppery hop and a dry, bitter, hoppy finish.

Nelson's Revenge

- **ABV 4.5%** ■ **BOTTLE SIZE 500 ml** ■ **SERVE cool**
- **INGREDIENTS Maris Otter pale malt/crystal malt/ Golding hops**

Nelson's Revenge reflects the famous admiral's associations with Norfolk (he was born in the county, at Burnham Thorpe in 1758). This brew started life as a house beer for the Limes Hotel at Fakenham but was later resurrected for the Norwich Beer Festival and now lives on.

Tasting Notes
With an appealing, spicy citrus fruit and pears aroma, this copper ale has bags of character right from the first sniff. A fine balance of zesty fruit (orange peel), malt and hop bitterness follows, with a dry, moreish, bittersweet finish.

Norfolk Nog

- **ABV 4.6%** ■ **BOTTLE SIZE 500 ml** ■ **SERVE cool**
- **INGREDIENTS Maris Otter pale malt/crystal malt/ chocolate malt/Fuggle and Golding hops**

Pre-dating the success of the brewery's Wherry by four years, Norfolk Nog was CAMRA's *Champion Beer of Britain* in 1992. To earn the supreme CAMRA accolade with two different ales is a remarkable achievement, especially for a small brewery. (For the record, only one other brewery, Fuller's, has claimed the top prize with more than one beer.) The only caveat when citing this achievement is that drinkers should be gently reminded that cask beer and bottled beer are not quite the same thing, even if the beer leaves the same cask, as in this case. The level of carbonation can make a difference to the nature of the beer, as can the maturing process in the bottle. A nog is thought to have been an East Anglian type of stock ale, stored for enjoyment many months after brewing.

Tasting Notes

This is a ruby-coloured, strong mild, without the deeper bitterness of a stout or the cloyingness of a heavy old ale. Its aroma is coffeeish and chocolatey, characteristics which continue lightly in the taste, alongside soft malt sweetness and a little fruit. Subtle roasted malt features in the bittersweet finish.

Admiral's Reserve

- **ABV 5%** ▪ **BOTTLE SIZE 500 ml** ▪ **SERVE cool**
- **INGREDIENTS Maris Otter pale malt/crystal malt/rye crystal malt/Golding hops**

First brewed in April 2002 to commemorate Woodforde's 21st anniversary, Admiral's Reserve is now a permanent member of the bottled range and is also available in cask form.

Tasting Notes

A dark golden strong ale with creamy malt and a hint of fruit in the nose, and a nutty, malty taste, together with a little sweetness, pear fruit and balancing bitterness. Bitter, nutty, malty notes hog the finish.

Headcracker

- **ABV 7%** ▪ **BOTTLE SIZE 500 ml**
- **SERVE at room temperature**
- **INGREDIENTS Maris Otter pale malt/caramalt/Golding hops**

Clearly in the first division of the appropriate names league, Headcracker is not a beer to treat lightly. Its origins are in the barley wine school. In fact, you could say it is now one of the class leaders, having won CAMRA's *Best Barley Wine* award on no less than three occasions (in cask form). This is one beer to experiment with over a longer period than the prescribed 12 months' shelf life to see how it matures and how the flavours mellow out in the bottle.

Tasting Notes

This complex barley wine has an orange-gold colour and a fruity (oranges and peaches) nose. The powerful, fairly sweet taste features fruit and a robust hop bitterness, while bitter fruit tingles away in the dry aftertaste.

Norfolk Nip

- **ABV 8.5%** ■ **BOTTLE SIZE 330 ml**
- **SERVE at room temperature**
- **INGREDIENTS Maris Otter pale malt/crystal malt/ chocolate malt/roasted barley/Golding hops**

Norfolk Nip closely follows a recipe dating from 1929 for a beer (also called Norfolk Nip) from the defunct Steward & Patteson brewery in Norwich. The original beer was phased out by Watney's in the early 1960s, but the brew was revived by Woodforde's in March 1992 to commemorate the tenth anniversary of the local CAMRA news journal, *Norfolk Nips*. Brewing now takes place annually on or around St Valentine's Day. The strength and high hop rate should enable this beer to mature long after bottling. Indeed, it has already enjoyed at least six months of maturation in the cask at the brewery prior to bottle filling.

Tasting Notes

Very dark ruby in colour, this barley wine has a hint of tropical fruit (pineapple) in its aroma, over a leathery, lightly treacly, malty base. Sweetness, dark malt, raisin fruit, pineapple, orange and fine hop bitterness combine in the complex taste, although it is not quite as full-bodied as expected. Gum-tingling, warm finish.

WYE VALLEY

Wye Valley Brewery, Stoke Lacy, Herefordshire HR7 4HG. Tel. (01885) 490505 Fax (01885) 490595
E-mail: sales@wyevalleybrewery.co.uk
Website: www.wyevalleybrewery.co.uk
Mail order service

Wye Valley Brewery began production in 1985 and, growing substantially, has since moved premises twice, taking up residence in Stoke Lacy in 2002. Wye Valley seasonal cask beers all roll out under the 'Dorothy Goodbody' title. There is not, and never has been, a real Dorothy: she is just a figment of the brewery's fertile imagination, a computer-generated 1950s blonde bombshell dreamt up to market the seasonal range. Three of these seasonal beers are regularly available in bottle-conditioned form, complete with a picture of the seductive Miss Goodbody on the front. Like the other offering, they are now bottled by Hop Back in Wiltshire or Hepworth & Co. in Sussex, having been filtered, re-seeded with fresh bottling yeast and kräusened to ensure good natural carbonation. Occasionally, seasonal and celebration beers may be bottled, too. Best before dates are set at 12 months. B United imports the beers (except for Golden Ale) to the US.

Dorothy Goodbody's Golden Ale

- **ABV 4.2%** ▪ **BOTTLE SIZE 500 ml** ▪ **SERVE cool**
- **INGREDIENTS Maris Otter pale malt/pale crystal malt/ wheat malt/East Kent Golding and Fuggle hops**

Available in cask-conditioned form March–August, Golden Ale was initially a filtered beer in bottle. However, it has been 'real' now for a number of years. Try it with fish, chicken or pasta dishes, the brewers suggest.

Tasting Notes

As its name implies, a dark golden ale with a lightly spicy, citrous nose, a bittersweet, fruity taste and a soft, malty mouthfeel, plus a dry, bitter hop finish.

Major stockists Local Spar and Waitrose

Butty Bach

- **ABV 4.5%** ▪ **BOTTLE SIZE 500 ml** ▪ **SERVE cool**
- **INGREDIENTS Maris Otter pale malt/crystal malt/wheat malt/flaked barley/East Kent Golding, Fuggle and Bramling Cross hops**

Mainly aimed at the brewery's Welsh customers, 'Little Friend' has been one of Wye Valley's most successful beers, its cask equivalent voted top beer at the Cardiff Beer Festival in the year it was first brewed, 1998.

Tasting Notes

A dark golden ale with fruity hop and spice in the aroma. On the palate there's a juicy, fruity hoppiness over a sweet, malty base, and the finish is also hop-fruity. Soft and easy- drinking.

Dorothy Goodbody's Wholesome Stout

- **ABV 4.6%** ▪ **BOTTLE SIZE 500 ml** ▪ **SERVE cool**
- **INGREDIENTS Maris Otter pale malt/roasted barley/ flaked barley/Northdown hops**

The label of this dark brew claims that Dorothy discovered the recipe in her grandfather's brewing books. The truth is that brewery founder, Peter Amor, once worked for a famous Irish brewery and was duly inspired to create this award-winning stout. Great with red meats and cheeses, is the brewery's recommendation.

Tasting Notes

A very dark red/brown stout with an aroma of chocolate, coffee and fruit. In the mouth it feels rich and nourishing, with an excellent smooth balance of chocolatey malt sweetness, fruit and crisp, bitter roast flavours. Roast and bitterness dominate the dry finish.

Dorothy Goodbody's Country Ale

- **ABV 6% ▪ BOTTLE SIZE 500 ml ▪ SERVE cool**
- **INGREDIENTS Maris Otter pale malt/crystal malt/amber malt/wheat malt/flaked barley/roasted barley/ Bramling Cross and Fuggle hops**

Tawny-hued Country Ale is a version of Wye Valley's Christmas Ale and was first bottled for export to the USA under the name of 'Our Glass'. Wye Valley advises you to drink it with cheeses or rich puddings.

Tasting Notes

A fruity, malty aroma leads to lots of sweet malt, hops and fruity flavours in the taste, including light pineapple. Big, malty finish with hops and bitterness.

YATES'

Yates' Brewery, The Inn at St Lawrence, Undercliff Drive, St Lawrence, Ventnor, Isle of Wight PO38 1XG.
Tel. (01983) 854689
E-mail: info@yates-brewery.fsnet.co.uk
Website: www.yates-brewery.co.uk

Dave Yates used to work for Burts Brewery on the Isle of Wight and also joined the shortlived Island Brewery. Since 2000, he's been brewing on his own, with a five-barrel plant based at The Inn at St Lawrence pub, near Ventnor. Bottled beers were launched in 2003 and are filled from a cask after being kräusened. Nine-month best before dates are applied.

Undercliff Experience

- **ABV 4.1% ▪ BOTTLE SIZE 500 ml ▪ SERVE cool**
- **INGREDIENTS Optic pale malt/crystal malt/chocolate malt/torrefied wheat/Golding and Fuggle hops**

The brewery's flagship bitter – taking its name from the brewery's address – is primarily seasoned with Golding hops, but a charge of Fuggles is added late in the boil. This is contrary to the method of most brewers who use this classic combination: the Goldings are usually added last for aroma.

Tasting Notes

An amber ale with a bittersweet, malt-and-hop taste and a dry, lemon edge that dominates the bitter finish.

Holy Joe

- **ABV 4.9%** ▪ **BOTTLE SIZE 500 ml** ▪ **SERVE cool**
- **INGREDIENTS Optic pale malt/crystal malt/torrefied wheat/Cascade hops/coriander**

A glance at the ingredients suggests that this is going to be a citrous beer, with the zesty inclusion of American Cascade hops and powdered coriander added late into the copper. The taste backs this up. The beer is named after a local character from the 1860s and is brewed throughout the summer months.

Tasting Notes

A golden beer with lots of citrus immediately evident in the aroma, and subtle malt emerging later. Plenty of bitterness features in the mouth along with slightly toasted, sweet malt flavours, pronounced tangy-citrous notes and spicy coriander. Bitter, hoppy, spicy and lightly toasted finish.

Wight Winter

- **ABV 5%** ▪ **BOTTLE SIZE 500 ml** ▪ **SERVE cool**
- **INGREDIENTS Optic pale malt/chocolate malt/roasted malt/torrefied wheat/Northdown hops**

This is the brewery's seasonal warmer, described by Dave Yates as a stout-like, very dark bitter. Other seasonal beers called A Little Bitter Spring/Summer/Autumn may also be bottled.

Tasting Notes

A ruby ale with malty milk chocolate at first in the nose, then plenty of orange fruit. It is mostly bitter, malty and roasted to taste, with a perfumed bitter orange note always present. Bitter, roasted, perfumed finish.

YSD (Yates' Special Draught)

- **ABV 5.5%** ▪ **BOTTLE SIZE 500 ml** ▪ **SERVE cool**
- **INGREDIENTS Optic pale malt/crystal malt/Fuggle and Cascade hops**

A strong ale replacing a beer of similar potency called Broadway Blitz in the Yates' range. 'A drink to be respected', declares the label.

Tasting Notes

Golden in colour, with a tart fruit nose, this strong beer has a dry, hoppy, bitter taste that belies its strength to some degree. Fruit notes emerge and linger in the dry, bitter, hoppy aftertaste.

YOUNG'S

Young & Co.'s Brewery PLC, The Ram Brewery, Wandsworth, London SW18 4JD.
Tel. (020) 8875 7000 Fax (020) 8875 7100
Website: www.youngs.co.uk

This popular London brewery has claims to being the oldest in the country, having been founded, it is believed, in 1581. The Young family first took an interest in 1831 and is still involved today, although Young's has been a publicly quoted company since 1898. The company now produces a wide range of bottled beers, two of which are bottle conditioned. In autumn 2002, it also brewed a special, bottle-conditioned beer called GBG 30, to commemorate the 30th edition of CAMRA's *Good Beer Guide*. This has been revived since for sales in Sainsbury under the name of GBG Celebration and may be seen again in future.

Champion Live Golden Beer

- **ABV 5% ▪ BOTTLE SIZE 500 ml ▪ SERVE cool**
- **INGREDIENTS Lager malt/Styrian Golding hops**

Lagered for five whole weeks at the brewery before being filtered, re-seeded with fresh yeast and kräusened with ale yeast, this new beer was the winner of the *Tesco Beer Challenge* in spring 2003 (hence the name). It proved so successful that it has outlived its initial six-month exclusive deal with Tesco.

Tasting Notes
A pale golden beer with spicy, citrous hops in the nose. The taste is floral and fruity-hoppy (elderflower notes), with plenty of buttery malt sweetness for balance. Dry, hoppy finish with lingering creamy malt sweetness.
Major stockists Asda, Tesco

Special London Ale

- **ABV 6.4 % ▪ BOTTLE SIZE 500 ml ▪ SERVE cool**
- **INGREDIENTS Maris Otter pale malt/crystal malt/Fuggle and Golding hops**

Special London Ale is the current name for Young's Export, an award-winning, originally filtered beer once targeted at the Belgian market and, for a while, brewed under licence in Belgium. This bottle-conditioned version was a few years in the planning, eventually arriving in off-licences in summer 1998. The beer is fermented for seven days in open fermenters and then warm conditioned for up to three weeks over a bed of whole Golding hops. A cold stabilisation period follows before the beer is filtered. The beer is then primed with a hopped wort extract and re-seeded with fresh yeast prior to bottling. A 12-month best before date is marked on the label, with the beer said to be at its prime three–four months after bottling. The high condition and heavy alcohol content allow it to be served with most foods. CAMRA's *Champion Bottle-Conditioned Beer* 1999 and overall champion at the 2002 *International Beer Competition.*

Tasting Notes

A bronze ale with a malt nose enlivened by hints of pineapple and orange. Smooth, rich and malty on the palate, it has a fine, tangy hop balance with bitter orange fruit notes. Good, bitter, fruity-hop finish.

Major stockists Asda, Co-op, Safeway, Sainsbury, Tesco, Unwins, Waitrose

International Selection

THE DRAMATIC RISE IN THE NUMBER of bottled real ales brewed in the UK is mirrored by an ever-expanding range of quality imported brews. Here is a selection of the most common bottle-conditioned beers found on UK shelves.

The Americas and Australia

Anything goes in America, Canada and even Mexico, as far as brewing is concerned. The craft brewers can turn their hands to beers of all international styles and have even produced outstanding variations of them. It's not all Bud and Miller, by any means. Australian brewers have a poor reputation on the world stage, thanks to the insipid lagers they export or have brewed under licence in other countries, but there is at least one brewery that proves that there is good beer Down Under.

Alaskan Smoked Porter 6.5%, Alaskan
Smoky, bittersweet, roasted porter with just a trace of fruit behind.

Blanche de Chambly 5%, Unibroue
Canadian white beer in the Belgian style, with lemon sharpness and malty-toffee undertones.

Coopers Original Pale Ale 4.5%, Coopers
A crisp, lagerish beer with light pear fruit and hops in the taste and an increasingly bitter aftertaste.

Coopers Sparkling Ale 5.8%, Coopers
An Adelaide beer with a sweetish, pear drop flavour, rounded off by a drying, bittersweet finish.

Coopers Stout 6.3%, Coopers
Crisp, clean and lightly bitter stout with roast grain character, although a touch thin for its strength.

Golden Monkey 9.5%, Victory
A Belgium-influenced, perfumed ale from Pennsylvania, incorporating spices for further mystery.

Goose Island IPA 5.9%, Goose Island
Glorious Chicago-brewed hopfest, filled with juicy fruit.

Honker's Ale 5%, Goose Island
A fresh, full-tasting ale with loads of hop-pocket character.

La Fin du Monde 9%, Unibroue
Canadian 'tripel' blonde, described as the 'beginning of paradise': orange-hoppy and pleasingly acidic.

Milennia 8%, Casta
A Trappist-style, spicy, malty ale with a liquorice-like bitterness that proves that not all Mexican beers need a slice of lime for character.

Raftman 5.5%, Unibroue
Whisky malt beer from Quebec, bittersweet, malty and with a lemon-hop overlay. Quite subdued in the smoke department.

Sierra Nevada Pale Ale 5.6%, Sierra Nevada
A crisp, refreshing Californian classic, marrying malt and bitterness with a dry, lime-flavoured hop bite.

Belgium

Belgium has been championing real ale in a bottle for decades. Many of the country's most famous beers are bottle conditioned, ranging from potent, nourishing brews supervised by monks in Trappist monasteries, to spicy, fragrant wheat beers (witbiers).

Abbaye des Rocs 9%, Abbaye des Rocs
Not from an abbey, but from a modern brewery set up in the 1980s close to the French border. Rich, fruity and spicy.

Achel Blonde 8%, Achel
The newest of the Trappist breweries, on the Belgian/Dutch border. The Blonde is peppery, bittersweet and dryish. Look out, too, for the maltier Brune.

Affligem Blonde 6%, Affligem
Soft, sweetish, spicy ale from an abbey-beer producer owned by Heineken. Stronger in its home market (6.8%).

Augustijn Grand Cru 9%, Van Steenberge
A bittersweet, powerful, golden ale with a tropical fruit character.

Barbãr 8%, Lefèbvre
A honey beer that manages to remain bitter rather than sweet, with heavy fruit and malt flavours.

Beersel 7%, Drie Fonteinen
A bittersweet, easy-drinking, citrous blonde containing wheat.

Blanche des Honnelles 6%, Abbaye des Rocs
A strong wheat beer.

Bon Secours Bière Vivante!! Blonde 8%, Caulier
A sweet, warming, slightly earthy, golden beer with a distinct gooseberry flavour.

Bon Secours Bière Vivante!! Brune 8%, Caulier
Spicy, malty and warming, with more than a suggestion of chocolate orange about it.

Brugs Tarwebier 4.8%, Alken-Maes
Quenching, scented, bitter lemon-accented wheat beer, with a dry 'tonic water' finish.

Celis White 5%, Van Steenberge
Pierre Celis, the man behind the early success of Hoegaarden, later created this witbier, now contract brewed: soft, dry, lemony, bittersweet and lightly spicy.

Chimay Rouge/Première 7%, Chimay
Sweetish, malty, spicy beer with a suggestion of cherry, from a Trappist monastery near the French border. Spot its red cap.

Chimay Blanche/Cinq Cents 8%, Chimay
Extremely hoppy, bitter orange and apricot-accented, zesty stablemate of Rouge, this time with a white cap.

Chimay Bleue/Grand Réserve 9%, Chimay
Blue-capped biggest of the Chimay brothers: full, smooth and malty with fruit notes and a renowned port-like finish.

Corsendonk Agnus 7.5%, Bocq
Commissioned brew for a wholesaler, using a defunct abbey name; classy, refreshing, bittersweet and lemony.

Corsendonk Pater 7.5%, Van Steenberge
A sweet, dark beer with a hint of raisin.

Delirium Tremens 9%, Huyghe
Jokey-named beer served in a stone-effect bottle but far from gimmicky in its mouth-numbing mix of fruit and hop flavours.

Dentergems Witbier 5%, Riva
One of Hoegaarden's spiced wheat beer competitors and similarly cloudy, but drier.

Duvel 8.5%, Moortgat
'Devil beer', deceptive in its blonde looks. Full zesty bitterness, subtle pear fruit and surprisingly light body for its strength.

Gouden Carolus Classic 8.5%, Het Anker
Mellow, toffeeish beer from 'The Anchor' brewery in Mechelen.

Hoegaarden 5%, Interbrew
Bittersweet, easy-drinking, fruity wheat beer, flavoured with coriander and curaçao. The style's market leader, with a gently peppery, bitter orange and stewed apple character.

Hoegaarden Grand Cru 8.7%, Interbrew
Strong, flowery, spicy, bittersweet strong beer, with hints of mango and orange and a suggestion of whisky.

Kasteelbier Blonde 11%, Van Honsebrouck
A big, alcoholic, almondy beer with a sweetish finish.

La Chouffe 8%, Achouffe
Coriandered blonde with bitter fruit notes.

McChouffe 8.5%, Achouffe
Ruby-coloured, malty merger of Belgian and Scottish styles.

Orval 6.2%, Orval
World classic amber ale from an Ardennes Trappist monastery: bitter, dry and fruitily acidic.

Reinaert Tripel 9%, Proef
A malty, bittersweet, pleasant tripel with light raisin character.

Reinaert Grand Cru 9.5%, Proef
Dry-finishing, burnished-copper brew, nicely balancing malty sweetness and light fruit, with pear in the aroma.
Rochefort 6 7.5%, Rochefort
Rarely seen away from its Ardennes Trappist homeland, but an amazing malty, spicy confection.
Rochefort 8 9.2%, Rochefort
Light-drinking for its strength, spicy, peppery and fruity.
Rochefort 10 11.3%, Rochefort
Dreamy, peppery and dry, with background fruit.
Silly Saison 5%, Silly
No-joke beer from Silly town, drinking sweet and light despite its deep raisiny, figgy fruit flavours and plenty of malt.
Tripel Karmeliet 8%, Bosteels
Abbey beer from a brewery better known for its 8% beer, Kwak. Sweet malt, strong toffee, hints of lemon, an oaty creaminess and spicy hops.
Val-Dieu Blonde 6%, Val-Dieu
A slightly chewy, lemon-accented, sweetish blonde.
Val-Dieu Brune 8%, Val-Dieu
A perfumed, sweet and malty, red-brown beer.
Val-Dieu Triple 9%, Val-Dieu
Golden, with jammy apricots and oranges in the sweet taste.
Vieille Provision 6.5%, Dupont
Crisp, herbal and gently bitter, with an orange acidity: a leading exponent of the saison style of quenching summer beers.
Westmalle Dubbel 7%, Westmalle
Complex, sweetish brown beer from the largest Trappist brewery. Spice, dark malt, rum and raisin.
Westmalle Tripel 9.5%, Westmalle
A pale, aromatic, classic tripel, with fruit and honey character.
Westvleteren Blonde 5.8%, Westvleteren
Full-flavoured blonde from a Trappist brewery near the Belgian hop fields, close to France.
Westvleteren 8 8%, Westvleteren
A melon-, almond- and liquorice-accented, slightly acidic, warming, ruby beer.
Westvleteren 12 10.2%, Westvleteren
A hearty, spicy, sweetish ale with a liquorice-like bitterness.

France

Although the French seem to be ensconced in copy-cat mode, emulating Belgian ales and wheat beers, they do have a classic beer style of their own in the bière de garde. Unfortunately, for purposes of this listing, most such beers – Jenlain, Ch'ti, Trois Monts being the best known – although beautifully matured, are conditioned at the brewery before bottling, rather than in the bottle itself, and are filtered.

Britt Blanche 4.8%, Britt
Spicy, Breton wheat beer, fruity and peppery.

Coreff Ambrée 5%, Deux Rivières
An amber Breton ale with a reasonable hop presence.

Duchesse Anne 6.5%, Lancelot
A strong blonde ale from Brittany.

Gavroche 8.5%, St-Sylvestre
A malty, herbal, fruity brew from close to the Belgian frontier.

L'Atrébate Brune 7%, Bécu
Spicy, malty, brown ale, the most impressive of a small series from the Pas-de-Calais.

La Fraîche de L'Aunelle 5.5%, Duyck
Organic, pale beer from the Nord-Pas-de-Calais brewers of the classic bière de garde, Jenlain.

Lancelot 6%, Lancelot
A Breton brew, featuring biscuity malt and tropical fruit.

Germany

Germany has a deserved international reputation for quality lager beers, in the hell, export, pils, Dortmunder and other styles, plus fascinating minor styles like Kölsch from Cologne and rauchbier smoked beer from Bamberg. However, when these are bottled they tend to be filtered and usually pasteurised, so it falls to the weissbier, the Bavarian-style wheat beer, to reveal how well Germans can present naturally-conditioned bottled beers. Look out, too, for own-label wheat beers authentically brewed in Germany for some of the leading British supermarkets.

Aventinus 8%, Schneider
Amazingly complex with a full, smooth, fairly sweet and malty taste, well supported by bananas and spice.

Erdinger Weissbier 5.3%, Erdinger
From the world's largest wheat beer brewery, just outside Munich: a mellow, quaffable, mildly clove-spiced, fruity brew.

Erdinger Dunkel 5.6%, Erdinger
A dark wheat beer offering a wonderful, sweet mix of mild clove, soft chocolate and a hint of liquorice.

Franziskaner Hefe-Weissbier 5%, Spaten-Franziskaner
A lightly spicy, fruity wheat beer from Munich.

Franziskaner Dunkel Hefe-Weissbier 5%, Spaten-Franziskaner
An apple-fruity, gently spicy, dark wheat beer.

Hopf Weisse 5.3%, Hopf
Award-winning, mellow and fruity weissbier from Bavaria.

König Ludwig Weissbier 5.5%, Kaltenberg
Castle-brewed, bittersweet, Bavarian favourite, now imported by Thwaites.
Löwen Weiss 5.2%, Löwenbräu
Quaffable, fruit-and-spice-fragranced Munich wheat beer.
Maisel's Weisse 5.7%, Maisel's
Easy-drinking, apple- and orange-fruity weissbier with warming hints of liquorice and clove.
Pikantus 7.3%, Erdinger
Complex, strong wheat beer, with sweet, mildly spicy, almond and raisin flavours.
Schneider Weisse 5.4 %, Schneider
Highly-rated Bavarian wheat beer from just north of Munich: spicy, dry and very fruity (banana), with a touch of sourness.
Schöfferhofer 5%, Binding
German national brand weissbier, with a pleasant clove-spice edge.
Weizenland Dunkel 5.1%, Weizenland
A nutty, spicy dark wheat beer with a mild lemon sourness and a hint of bubblegum.
Weizenland Hefetrüb 5.3%, Weizenland
A fruity, chewy, bittersweet wheat beer.

The Netherlands

The Netherlands shares many of the beery qualities of its near-neighbour Belgium, even if it is best known around the world for its sweetish lager beers.
Korenwolf 5%, Gulpener
Named after the Dutch for a hamster (literally 'corn wolf'): a spiced beer in the Hoegaarden mould, brewed with four different cereals. Imported into the UK by Coors.
La Trappe Dubbel 6.5%, Schaapskooi
Recently defrocked Trappist beer (the monks sold the brewery to Dutch giant Bavaria): sweet, malty, spicy and nourishing.
La Trappe Tripel 8%, Schaapskooi
A well-regarded, bittersweet, fruity tripel.
La Trappe Quadrupel 10%, Schaapskooi
Sweetish, spicy, malty and warming, with marzipan undertones.
Wieckse Witte 5%, Ridder
Refreshing, lightly lemony, slightly toffeeish, spicy wheat beer, Heineken's bid to steal away Hoegaarden drinkers.
Zatte Tripel 8%, IJ
A tasty, fruity (bitter orange) tripel with a gently bitter aftertaste.

The Champions

Below is a list of all the winners of CAMRA's *Champion Bottle-Conditioned Beer of Britain* contest, which is now sponsored by *The Guardian* newspaper. Judging takes place at the Great British Beer Festival in August each year.

1991
1 Bass Worthington's White Shield
2 Guinness Original Stout
3 Eldridge Pope Thomas Hardy's Ale

1992
1 Gale's Prize Old Ale
2 Eldridge Pope Thomas Hardy's Ale
3 Bass Worthington's White Shield

1993
1 Eldridge Pope Thomas Hardy's Ale
2 Courage Imperial Russian Stout
No 3rd place declared.

1994
1 Courage Imperial Russian Stout
2 King & Barnes Festive
3 Shepherd Neame Spitfire

1995
1 King & Barnes Festive
2 Gale's Prize Old Ale
3 Bass Worthington's White Shield

1996
1 Marston's Oyster Stout
2 Bass Worthington's White Shield
3 Courage Imperial Russian Stout

1997
1 Hop Back Summer Lightning
2 King & Barnes Festive
3 Fuller's 1845

1998
1 Fuller's 1845
2 Burton Bridge Empire Pale Ale
3 Hampshire Pride of Romsey

1999
1 Young's Special London Ale
2 Salopian Entire Butt
3 Hampshire Pride of Romsey

2000
1 King & Barnes Worthington's White Shield
2 Hampshire Pride of Romsey
3 King & Barnes Festive

2001
1 RCH Ale Mary
2 Hop Back Summer Lightning
3 Fuller's 1845

2002
1 Fuller's 1845
2 Brakspear Live Organic
3 Hop Back Summer Lightning

2003
1 O'Hanlon's Original Port Stout
2 Fuller's 1845
3 RCH Old Slug Porter

Bottled perfection at ASDA

Pick up your favourite beer when you do your shopping. ASDA have over 100 speciality beers and real ales all at great Low Prices. Cheers!

ASDA

Some products available in selected stores.

Beer Shops

The variety of bottled beers sold in British supermarkets has increased dramatically in recent years. No longer do you visit your local store and expect to find only bland national beers in ugly, cheap cans. Special mention must be given to Safeway (although the take over by Morrisons may see a decline in the number and variety of bottled beers it stocks) and to Booths in the North-West, although other supermarkets, notably Asda and Sainsbury, are improving their range on a regular basis. For an even wider selection, it may pay to seek out a specialist independent off-licence. The following shops all have a reputation for stocking bottle-conditioned beers and should prove a useful starting point. Some of these also offer mail order services, as indicated by the abbreviation (MO) after the address. There are also a small number of internet-based companies that offer mail order beer sales. The most prominent of these are listed at the end of this section.

Bristol

The Bristol Wine Company,
Transom House, Victoria Street,
Bristol. (MO)
Tel. (0117) 373 0288
www.thebristolwinecompany.co.uk

Humpers Off-Licence,
26 Soundwell Road, Staple Hill.
Tel. (0117) 956 5525

Cambridgeshire

Bacchanalia, 79 Victoria Road,
Cambridge. (MO)
Tel. (01223) 576292

Bacchanalia, 90 Mill Road,
Cambridge. (MO)
Tel. (01223) 315034

Wadsworth's, 34 The Broadway,
St Ives.
Tel. (01480) 463522

Cheshire

deFINE Food & Wine, Chester Road,
Sandiway, Northwich. (MO)
Tel. (01606) 882101
www.definefoodandwine.com

Cumbria

Open All Hours, 5 St Johns Street,
Keswick. (MO)
Tel. (0176 87) 75414
www.personalbeer.co.uk

Derbyshire

Chatsworth Farm Shop, Pilsley,
Bakewell.
Tel. (01246) 583392

Goyt Wines, 1A Canal Street,
Whaley Bridge.
Tel. (01663) 734214
www.goytwines.co.uk

The Original Farmer's Market Shop,
3 Market Street, Bakewell.
Tel. (01629) 815814

Devon

Green Valley Cider at Darts Farm,
Topsham, Exeter. (MO)
Tel. (01392) 876658

Tucker's Maltings, Teign Road,
Newton Abbot. (MO)
Tel. (01626) 334734
www.tuckersmaltings.com

Durham

Binns Department Store,
1–7 High Row, Darlington.
Tel. (08701) 607237

Essex

Beers Unlimited, 500 London Road,
Westcliff-on-Sea. (MO)
Tel. (01702) 345474
www.beersunlimited.co.uk

Bottles, 37 Broomfield Road,
Chelmsford. (MO)
Tel. (01245) 255579
www.onlyfinebeer.co.uk

Hampshire

Bitter Virtue, 70 Cambridge Road,
Portswood, Southampton. (MO)
Tel. (023) 8055 4881
www.bittervirtue.co uk

Herefordshire

Orchard, Hive & Vine,
4 High Street, Leominster. (MO)
Tel. (01568) 611232
www.orchard-hive-and-vine.co.uk

Hertfordshire

Boxmoor Vintners,
25–27 St John's Road, Boxmoor.
Tel. (01442) 252171

Isle of Wight

Scarecrow Brewery and Beer Emporium, Arreton Craft Village, Arreton.
Tel. (01983) 856161 (Ventnor Brewery)

Kent

The Bitter End, 107 Camden Road, Tunbridge Wells. (MO)
Tel. (01892) 522918
www.thebitterend.biz

The Cask & Glass, 64 Priory Street, Tonbridge.
Tel. (01732) 359784

Lancashire

Rainhall Drinks,
18–22 Rainhall Road, Barnoldswick.
Tel. (01282) 813374
www.rainhalldrinks.co.uk

Real Ale Shop, 47 Lovat Road, Preston.
Tel. (01772) 201591

Leicestershire

Melton Wines, Unit 5, Bell Centre, Nottingham Street, Melton Mowbray.
Tel. (01664) 410114

The Offie,
142 Clarendon Park Road, Leicester. (MO)
Tel. (0116) 270 1553
www.the-offie.co.uk

Lincolnshire

The Beer Cellar, 2 Gordon Road, Bailgate, Lincoln.
Tel. (01522) 524948

Poachers Off-Licence,
457 High Street, Lincoln.
Tel. (01522) 510237

Greater London

The Beer Shop, 14 Pitfield Street, Hoxton, N1. (MO)
Tel. (020) 7739 3701
www.pitfieldbeershop.co.uk

The Bitter End, 139 Masons Hill, Bromley. (MO)
Tel. (020) 8466 6083
www.thebitterend.biz

Cave Direct, 40 Parkview Road, Welling.
Tel. (020) 8303 5040

Hops 'n' Pops Wine Merchant,
538 Holloway Road, Holloway, N7.
Tel. (020) 7272 1729

Nelson Wines, 168 Merton High Street, Merton, SW19.
Tel. (020) 8542 1558

Utobeer: The Drinks Cage, Unit 24, Borough Market, London Bridge, SE1. (Fri pm and Sat only)
Tel. (020) 7394 8601
www.utobeer.co.uk

Greater Manchester

The Bottle Stop, 136 Acre Lane, Bramhall, Stockport.
Tel. (0161) 439 4904

Carringtons, 322 Barlow Moor Road, Chorlton. (MO)
Tel. (0161) 881 0099

Carringtons, 688 Wilmslow Road, Didsbury. (MO)
Tel. (0161) 446 2546

Unicorn Grocery, 89 Albany Road, Chorlton-cum-Hardy. (organic beers)
Tel. (0161) 861 0010
www.unicorn-grocery.co.uk

Norfolk

Beers of Europe, Garage Lane, Setchey, King's Lynn. (MO)
Tel. (01553) 812000
www.beersofeurope.co.uk

Breckland Wines, 80 High Street, Watton.
Tel. (01953) 881592

Castles, 2 Mere Street, Diss.
Tel. (01379) 641863

Elveden Ales, Elveden Courtyard, Elveden Estate, Thetford.

Iceni Brewery, 3 Foulden Road, Ickburgh.
Tel. (01842) 878922

The Real Ale Shop, Branthill Farm, Wells-next-the-Sea.
Tel. (01328) 710810
www.therealaleshop.co.uk

Oxfordshire

Classic Wines and Beers,
254 Cowley Road, Oxford. (MO)
Tel. (01865) 792157

SH Jones & Co. Ltd., 27 High Street, Banbury. (MO)
Tel. (01295) 251179
www.shjones.com

SH Jones & Co. Ltd.,
9 Market Square, Bicester. (MO)
Tel. (01869) 322448
www.shjones.com

The Grog Shop, 13 Kingston Road, Oxford.
Tel. (01865) 557088

Shropshire

The Marches Little Beer Shoppe,
2 Old Street, Ludlow. (MO)
Tel. (01584) 878999
www.beerinabox.co.uk

Somerset

Open Bottles, 131 Taunton Road, Bridgwater.
Tel. (01278) 459666

Suffolk

Barwell Foods, 39 Abbeygate Street, Bury St Edmunds.
Tel. (01284) 754084

Memorable Cheeses, 1 The Walk, Ipswich.
Tel. (01473) 257315

Post Office & Farm Shop,
The Queen's Head, Rede Road, Hawkedon.
Tel. (01284) 789218

Surrey

Arthur Rackham Emporia,
216 London Road, Burpham, Guildford. (MO)
Tel. (0870) 870 1110
www.ar-emporia.com

Hogs Back Brewery Shop,
Manor Farm, The Street, Tongham. (MO)
Tel. (01252) 783000
www.hogsback.co.uk

Sussex (East and West)

The Beer Essentials,
30A East Street, Horsham.
Tel. (01403) 218890

Southover Wines,
80–81 Southover Street, Brighton.
Tel. (01273) 600402

Trafalgar Wines,
23 Trafalgar Street, Brighton.
Tel. (01273) 683325

Warwickshire

SH Jones & Co. Ltd.,
121 Regent Street, Leamington Spa. (MO)
Tel (01926) 315609
www.shjones.com

West Midlands

Alexander Wines,
112 Berkeley Road South, Earlsdon, Coventry. (MO)
Tel. (024) 7667 3474
www.alexanderwines.co.uk

Bernie's Real Ale Off-Licence,
266 Cranmore Boulevard, Shirley.
Tel. (0121) 744 2827

Da'Costa Wines and Beers,
84–86 Edgewood Road, Rednal, Birmingham.
Tel. (0121) 453 9564

Global Wines, 2 Abbey Road, Smethwick, Birmingham.
Tel. (0121) 420 3694

Global Wines,
243 Eachelhurst Road, Sutton Coldfield.
Tel. (0121) 351 4075

Laurel Wines, 63 Westwood Road, Sutton Coldfield.
Tel. (0121) 353 0399

Stirchley Wines and Spirits,
1535–37 Pershore Road, Stirchley, Birmingham.
Tel. (0121) 459 9936
www.stirchleywines.co.uk

Wiltshire

Magnum Wines, 22 Wood Street, Old Town, Swindon.
Tel. (01793) 642569

Worcestershire

Hop Pocket Wine Company, The Hop Pocket Craft Centre, New House, Bishops Frome.
Tel. (01531) 640323
www.hoppocketwine.co.uk

Tipplers, 70 Load Street, Bewdley.
Tel. (01299) 402254

Weatheroak Ales, 25 Withybed Lane, Alvechurch.
Tel. (0121) 445 4411
www.weatheroakales.co.uk

Yorkshire

Ale Shop, 79 Raglan Road, Leeds.
Tel. (0113) 242 7177

Archer Road Beer Stop, 57 Archer Road, Sheffield.
Tel. (0114) 255 1356

Beer-Ritz, 17 Market Place, Knaresborough. (MO)
Tel. (01423) 862850
www.beerritz.co.uk

Beer-Ritz, Victoria Buildings, Weetwood Lane, Far Headingley, Leeds. (MO)
Tel. (0113) 275 3464
www.beerritz.co.uk

Dukes of Ingleton, Albion House, 6 High Street, Ingleton. (MO)
Tel. (0152 42) 41738

Fabeers, 31 Goodramgate, York. (MO)
Tel. (01904) 628344
www.fabeers.com

Fabeers, 39 High Street, Wetherby. (MO)
Tel. (01937) 588800
www.fabeers.com

Jug and Bottle, Main Street, Bubwith.
Tel. (01757) 289707

Mitchells Wine Merchants, 354 Meadowhead, Sheffield.
Tel. (0114) 274 0311

Wells Wine Cellar, 94–100 St Thomas Street, Scarborough.
Tel. (01723) 362220

York Beer and Wine Shop, 28 Sandringham Street, York.
Tel. (01904) 647136
www.yorkbeerandwineshop.co.uk

Scotland

Peckham's (licensed delicatessen with several branches in Glasgow, Edinburgh and Stirling: MO)
Tel. (0141) 445 4555
www.peckhams.co.uk

Peter Green and Co., 37A/B Warrender Park Road, Edinburgh.
Tel. (0131) 229 5925

The Wine Basket, 144 Dundas Street, Edinburgh. (MO)
Tel. (0131) 557 2530

Wales

Thirst for Beer, Unit 2, Y Maes, Pwllheli, Gwynedd.
Tel. (01758) 701004

Northern Ireland

The Vineyard, 375 Ormeau Road, Belfast.
Tel. (028) 9064 5774
www.vineyardbelfast.co.uk

The Vintage, 33 Church Street, Antrim.
Tel. (028) 9446 2526

Internet Sites

The following internet companies sell beer via the web, but check also the websites of the shops listed above.

www.artfuldrinker.co.uk
www.beersinabox.com
www.euro-beer.co.uk
www.livingbeer.com

Bottled Beer Dictionary

A quick reference guide to the technical terms used in this book and to the language used on the labels of bottled beers.

ABV: Alcohol by Volume – the percentage of alcohol in a beer.

Abbey beer: a strong beer brewed in the fashion of monastic beers but by commercial companies rather than monks. Only authentic Trappist monasteries have the legal right to call their beers 'Trappist'; others producing beers in a similar style under licence from a clerical order have adopted the term 'Abbey'.

adjuncts: materials like cereals and sugars which are added to malted barley, often to create a cheaper brew but sometimes for special flavours or effects.

aftertaste/afterpalate: see finish.

ale: a top-fermenting beer (the yeast generally sits on top of the wort during fermentation).

alpha acid: the bittering component of a hop; the higher the alpha acid content, the fewer hops are needed for bitterness.

aroma: the perfumes given off by a beer.

barley: the cereal from which malt is made, occasionally used in its unmalted form in brewing, primarily to add colour.

barley wine: a very strong, often sweetish beer.

bitter: a well-hopped ale.

body: the fullness of the beer, generally indicative of the malt content.

bottle-conditioned: beer which undergoes a secondary fermentation in the bottle ('real ale in a bottle').

brewery-conditioned: beer with a fermentation completed at the brewery and usually pasteurised.

bright: filtered (and usually pasteurised) beer.

burtonise: to adjust the salts in brewing water to emulate the natural, hard waters of Burton upon Trent.

CAMRA: The Campaign for Real Ale – Britain's beer and pubs consumer organisation, founded in 1971.

carbon dioxide: a gas naturally created by yeast during fermentation and vital to the drinkability of a beer; see also condition.

cask: container for storing unpasteurised beer.

cask-conditioned: beer which undergoes a secondary fermentation in a cask ('real ale').

condition: the amount of dissolved carbon dioxide in a beer. Too much condition and the beer is gassy; too little and the beer is flat.

decoction: a continental mashing system in which parts of the mash extract are transferred into a second vessel and subjected to a higher temperature, before returning to the original vessel. The aim is better starch conversion into sugar.

dry hopping: the process of adding hops to a beer after it has been brewed, usually in the cask or in a conditioning tank prior to bottling, in order to enhance the hop character and aroma.

dubbel: a Belgian/Dutch Trappist or Abbey 'double' ale of about 7% ABV, generally dark brown and malty, with low hop character. Tripel ('triple') beers are stronger (around 8–9%), fruity and often pale in colour.

80/-: see shilling system.

esters: organic compounds comprised of an alcohol and an acid which are produced during fermentation. These have unusual – often fruity – aromas and flavours.

filtered: a beer with its yeast and other sediment extracted; sterile-filtered beer has been passed through a particularly fine filter.

fine: to clear a beer by adding an amount of glutinous 'finings'. Finings attract yeast particles like a magnet and draw them to the bottom of a cask of beer (or a conditioning tank in the case of many bottled beers), leaving the beer clear. Finings are usually made from the swim-bladder of a tropical fish. Also known as isinglass.

finish: the lingering taste in the mouth after swallowing beer.

framboise/frambozen: see kriek.

green beer: beer that is not fully matured.

green hops: hops picked fresh from the bine and used in brewing without undergoing the traditional drying process that allows hops to be stored for months. Green hops provide a more pungent, sappy character.

grist: crushed malt ready for mashing. The term also refers to a mix of cereals, or hops, used in the brew.

gueuze: see lambic.

head: the froth on top of a beer.

hop: fast-growing plant, a relative of the nettle and cannabis. Its flowers are used to provide bitterness and other flavours in beer. Hops also help preserve beer.

isinglass: see fine.

keg: a pressurised container for storing usually pasteurised beer. Brewery-conditioned beers are known as 'keg' beers and need gas pressure to give them artificial fizz.

kräusen: to add a small quantity of partially fermented wort to a beer in order to provide fresh sugars for the yeast to continue fermentation. It helps generate extra condition.

kriek: a Belgian lambic beer undergoing a secondary fermentation with the addition of cherries or cherry juice. Similar beers incorporate raspberries ('framboise'/'frambozen'), peaches ('pêche'), blackcurrants ('cassis') and other fruits. See also lambic.

lager: a bottom-fermented beer (the yeast sinks to the bottom of the wort during fermentation) that is matured for several weeks (months in the best instances) at low temperatures before going on sale.

lambic: a Belgian wheat beer fermented by wild yeasts and aged in casks. Blended lambic is known as gueuze. See also kriek.

late hopping: the process of adding hops late to the copper boil, to compensate for any aroma that may have been lost from hops used earlier in the boil.

malt: barley which has been partially germinated to release vital sugars for brewing, then kilned to arrest germination and provide various flavours.

malt extract: commercially-produced concentrated wort, used by some brewers to save mashing, or to supplement their own wort.

mash: the infusion of malt and water in the mash tun which extracts fermentable materials from the grain.

mild: a lightly-hopped, usually lowish-strength ale, often dark in colour.

mouthfeel: the texture and body of the beer.

nitrokeg: keg beer dispensed with a mix of carbon dioxide and nitrogen gas, to soften the gassiness associated with other keg beers. Such beers are filtered and pasteurised, 'dead' products.

nose: see aroma.

OG: Original Gravity – a reading taken before fermentation to gauge the amount of fermentable material in a beer. The higher the OG, the more fermentables and the greater the likely strength of the finished brew.

old ale: a strong, dark beer; traditionally, a beer set aside to mature.

original gravity: see OG.

oxidation: the deterioration in beer caused by oxygen. This is usually manifested in a wet paper or cardboard taste.

palate: the sense of taste.

parti-gyle: method of brewing more than one beer at the same time, using one standard brew that is then adapted – often by adding water to change the strength, or by using the first runnings from the mash tun to make a heavy beer and later runnings to produce a lighter beer.

pasteurised: beer which has been heat treated to kill off remaining yeast cells and prevent further fermentation.

porter: a lighter-bodied predecessor of stout, usually dry, with some sweetness in the taste.

rack: to run beer from a tank into a cask or bottles.

real ale: an unpasteurised, unfiltered beer which continues to ferment in the vessel from which it is dispensed ('cask-conditioned' or 'bottle-conditioned').

sediment: solids in beer, primarily yeast but also possibly some proteins.

shilling system: a Scottish system of branding beers according to style and strength, derived from Victorian times when the number of shillings stated referred to the gross price payable by the publican on each barrel. 60/-, or light, is the Scottish equivalent of a mild; 70/-, or heavy, is a Scottish bitter; and 80/-, or export, is a stronger beer again.

SIBA: The Society of Independent Brewers, a trade body representing the interests of the small brewing sector.

single-varietal: a beer using just one strain of hops or one type of malt.

sterile-filtered: see filtered.

stock ale: traditionally, a very strong beer intended to be kept and matured for several months.

stout: a heavy, strongish beer, usually dark in colour and tasting dry and bitter, often with roasted barley flavour.

sunstruck: beer which has been over-exposed to bright light. This can cause a chemical reaction, leading to unsavoury aromas and flavours.

Trappist ale: a bottle-fermented strong beer brewed by certain monks in Belgium. See also Abbey beer.

tripel: see dubbel.

weissbier: a Bavarian style of wheat beer, known for its fruit-and-spices character. Hefeweissbiers are naturally cloudy; kristalweissbiers are filtered to be clear. Also called weizenbiers.

wheat beer: a style of beer originating in Germany and Belgium, brewed with a high percentage of wheat and often served cloudy with yeast in suspension.

witbier: a Belgian-style, spiced wheat beer; also known as bière blanche.

wort: the unfermented sweet liquid produced by mashing malt and water.

yeast: a single-celled micro-organism which turns sugar in wort into alcohol and carbon dioxide – the cause of fermentation.

Real Ale in a Bottle Index

Q–R

S

Breweries Index

Books for Beer Lovers

CAMRA Books, the publishing wing of the Campaign for Real Ale, offers an excellent choice of books for beer lovers, cider fans and home brewers. Three new titles stand out in the latest selection.

Good Beer Guide 2005
Editor: Roger Protz

The *Good Beer Guide* is the only guide you will need to find the right pint, in the right place, every time: the original and the best independent guide to around 4,500 pubs throughout the UK, rated by *The Sun* newspaper in the top 20 books of all time!

Established for more than 30 years, the guide is fully revised and updated each year, with authoritative, meticulously-researched entries provided by dedicated CAMRA members throughout the country. It is also the only guide with a comprehensive and thoroughly up-to-date listing of the country's breweries.

Now in two colours throughout, the *Good Beer Guide* provides even more detailed information about pubs serving real cask beer, the food they offer, pub history, beer gardens, accommodation, transport links, invaluable maps and more.

£13.99
ISBN 1 85249 196 5

The Book of Beer Knowledge
Essential Wisdom for the Discerning Drinker
Author: Jeff Evans

The Book of Beer Knowledge is a perfect gift for beer lovers everywhere. An indispensable collection of facts, figures and wisdom that entertains, informs and amuses.

It's a beer buff's dream, a fact-checker's delight and a fantastic drinking companion at home, in the pub garden or by the bedside.

Around 250 entries cover everything from the landlords of soap pubs, foreign words for 'cheers' and the world's biggest brewers to bizarre beer names, beer in the movies and Homer Simpson's drinking buddies.

£9.99
ISBN 1 85249 198 1

CAMRA'S Good Cider Guide
Available in 2005

CAMRA's Good Cider Guide, now in its 5th edition, features more than 600 traditional cider producers and outlets in the UK and is an essential volume for anyone wishing to become a cider connoisseur.

The popularity of real cider is continually rising, as more and more people discover how deliciously mellow, aromatic and intoxicating the flavours of naturally-produced cider can be. *CAMRA'S Good Cider Guide*, revised and updated, offers a county-by-county directory of UK cider producers and retail outlets, and provides unique, in-depth knowledge for the discerning cider consumer.

In addition, cider experts provide features on production techniques, community orchards, traditional cider varieties, new cooking with cider recipes and regional specialisations, from Normandy in France, to the celebrated orchards of Asturias in Northern Spain and North America.

£10.99
ISBN 1 85249 195 7

Order these and other CAMRA books online at www.camra.org.uk (overseas orders also taken), ask at your local bookstore, or contact: CAMRA, 230 Hatfield Road, St Albans AL1 4LW. Tel. (01727) 867201 Fax (01727) 867670

CAMRA

It takes all sorts to campaign for real ale

CAMRA, the Campaign for Real Ale, is an independent, not-for-profit, volunteer-led consumer group. We actively campaign for full pints and longer licensing hours, as well as protecting the 'local' pub and lobbying government to champion pub-goers' rights.

Join today and receive all the great benefits of membership, which include the Campaign's lively, monthly newspaper, *What's Brewing*, free or reduced-price entry to over 140 annual beer festivals, and money off many CAMRA publications, including the *Good Beer Guide* and the *Good Bottled Beer Guide*.

Do you feel passionately about your pint? Then why not join CAMRA?

Choose from the following membership options by ticking the appropriate box.

Single Membership (UK & EU)	**£16**	☐	From 1st January 2005	**£18**	☐
Under-26 membership	**£9**	☐	From 1st January 2005	**£10**	☐
Over-60 membership	**£9**	☐	From 1st January 2005	**£10**	☐

- For joint membership add £3 (for concessionary rates both members must be eligible for the membership rate).
- Life membership information is available on request.

If you join by Direct Debit you will receive three months' membership extra, free!

Just fill in the application form below (or a photocopy of it) and the Direct Debit form overleaf to receive three months' membership FREE! If you do not want to pay by Direct Debit, please fill in the application form below and send a cheque payable to CAMRA.

Name(s)

Address

Postcode

Date of Birth

E-mail

Signature(s)

Please return to: CAMRA, 230 Hatfield Road, St Albans, Hertfordshire, AL1 4LW.
For more information on CAMRA, visit us at www.camra.org.uk

Instruction to your Bank or Building Society to pay by Direct Debit

Please fill in and send to the Campaign for Real Ale Limited, 230 Hatfield Road, St Albans, Herts AL1 4LW

DIRECT Debit

Name and full postal address of your bank or building society

To The Manager Bank/Building Society

Address

Postcode

Name of Account Holder(s)

Bank/Building Society account number

Branch Sort Code

Reference Number

Banks and Building Societies may not accept Direct Debit instructions for some types of account

Originator's Identification Number

9	2	6	1	2	9

FOR CAMRA OFFICIAL USE ONLY
This is not part of the instruction to your Bank or Building Society

Membership Number

Name

Postcode

Instructions to your Bank or Building Society
Please pay CAMRA Direct Debits from the account detailed on this instruction subject to the safeguards assured by the Direct Debit Guarantee. I understand that this instruction may remain with CAMRA and, if so, will be passed electronically to my Bank/Building Society

Signature(s)

Date

Direct Debit

This Guarantee should be detached and retained by the payer

- This Guarantee is offered by all Banks and Building Societies that take part in the Direct Debit Scheme. The efficiency and security of the Scheme is monitored and protected by your own Bank or Building Society.
- If the amounts to be paid or the payment dates change CAMRA will notify you 7 working days in advance of your account being debited or as otherwise agreed.
- If an error is made by CAMRA or your Bank or Building Society, you are guaranteed a full and immediate refund from your branch of the amount paid.
- You can cancel a Direct Debit at any time by writing to your Bank or Building Society. Please also send a copy of your letter to us.